Interracial Encoun

INTERRACIAL ENCOUNTERS

Reciprocal Representations in African American
and Asian American Literatures, 1896–1937

JULIA H. LEE

New York University Press

NEW YORK AND LONDON

NEW YORK UNIVERSITY PRESS
New York and London
www.nyupress.org

LIBRARY OF CONGRESS CATALOGING-IN-PUBLICATION DATA
Lee, Julia H.
  Interracial encounters : reciprocal representations in African American and Asian American literatures, 1896–1937 / Julia H. Lee.
    p. cm.
  Includes bibliographical references and index.
  ISBN 978-0-8147-5255-5 (cloth : acid-free paper)
  ISBN 978-0-8147-5256-2 (pbk.   )
  ISBN 978-0-8147-5257-9 (e-book)
  ISBN 978-0-8147-5328-6 (e-book)
  1. American literature—African American authors—History and criticism.   2. American literature—Asian American authors—History and criticism.   3. Identity (philosophical concept) in literature.   4. African Americans in literature.   5. Asian Americans in literature.   I. Title.
PS153.N5L39   2011
810.9'896073—dc22

                                                                2011015709

References to Internet websites (URLs) were accurate at the time of writing. Neither the author nor New York University Press is responsible for URLs that may have expired or changed since the manuscript was prepared.

New York University Press books

Manufactured in the United States of America

c 10 9 8 7 6 5 4 3 2 1
p 10 9 8 7 6 5 4 3 2 1

THE
AMERICAN
LITERATURES
INITIATIVE
A book in the American Literatures Initiative (ALI), a collaborative publishing project of NYU Press, Fordham University Press, Rutgers University Press, Temple University Press, and the University of Virginia Press. The Initiative is supported by The Andrew W. Mellon Foundation. For more information, please visit www.americanliteratures.org.

CONTENTS

Acknowledgments

The intellectual and personal debts I incurred while writing this book are too numerous to be recounted here, but I at least know where to begin. This project began as dissertation under the remarkable direction of King-Kok Cheung, whose wisdom and support was the bedrock of my graduate experience. I will always be grateful for the unwavering confidence she had in my research and career, especially at those low moments when it seemed to me that such faith was seriously misplaced. Eric Sundquist offered wise counsel regarding my project and generously helped me countless times at a moment's notice. I also wish to express my gratitude to Valerie Smith, who first guided me down the path of early twentieth-century African American literature, and Richard Yarborough and Cheryl Harris, who provided rigorous commentary that helped this project in its early stages. Chris Looby and the members of the UCLA Americanist Research Colloquium provided new directions for the project. Tammy Ho, Susan Hwang, Lynn Itagaki, Bonnie Foote, James Masland, Holly Crawford Pickett, Jessica Pressman, and Melissa Sodeman were my first readers and the most generous that any writer could ask for. Amanda Botticello, Brad Lupien, Jamie Nyez, and Jessica Pressman lightened the pressures of graduate school by filling my life with pasta, Korean BBQ, and laughter; I am lucky to have them as friends. For their friendship in Los Angeles, and for getting me out of the house, I must thank Andy Chang, Kevin Cooney, Melanie Ho, Joyce Lee, La'Tonya Rease Miles, Derek Pacheco, Nush Powell, Joanne Tong, and Jiyeon Yoo.

I want to express my deepest thanks to the administrators, faculty, staff, and fellows in the University of California's President's Postdoctoral Fellowship Program; without the generous support of this noble and far-sighted program, my struggle to revise would have been infinitely more difficult. Brook Thomas at UC Irvine offered a fresh set of eyes to my work and a sympathetic ear in the seemingly Herculean task of transforming the dissertation into a book. James Masland, Christine Wooley, and Caroline Yang took time out of their own busy schedules to comment on chapters at a critical point in the revision process. Jim Lee has read my work and always provided the most rigorous assessment of its strengths and weaknesses; he has also mentored me through many an academic quandary, and I am proud to walk in his giant footsteps. I would also like to thank Eric Zinner at New York University Press for his interest in and enthusiasm for the project, as well as his assistant Ciara McLaughlin for being ready to answer my questions about the publication process. Two anonymous readers at NYU Press strengthened this project in ways too numerous to recount; my appreciation to Priscilla Wald for showing her support and asking questions that were difficult but absolutely necessary to answer.

At the University of Texas at Austin, Elizabeth Cullingford and Madeline Hsu have made me feel like the most valued and protected assistant professor on the planet. Madeline also provided insightful and speedy feedback on this book's second chapter, for which I am eternally grateful. The College of Liberal Arts provided a semester's leave, which enabled me to finish the manuscript, and the Center for Women and Gender Studies New Faculty Colloquium offered support and a space for me to present my work. My thanks to Kim Alidio, Kenyatta Dawson, Madeline Hsu, Barbara Jann, Shanti Kumar, Nhi Lieu, Madhavi Mallapragada, and Sharmila Rudrappa at the Center for Asian American Studies for encouraging me whenever possible. Colleagues in English have also provided wise professional counsel and personal support: J. K. Barret, Phil Barrish, Dan Birkholz, Mia Carter, Ann Cvetkovich, John Gonzalez, Richard Heyman, Neville Hoad, Coleman Hutchison, Meta Jones, Martin Kervorkian, Lisa Moore, Gretchen Murphy, Frank Whigham, and Jennifer Wilks.

Since the first day of graduate school, Jane Degenhardt has been a dear friend and my most stimulating interlocutor—without her intellectual rigor, generosity, and madcap ways, I am quite certain that I would not be where I am today. Although we have been separated by a continent for most of our professional careers, she will be forever linked in my mind with the ideas behind this project.

My grandparents—Lee Young Kyoon, Hong Woon Jun, Lee Chong Kun, and Kim Ok Ran—are a part of everything I do, even though they are always so far away. My thanks to Vivien, Amy, and Sarah for reminding me that the bonds of sisterhood cannot be unraveled, no matter how old we get, and to my brother-in-law Paul Segerstrom for enduring my bossy ways. Although she arrived on the scene after this manuscript was completed, it is impossible for me not to mention the most important person in the Lee family, Keely YunAh Segerstrom, whose presence has filled all of our lives with joy. I lovingly dedicate this book to my parents, Kee Chin Lee and Joung Hwan Lee. I thank them for all the sacrifices they have made—and continue to make—in order to ensure all of us the best life possible.

1 / Introduction

In a speech delivered to the Cleveland Council of Sociology in 1906 on the subject of the "problem" of race, Charles Chesnutt describes the nation's attitude toward African Americans by comparing them to another racial group: "The Negro is a hard pill to swallow. The Chinese we have sought to keep out—the Negro is too big to throw up" ("The Future American," 248). Chesnutt's enshrinement in the canon is based in part on his fiction's nuanced and complex representations of black-white race relations, but this quotation is striking because it suggests that African American identity is structured in part by its relationship to an Asian other. To put it another way, these lines suggest how closely connected African Americans and Asians are to each other, not just in the nation's mind but within the author's own. Far from being a straightforward comparison, however, this linkage prompts an ambivalent and even contradictory response from Chesnutt. On the one hand, Chesnutt uses an alimentary metaphor to link black and yellow bodies as foreign objects that the national body politic either refuses to ingest or wishes to "throw up." His formulation of race relations as a form of both absorption and rejection indicates how deeply and ambivalently embedded the racial other is in the formation of an ego identity, a process that Anne Cheng calls racial melancholia.[1] At the same time, Chesnutt subtly distances the two groups by using the pronoun "we" to describe those who have striven to keep the Chinese out. The distinction Chesnutt makes recognizes the fact that the two groups were often treated in radically different ways. The Chinese can be thrown out in a way that Negroes cannot, the implication being that the latter have been in the United States too long and in numbers too large to expel successfully.

The ambivalence that permeates Chesnutt's brief description of the Afro-Asian relationship and the confluences and divergences that it constructs between the two groups are characteristic of writings by both African American and Asian American writers from the early twentieth century and form the backbone of my study. *Interracial Encounters* traces a series of Afro-Asian encounters and relationships that appear in African American and Asian American texts, examining the aesthetic effects they have on those productions and the politically diverse work they do in an era when the nation's racial philosophy presumed, to quote W. E. B. Du Bois, the "high civilization of the whites, the lack of culture among the blacks, the apparent incapacity for self-rule in many non-Europeans, and the stagnation of Asia" ("First Universal Races," 45). The fact that the two communities were often defined, compared, or contrasted against each other in national discourses plays a formative role in understanding how they portrayed each other in fiction and essays from the period. This book tracks the various ways that Asian American and African American textual productions responded to this perception of racial difference and the relationship that the nation conceived as existing between the two groups. The intersectional quality of racial relations, which Chesnutt's speech captures, is central to my book's critical project of mapping the fertile but uneven terrain from which African American and Asian American interracial representations emerged.

As the passage from Chesnutt's speech suggests, African Americans and Asian Americans in the early twentieth century depicted each other in wide-ranging and decidedly conflictual ways. The "Negroes," "Mulattoes," "Africans," "Asiatics," "Orientals," "Indians," and "Chinamen" who mingle and interact with each other in texts by Chesnutt, Wu Tingfang, Nella Larsen, Edith Eaton, Winnifred Eaton, W. E. B. Du Bois, and Younghill Kang fulfill a range of artistic and political purposes, reminding the nation to comply with its democratic principles, pointing to the failures of a racial community, shoring up a racial identity, imagining themselves as aesthetic objects emptied of historical meaning, embodying a gendered conception of the exotic or foreign, exposing the impossibilities of inclusiveness under the rubric of the nation-state, allying with each other in the struggle for social justice and political action, and symbolizing the link between racism within the United States and imperialist projects abroad. The range of attitudes expressed in these texts indicates the complexity of the interracial relationship between African Americans and Asians in the early twentieth century.

The diversity of these textual interactions also belies a late twentieth-century narrative of Afro-Asian interactions that tends to imagine the relationship in monolithic terms. Since the late 1960s, with increasing racial turmoil and unrest and the emergence of race-consciousness movements, the relationship between the two communities has often been either dismissed as irrevocably antagonistic or romanticized as intrinsically linked by a shared history of racism.[2] As many critics have pointed out, the popular press has been particularly invested in representing the relationship as inherently oppositional, basing this assessment on a highly essentialized view of cultural differences, and clinging to the notion of Asians as the model minority, implying none too subtly that blacks are the marred minority. As Keith Osajima notes, the emphasis placed on Afro-Asian hostility strengthened the notion that the two groups were insuperably different and insinuated that African American culture was somehow lacking when compared to Asian American experiences: "[The] delineation of good and bad culture deflected attention away from societal factors and placed blame for racial inequality on minorities" (217).

Meanwhile, in progressive and academic circles, the tendency has been to counter such popular images with narratives of Afro-Asian kinship and affiliation. One of the cornerstones of ethnic studies is its "coalitional and collaborative ethos" (D. Kim, *Writing Manhood*, xviii), an institutional commitment that has both supported and in turn been supported by a scholarship that emphasizes the bilateral potential of Afro-Asian relations. One must be cautious, however, that the legitimacy and urgency of this anti-racist project does not obscure the disharmonies and suspicions that are as integral and formative a part of interracial histories as the convergences. In his foundational essay "Is Yellow Black or White?" Gary Okihiro asserts of Asians and Africans, "We are a kindred people [who] know each other well," sharing a history of colonization and racial oppression, as well as "migration, interaction and cultural sharing, and commerce and trade" (34). The radical potential of such coalitions, which, as George Lipsitz points out, can be "powerful weapons against white supremacy" (210), does not mean that any Afro-Asian alliance—whether personal, cultural, or political—is by its very essence or existence resistant to racial, gender, or sexual hegemonies. The claim that Asians and Africans have a kinship based on intersecting histories of commerce and oppression operates with the same logic as the notion, propagated in the past forty years, that African Americans and Asians feel an implacable animosity toward each other. Vijay Prashad reminds us that even interracial relationships can be incorporated into the service of a "color-blind capitalism" and cites as examples films like *Rush Hour* and *Martial Law*, in which Asian and African American identities are commodified in conjunction with each other in order to explore "two ethnic niche markets" ("Bandung," xiv).[3] Daniel Kim argues in *Writing Manhood* that by paying as close attention to the antagonisms between the two groups as to the affiliations, critics can advance the goal of "more progressive forms of interracialism, for [these antagonisms] speak to the question of why such coalitions seem to emerge with such infrequency and difficulty" (xx).

In looking at the early twentieth century, *Interracial Encounters* complicates these grand narratives of interracial relations by foregrounding the fact that Afro-Asian relations actually have a long and densely complicated history that predates our contemporary moment and that these relationships have been surprisingly ecumenical in their politics. My analysis of the texts in this study is informed by three interconnected points. First, this book is a historicizing project; it assumes that literary representations of interracial relationships are most fully understood by examining the historical circumstances surrounding their production. I ask what kinds of Afro-Asian representations emerged in light of the shifting levels of economic exploitation, physical violence, and political exclusion from the nation's imagined community that each group endured in the early twentieth century. In other words, Afro-Asian representations are informed by the specific discourses that the early twentieth century's national anxieties surrounding citizenship and global relations produced. The incredible diversity and surprising ambivalence of these interracial representations notwithstanding, the justification for linking these works emerges from the texts themselves and the buried history of Afro-Asian relations to which they allude but never fully describe. Evidence of a long history of interracial relations between these two groups has always been present in these texts and other historical or cultural documents, but it is only in the past few decades that readers and critics have begun to rethink their adherence to the prevalent racial binary of white/other and adjust their interpretive lenses to detect alternative racial histories. Historicizing Afro-Asian relations and theorizing the importance of such an approach forms the backbone of this book.

The time period of this study illustrates how rich a comparative analysis of African American and Asian American cultural production can be. My analysis begins in 1896, a time when anti-Chinese sentiment was at its height and the year that the Supreme Court codified black inferiority in *Plessy v. Ferguson*, and ends in the late 1930s, just before the outbreak of World War II would again dramatically alter the way the United States imagined itself, its citizens, and its interactions with the world. This historical context matters in interracial relations if we are to avoid essentializing race (i.e., claiming that all minority groups are similar because they have experienced racism) or reinscribing racial hierarchies (i.e., claiming that African Americans and Asians have the most complicated relationship and therefore are the most worthy of attention), about which I will say more later.

Early twentieth-century America's troubled and multifaceted pairing of African and Asian bodies in a variety of legal, cultural, political, and scientific discourses maintained the racial exclusivity of American identity; at the same time, this pairing embodied the nation's general apprehension about the racialized body's relationship to American identity. This chapter is devoted to explaining this historical context in greater detail, but for now, it is important to emphasize that the literary texts in this study revise a potent national narrative in which American identity emerges from the interplay between the fantasies of the "Negro Problem" and the "Yellow Peril." It is because blackness and yellowness are so intertwined in the early twentieth-century's national imagination that Asian American and African American authors confront that issue through reciprocal representations in their own writings. The interracial representations I scrutinize emerged from the multiple associations that the nation imagined between African Americans and Asians in the early twentieth century, a time that witnessed America's emergence as a colonial power with global reach, a massive influx of foreigners onto its shores, the migration of African Americans from the South to the North, Midwest, and West, and the increasing industrialization of its economy and urbanization of its populace. In my chapters on these writers and their texts, I pay particular attention to what kinds of rhetorical tropes and representational strategies they used when depicting these moments of interracial encounter. However, I also argue that Asian American and African American texts of the early twentieth century acknowledge that multiple logics of exclusion are being constructed and mobilized in order to marginalize not only their own group but the other as well.[4] Because of the way that American popular and legal culture frequently paired the figure of the Negro with that of the Chinaman or Asiatic—or the Negro problem with the "Chinese question" or the Yellow Peril—Asian

American and African American cultural producers acknowledge that tackling the question of inclusion in their work means engaging, however obliquely, with each other.[5]

This leads me to my second point: that these interracial representations express and reveal the extent to which Asian American and African American identities are mutually constituted within these historical moments. The representations of these encounters are also instrumental in understanding how authors from both groups conceptualized their respective communities, their relationship to the nation-state, and their solutions for the problem of race-based exclusion. Being African American in America means negotiating a relationship of some kind with the figure of the Asian; conversely, Asians must take into account the role of blackness in constituting their identities. Blackness played a key role, not only in how Asians were perceived, but also in how Asian authors imagined themselves within a national and then a global framework; similarly, the figure of the Asian was vital in the construction of an African American identity and became an important trope in African American literary texts for expressing black America's relation to the nation and the world. The interracial encounters and relationships that are portrayed in these works capture the extent to which Africans and Asians are imbricated in their identity constructions. That is, racial identity is constantly being shaped and informed by a panoply of forces, and to imagine the formation of a racial identity solely as a contrast to "whiteness" renders other racial identity markers in monolithic terms and reaffirms the power of established racial hierarchies.

Again and again, the texts I examine reveal that Asian American and African American subjectivities require the other's presence in order to articulate themselves as national and racialized subjects. The Chinese passenger riding in the whites-only train car in Justice John Harlan's famous dissent to *Plessy v. Ferguson* and Charles Chesnutt's novel *The Marrow of Tradition* highlights the hypocrisy of Jim Crow exclusion and also suggests that African Americans occupy a superlative outsider position in relation to other racial groups. The oriental objects in Nella Larsen's *Quicksand* become the models with which Helga Larsen attempts to shield herself from the discursive violence that African American women have endured. The black Jamaicans that appear in the memoirs of the Eaton sisters provide a contrast and lend depth to their respective struggles to locate their own biracial subjectivities. The political struggle against global oppression that W. E. B. Du Bois and Younghill Kang write of in their novels requires a multiracial and multi-ethnic cast of characters.

Thus, the complex relationship that the nation imposed upon African Americans and Asians heavily informed the mutual cultural representations that African Americans and Asian American authors produced.

So what kind of interracial representations emerge when two groups are constantly paired with or pitted against each other to symbolize all that America is—or does not want to be? How do African American and Asian American authors respond to myths of the ideal national subject that are polychromatic in their exclusionary practices? Or, to restate Du Bois's famous question in terms more relevant to this project (if much less eloquent), "How does it feel to be *part* of a problem?" To answer these questions and describe how the literary representations of interracial encounters interact with racial identities and political institutions, I rely on two theories of racial identity, one put forth by Robin Kelley and one by Michael Omi and Howard Winant, to elucidate the relationship between African American and Asian American cultural histories. The theories of polyculturalism and racial formation are useful models for thinking outside the white/other or majority/minority binaries of racial identity and interaction that have prevailed in literary studies; although I do not apply these theories in a systematic way to every text under consideration in this book, I do think they provoke a broad set of questions that ultimately make comparative racial cultural studies not only possible but also exciting. Kelley's polyculturalism focuses on the often unspoken ways that different racial groups influence and borrow from each other, particularly in the realm of culture. I find polyculturalism to be useful in articulating my argument for the relationship between African Americans and Asian Americans in the early twentieth century. Kelley argues for the impurity of all racial identities, both in terms of lines of descent and cultural histories, and suggests that polyculturalism happens everywhere, without a sense of self-consciousness on the part of those individuals who are the products of or borrow from other cultures. In this regard, Kelley is drawing a pointed contrast between his idea of polyculturalism and multiculturalism, a term he dislikes because it "implies that cultures are fixed [and] discrete entities" ("People in Me"). Like Kelley's work, this book counters the multicultural project of the late twentieth century, in which the emphasis was on extrapolating the similarities or equivalences between various racial groups constructed within rigid borders. This study attempts to capture how various racialized groups were shaped and influenced by each other in their struggles to negotiate the reality of the exclusionary nature of the nation and in their imagining of political structures that might rectify that injustice.

Perhaps more than Kelley's, Omi and Winant's thesis on racial formation has played a foundational role in my approach to comparative racial
analysis. Their theory of racial formation analyzes how racial identity
is constructed by the continuous negotiation between national institutions and discourses and the racialized groups themselves. The identities of these writers as African Americans or Asian Americans emerged
not only from their multifaceted interactions with each other, as Kelley
suggests, but also from a mythology of national identity that was deeply
implicated in anxieties about racial difference. According to Omi and
Winant, "Race is a matter of both social structure and cultural representation"; therefore, racial formation is the dialectical process that occurs
between institutions of power and ethnic or racial groups (56). One of
the "racial projects" that informed how African Americans and Asian
Americans viewed their own identities was the pervasive mythology of
the "American" so endemic in the early twentieth century. In the words
of Omi and Winant, this fantasy of national identity narrates "an interpretation, representation, or explanation of racial dynamics [in] an
effort to reorganize and redistribute resources along particular racial
lines" (56). The racial project of defining American identity in the early
twentieth century was neither trivial nor merely theoretical; many believed that the very survival of the nation depended on who could and
should be considered American. Although Theodore Roosevelt's menacing warning in a 1915 speech that "there is no room in this country for
hyphenated Americans" refers explicitly to the threat posed by the influx
of southern and eastern European immigrants, it also reflects the nation's anxieties that the increasing physical, political, and social mobility
of the country's black citizens and the influx of immigrants from other
countries, especially Asia, would somehow destroy the natural coherence of the American nation and subject ("Roosevelt Bars the Hyphenated"). This anxiety about American identity can also be seen in Woodrow
Wilson's comment in 1914 that "some Americans need hyphens in their
names, because only part of them has come over; but when the whole
man has come over, heart and thought and all, the hyphen drops of its
own weight out of his name" (quoted in Robinson et al., 217). The image
of the hyphen dropping out of an identity because of "its own weight"
suggests it is a burden that any reasonable person would want to shed at
the first available opportunity. The weightiness of the hyphen stands in
contrast to the weightlessness of American identity itself, as something
natural, dominant, and an end in itself.

Constructing American identity as weightless is also a double-edged sword; the metaphor itself betrays the anxieties that inspired discussions about what it means to be an American. On the one hand, American identity can easily be taken up and worn without any trouble; on the other hand, its lack of heft suggests that it might be lacking in substance. In other words, despite the "naturalness" of such an identity, it is also, ironically, extraordinarily fragile if it can be obliterated by the existence of a hyphen. Roosevelt alluded to that fragility when he thundered in the same 1915 speech, "The one absolutely certain way of bringing this nation to ruin, of preventing all possibility of its continuing to be a nation at all, would be to permit it to become a tangle of squabbling nationalities" ("Roosevelt Bars the Hyphenated"). With his apocalyptic vision of a nation on the brink of ruin, Roosevelt no doubt means to evoke the memories and fears associated with the chaos of the Civil War, which was at that point a fairly recent memory, as well as point to the horrors unfolding overseas during the First World War; however, his language also suggests that being American as such endows its citizens' lives and their nation with a unique and transformative meaning that is more than just the sum of its parts. Within the operative mythology of the nation, being American meant something more than one's legal status; it constituted the core of one's identity as a citizen and as a person and was inextricable from one's essential self.

Omi and Winant's theory of racial formation takes into account the power of these kinds of foundational cultural narratives to structure a racial community's (and by extension the nation's) thinking about identity and difference; whether or not we like it politically, it is through the interplay between communities and institutions that racial identities are formed and re-formed. I have located my own work within the dynamic between social structure and cultural discourse that Omi and Winant and Kelley theorize. The cultural, historical, and legal texts that pair African Americans and Asians within their pages reveal how closely linked the histories of these two racial groups are and also influence how the two groups view themselves and each other. Each writer examined in this study positions his or her text differently vis-à-vis American identity, but each position pressures others and alters the terms of the entire discourse. Through these representations, these texts explore the common ground and tensions that exist between Asians and African Americans because of their uniquely linked and imbricated positions in the national fantasy of American identity. At this specific moment in history and on this particular issue, African Americans and Asian Americans were responsive to prevailing notions of citizenship and American identity in such a way that one *cannot* understand the history of national identity in this country without examining both groups' responses. As John Torok argues in "Reconstruction and Racial Nativism," his analysis of the congressional debates surrounding the Reconstruction amendments, the history of Chinese exclusion "cannot be understood outside the context of the late nineteenth century evisceration of the protections extended to black freedmen and women by the Reconstruction amendments and laws" (69); conversely, the slow judicial and legislative erosion of black civil liberties in the post-Reconstruction era was also informed by anxieties surrounding the presence of the "foreign" Chinese in the United States.[6]

My third and final point is that while inclusion into a national body politic preoccupies the writers under examination, it is equally important to emphasize that several of the authors included here question the nation-state as the only option for political organization. So while the writers I discuss often represent the Afro-Asian encounter in ambivalent, contradictory, and conflicted terms, they share an awareness that the nationalist fantasy of "American identity" from which they have been barred vitally depends upon the complicated juxtaposition and joint exclusion of both African Americans and Asians. The novels of Du Bois and Kang and to a lesser extent the works of the Eatons and Larsen respond to the assumptions articulated by Roosevelt and Wilson specifically and by the culture more generally: that an American national identity was natural, desirable, universal—and utterly impossible for African Americans and Asians to attain. Instead, the nation situates Africans and Asians in a series of shifting interrelationships in order to support its political need for a mythic, racially homogeneous civic population and its economic need for a readily available, racially stratified pool of labor.[7]

The engagement with another racial group within the nation, ironically enough, serves as a launching point for imagining the limits of and alternatives to the nation. Some of the texts under consideration go so far as to imagine alternatives to the nation-state, different kinds of spaces where Africans, Asians, and other traditionally oppressed peoples can claim political power while contesting racism and colonialism. Almost all of the texts, however, push against a binary that insulates the domestic from the global.[8] The relationship between Africans and Asians has never been bounded geographically. The colonial exploitation that characterized the nineteenth century, America's rising position as a global, economic, and political power, and the Third World's emerging independence and resistance campaigns all contributed to a growing sense that any Afro-Asian American relationship might have implications that exceeded U.S. borders. One of the threads I follow in this project is how these authors and texts recognize and represent the inextricable, if unseen, links between racial exclusion within this country and the colonizing efforts of the United States and Europe in the Third World. The interest in the nation-state's exclusionary policies and mythologies did not prevent most of these authors from critiquing its ideological requirements and even from imagining alternatives to it. If being an American national subject and being of African or Asian descent were mutually exclusive, then perhaps the problem was with the concept of the nation itself. Thus, the depiction of Afro-Asian encounters also signals the materialization of a kind of postnational awareness. The postnational is figured in two ways in several of the texts: as a globalized site outside of but intimately tied to the nation-state, in which Western colonizers can practice on a global scale the economic persecution and racial stratification that they advance at home, and conversely, and ironically, as a geopolitical space that makes possible interracial resistance and communities.

These three threads of Afro-Asian literary representations—historicity, mutual constitution, and postnational imaginings—are woven through the close readings I perform throughout the book, with some chapters emphasizing a particular thread more heavily than others. Later, I describe in more detail what each chapter aims to accomplish, but for now, I would like to pause and note two important clarifications of my argument. First, although I am focusing on the literary dialogue that emerged between African American and Asian Americans authors as a result of the mutual relationship imposed upon them by the nation, it bears repeating that I am not suggesting that their histories within the United States are the same, parallel, or analogous, or that what might be pertinent to one group is equally pertinent to the other. For example, Asian American authors routinely depict characters debating whether or not they should return to their country of origin (whether or not the authors themselves have actually ever been there), and several of the texts in this study represent or take up the question of the differences between Asian national groups, often in terms of their treatment within the United States, but also to depict certain groups as more deserving of inclusion than others. The African American authors I focus on do not address ethno-national distinctions within the black community or agonize over a return to Africa. Likewise, the long history of chattel slavery obviously looms large in African American writings of the early twentieth century in a way that is specific and unique to that community. I highlight these very different histories—without falling prey to what Grace Kyungwon Hong has called a "logic of similarity"[9]—while exploring what it means that the nation insisted upon seeing the two groups as connected to each other. The anxiety that a comparative analysis might wind up reifying racial categories is addressed by Werner Sollors in his study of how prohibitions against interracial marriage constructed racial identity and communities. Sollors wonders whether what he calls an "interracial focus" might "inadvertently [strengthen] a biological concept of 'race' that it promises to transcend" (3). I take Sollors's warning to heart, but I agree with him when he argues that such a risk must be taken if the critic is to understand "the cultural operations which make [categories of race] natural or self-evident" (3). One of the ways I avoid this pitfall is by acknowledging, capturing, and historicizing thoroughly the variations in attitudes between and within this set of African American and Asian American texts. My goal is to analyze how Asian American and African American cultural representations responded to an imposed narrative of Afro-Asian racial difference while at the same time recognizing and insisting upon the incommensurable histories that make up and distinguish Asian American and African American experiences. These historically contingent depictions of interracial relations also meant that Africans and Asians constructed America in vastly different ways. In other words, while "Negroes" and "Asiatics" were often imagined in relational terms by the nation, the distinctive histories of Africans and Asians in the United States meant that each group put different pressures on what it meant to be American, or on what it meant to be one who was excluded from the American identity.

The second aspect of my argument that requires clarification pertains to my choice to focus on the links between African American and Asian American literary productions, as opposed to looking at another interracial pairing or including several racial groups into the mix. Needless to say, the kind of relational positioning that I have described thus far has never been limited to just Asian Americans and African Americans. The literatures of Native Americans, Mexican and Latin Americans, non-Anglo ethnic groups such as the Irish, Jewish Americans, and even Anglo-Americans are always complicit in the kind of interracial formation that I am examining. African Americans and Asians were two of the racial groups that were excluded from claiming an idealized national identity, but they were by no means the only two, and each of them was also scrutinized and constructed by the nation in relation to other groups who were perceived as being "other" whether racially, ethnically, or religiously. The scholarship that performs this kind of comparative analysis, whether between two groups or among several, is impressive and growing in the humanities and social sciences.[10] In delimiting the boundaries of my study to African Americans and Asian Americans, I do not mean to reify racial identities and racial communities, nor do I mean to privilege Afro-Asian interactions as more complete, progressive, or revelatory of American racial dynamics than other kinds of interracial contact. Neither do I wish to suggest that the racial binary of black-white relations that has so long dominated the national consciousness (at times to the exclusion of other narratives of racial difference) should be replaced by a racial trinary that automatically includes Asians or Asian Americans.

My justification for looking at this particular relationship as it played out through African American and Asian American works is rooted in the extent and depth to which the two groups were paired with or pitted against each other *in this period*. In other words, I am not suggesting that this interracial relationship is representative of interracial dynamics so much as it exemplifies a particular historical narrative of racial difference and national identity that has a long and deep past in the United States and that continues to be relevant today. One of the premises of this book is that the persistence and intensity of this pairing during the approximately forty-year span of my study explains why black characters appear so frequently in Asian American literary works and Asian figures in African American literary works in the early twentieth century. In other words, my argument for reading Asian American and African American literatures in relation to each other in the early twentieth-century is historical and textual—historical because the two groups were linked in and through national dialogues about what constituted the limits of American identity, and textual because the prevalence of these discourses meant that Asian American and African American authors who were interested in issues of inclusion and exclusion inevitably had to grapple with each others' communities. Not only do these authors represent the Afro-Asian relationship more frequently than other kinds of interracial relationships, but they seem to invest those relationships with a tremendous amount of political capital.

Of course, every scholarly endeavor must make choices about what or who will be its focus. Comparative research projects, including this one, must be transparent about their rationale for yoking together its objects of inquiry; as Sollors suggests, this vigilance is necessary in order to avoid unwittingly reinscribing the racial hierarchies or binaries that they are attempting to dismantle in the first place. However, I believe that this kind of scholarship is worth the intellectual risks it poses because it can deepen and enrich our notions of what makes up American literature as well as present us with an array of compelling and significant alternative literary histories that do not fit easily or at all into the norms of the canonical narrative. In the past decade or so, there have been many works that, like this one, attempt to unearth the potential for interracial dialogue that has long been embedded in traditional literary scholarship. These works participate in a rich critical dialogue currently ongoing in American literature that seeks to identify the interrelationships between various racialized groups in cultural productions. I consider my own work to be enabled by critics such as King-Kok Cheung, Daniel Kim, George Lipsitz, James Lee, Lisa Lowe, Bill Mullen, Gary Okihiro, Vijay Prashad, Brook Thomas, and Penny Von Eschen, all of whom have written about the intersections between African and Asian diasporas in the United States and elsewhere. While I might take issue with some of their claims about the politics that drive Afro-Asian encounters, I consider my work to be very much in sympathy with their aim of elaborating a history of interracial relations that has been obscured or ignored. I also consider my work to be in line with those literary scholars who promote the idea that no one group (minority or majority) can narrate a definitive account of race in America. For example, in *To Wake the Nations* Eric Sundquist argues that neither a black nor a white perspective alone can "account for the ongoing crisis over race in American cultural and political life, just as neither black nor white authorship guarantees any sort of univocal vision or moral advantage" (7); his study thus focuses on the interplay between African American and Anglo-American writers and their texts. Less than a decade later, Wai Chee Dimock, advocating for a more globalized understanding of canonical American literature, echoes Sundquist's sentiment when she states, "Neither a single nation nor a single race can yield an adequate frame for literary history" (757). Speaking more particularly for American literary studies, Daniel Kim, in his reading of the novel *Native Speaker* by Chang-rae Lee, speaks of challenging an "optics of racial politics that is calibrated to register only shades of black and white" ("Do I, Too, Sing America," 233). In this book, I take up that challenge, recognizing not only that Asian communities existed in the United States between the nineteenth and twentieth centuries but also that they affected the discourse of citizenship and American identity and produced work that dealt with other racial minorities, whether directly or indirectly. Kim's point about recalibrating the lens of criticism to register more than black and white is a response to a history that has often deemed Asians "tangential" to American anxieties about race and culture.[11] The question of interracial relations between African Americans and Asians has only recently been asked.[12] Similarly the overwhelming reality of white violence and oppression against African Americans has meant a steady and important emphasis on black responses to white racism. Like the critics I cited earlier, I argue for a more complicated investigation of American literature, one that minimizes the binary narrative of racial contact and oppression and instead takes into account the cultural productions and histories of communities that do not fit into the binary. I hope my research exposes the limits of any kind of master narrative of race and that it reveals the necessity of historicizing the racial differences that we take for granted. More critical work needs to be done to investigate the various ways that America perpetuated its project of exclusion, even while it maintained its rhetoric and mythology of inclusion and individual rights. My project aims to do just that; it points to the ways African American and Asian American writers were aware of each other and interested in examining how the other group's plight affected their own. If we are to look at the early twentieth century as a moment in which the shifting relationship between politics, demographics, and economics profoundly affected how Americans viewed themselves, then we absolutely need to understand how African Americans and Asians were influencing that narration of American identity. By focusing on two so-called minority cultural traditions, I de-privilege European American culture as the dominant tradition in interracial relationships and discourses, against which all other cultural productions must measure themselves.

The complex interracial dynamics between African Americans, Asian Americans, and the nation that juxtaposed them inform my project's literary analysis. That is, I am setting forth an argument about the relationship between these two literary cultures that is grounded in a very particular if complicated historical period of racial relations in early twentieth-century America. This period marks an important juncture in the histories of both African American and Asian American literary production; it offers a fruitful and heretofore underappreciated site for cross-cultural literary study. Once dismissed as a time when African American and Asian American cultural works were aesthetically unformed and politically suspect, both African American and Asian American literary scholars have increasingly come to understand the first third of the century as of central importance in understanding the ebb and flow of their respective literary traditions.

Within the past several years the significance of this time period has been well established in African American literature. Although this period has often been called "the nadir" because of the violence and political backlash that blacks faced, African American arts and letters were thriving and exploring new avenues in the wake of Reconstruction. The rise of Paul Laurence Dunbar (the first African American able to make a living as a writer), the proliferation of magazine culture, the popularity of dialect and plantation tales, the public's curiosity about ethnography, the growing presence of African Americans in American cities, and the increasing embourgeoisement of certain segments of the black community—these were just some of the factors that contributed to the flourishing state of African American literature at this time. Writers such as Dunbar, Chesnutt, Du Bois, Frances Harper, Pauline Hopkins, and James Weldon Johnson were at the height of their creative powers at the turn of the century; many went on to influence the next wave of prominent African American writers during the Harlem Renaissance.

In particular, the rise of black women's domestic fiction signals the proliferation of a black, middle-class readership but also speaks to the determination of black writers to produce narratives that were engaged in the political and social struggles of their communities. Speaking of the genre that she calls novels of "genteel domestic feminism," Claudia Tate reminds her readers that the post-Reconstruction period is often called one of the "most violent periods of white/black race relations" (*Domestic Allegories*, 4). In the past, critical inquiry into this particular historical moment has tended to paint the literature produced as operating under "the influence of white America, creating inauthentic light-skinned mulatta characters designed to accommodate their white readers' tastes in heroines" (duCille, 7). However, a new wave of critics has questioned the easy dismissal of these works based on their distinctly non-revolutionary political moorings. Ann duCille, for one, argues persuasively that these sentimental novels force readers to see "the humanity of a people they otherwise constructed as subhuman—beyond the pale of white comprehension" (8). The importance of this particular moment in literary history has been recognized because critics have come to understand that black writers were using a multitude of aesthetic strategies to convey their political point. The trope of "racial uplift," once dismissed because of its supposed devotion to middle-class values and goals, has garnered the renewed interest of African American literary and feminist scholars invested in re-examining such works.

Asian American literature follows a very different trajectory, and my privileging of this particular moment in Asian American literary history might be considered unusual. Critics often consider the publication in 1912 of Edith Eaton's collection of short stories, Mrs. Spring Fragrance, to be the first important marker in the history of Asian American literature. Mrs. Spring Fragrance is the first work of fiction by an author of Asian descent about Asians in America.[13] Edith's sister, Winnifred (whose pen name was Onoto Watanna), was the first North American of Asian descent to write a novel, Miss Numé of Japan (1899). As the title suggests, the narrative is set in Japan and contains American and Japanese national characters. Other known works by Asian American authors in this time period are few and far between.[14] That absence stems from a combination of factors: the relatively small size of the Asian population in the United States, which was kept low due to exclusion and anti-miscegenation laws; the labor-intensive nature of the work that most Asians were forced to accept; and the hostile environment that Asians faced in their daily lives.

However, despite the absence of texts by Asians and Asian Americans in English, Victor Bascara rightly points out that Asian American literary critics should not ignore the importance of this time period in understanding Asian American literature. He states that the late nineteenth century and early twentieth set "the terms and conditions of Asian incorporation into the national collective" ("Following the Money") and that the significance of this era in Asian American literature stems from the emergence of U.S. imperialism. American imperialism abroad and racism at home "persist[ed] in the regulative narrative forms of U.S. national culture and in the place of Asian racialization in the new empire's management of difference." Bascara's formulation relies in part on the scholarship of Lisa Lowe, who argues that Asian American cultural productions constitute a site of resistance to American capitalist and imperialist projects. Lowe posits that nineteenth-century America racialized and gendered Chinese male immigrants in order to mask the differences between America's capitalist and political projects; thus, one can assume that it is only by knowing the racializing and gendering imperative of Chinese immigrants in the late nineteenth century that the literature published after 1965 can be understood (16). The conflict between capitalism and nationalism that Lowe chronicles in Immigrant Acts has its beginnings at the turn of the century. This conflict informs Asian American literary works of this period and afterward because they, as Lowe puts it, remember that which the "U.S. nation seeks to forget" (17). But this period in Asian American cultural history operates as more than a mere barometer for the work that followed. Within it, we can see how modern American notions of race, citizenship, identity, and racial difference were emerging.

Chapter 2 delineates in further detail how the late nineteenth century and early twentieth juxtaposed African American and Asian bodies in a variety of historical and cultural productions. That chapter ends with an analysis of Justice John Harlan's dissent to the Supreme Court case *Plessy v. Ferguson*, which I argue is a foundational document in understanding how the relationship between African American and Asian figures was constantly shifting depending upon how the nation and its citizenry were constructed. Chapter 3, "Estrangement on a Train: Race and Narratives of American Identity," introduces the terms and conflicts that the following chapters will explicate by exploring how the dynamics of interracial triangulation that first appears in Harlan's dissent are taken up by Charles Chesnutt in his novel *The Marrow of Tradition* (1901) and by Wu Tingfang in his memoir *America through the Spectacles of an Oriental Diplomat* (1914). Both Chesnutt and Wu describe a scene in which a black man is forced to ride in a colored train car while a Chinese man is permitted to ride in the white section. Chesnutt and Wu explore the sense of estrangement that arises when African Americans and Chinese confront each other in a space that is a symbol for the nation's progress and freedom and yet is unjust in its spatial division of blacks and whites, as well as inadequate in accounting for race outside of a black-white binary. My focus in this chapter is examining how the estranging effects of train travel intersected with the estrangement produced by interracial recognition in *The Marrow of Tradition* and *America*. This moment reveals how African Americans and Chinese are alienated from each other as communities with potential political common ground in order for an ideal American identity to maintain its racial exclusivity. Chesnutt and Wu expose the chasm between America's rhetoric of equality and inclusion and the reality of race-based exclusion, but they also betray their own unease over the possibility of presenting an alternative model for American subjecthood that can include *both* Africans and the Chinese. I argue that neither of the texts can imagine a resolution to this scene of direct racial confrontation.

Direct racial confrontations seem to play minor roles in the memoirs of the Anglo-Chinese North American authors and sisters Edith and Winnifred Eaton, who are the subject of chapter 4, "The Eaton Sisters Go to Jamaica." And yet, these face-to-face meetings, which are deployed in radically different ways in each author's text, play crucial roles in how each woman attempts to represent her biracial subjectivity. In her memoir *Me: A Book of Remembrance* (1915), Winnifred Eaton uses black figures to solidify her claim to the privileges of white womanhood and authorship—a claim that would have been rendered tenuous historically by her biracial status. In particular, she describes several scenes in which she is the object of black Jamaican male sexual desire. If white woman-hood is defined by the desirous gaze of the black man, then Winnifred's constant staging of situations in which she flees the advances of black men strengthens her claim to white womanhood and the privileges as-sociated with it. Edith's interactions with Afro-Jamaicans in "Leaves from the Mental Portfolio of an Eurasian" (1909) have quite the opposite effect from Winnifred's; rather than shoring up her sense of entitlement as a white woman, Edith's interactions with Afro-Jamaicans remind her how contingent and imperfect her own mimicry of white womanhood is. Keeping in mind the postcolonial critique that pervades "Leaves," the second half of this chapter foregrounds the links between the rac-ist domestic practices of the United States with the colonial project of exploitation in Jamaica. Within this transnational context, I then focus on the linguistic and rhetorical strategies employed by Edith in the short stories "Mrs. Spring Fragrance" and "The Inferior Woman" (1912). Edith calls into question terms such as "inferior," "superior," "romance," and "American"—concepts that are central not only to the progress that un-dergirds the narrative of Americanization, but also to the racialized biol-ogy and anthropology of the time. By including in her critique the (lit-eral) science behind racism, which was being employed against multiple minority groups, Edith implicitly includes Africans in her defense of the Chinese. I argue that by uncovering the racialization behind the rhetoric of American identity, Edith critiques the laws and hierarchies that keep both African Americans *and* Chinese out of America.

Although the black Jamaicans who populate the Eatons' works are allegorical figures rather than fully drawn flesh-and-blood characters, they are characters with whom our authors can interact, no matter how briefly. But my analysis of the Eatons raises this question: Can an inter-racial encounter occur without the appearance of a second, racialized character? In chapter 5, I argue that it can. "*Quicksand* and the Racial Aesthetics of Chinoiserie" examines how Nella Larsen's novel, published in 1928, uses figurations (rather than actual figures) of the Orient to ex-plore Helga Crane's biracial, gendered, and transnational identity. This chapter explores a question that has yet to be articulated in scholarly accounts of Larsen's novel: What is the significance of the oriental images that Larsen inserts throughout the narrative? I claim that the chinoiserie in the novel offers Helga Crane an alluring, if ultimately deceptive, model for subjecthood that decouples her black female body from its history of sexual, economic, and racial oppression. Helga realizes, to her dismay, that such a radical decontextualization of herself from a racial and gender history represents another kind of discursive violence. Her orientalism represents a search for safety from racial, sexual, and gendered prerogatives; despite her failure to find such a refuge, the novel forges a connection between the histories of African Americans and the Chinese. Significantly Helga's attempt to aestheticize and deracinate herself begins domestically but reaches its apotheosis in Europe. *Quicksand* differentiates the racism that Helga encounters in Denmark from what she experiences in the United States, but by setting a substantial portion of the novel in Europe Larsen underscores the connection between the local and global in projects of racial oppression. Helga's inability to escape racist economies suggests that any solution that does not recognize the global and transnational effects of race will be inadequate for dismantling the hierarchies of West over East or citizen over savage.

Chapter 6, "Nation, Narration, and the Afro-Asian Encounter in W. E. B. Du Bois's *Dark Princess* and Younghill Kang's *East Goes West*," tackles the question of what Afro-Asian political alliances and personal relationships might look like, and in what kinds of spaces they might exist and flourish. I argue that *Dark Princess* (1928) and *East Goes West* (1937) imagine an Afro-Asian alliance in the early twentieth century through their revisions of novelistic conventions. This chapter makes the case that the Afro-Asian encounters depicted in these novels are deeply invested in bringing a transnational perspective to explicating and resolving tensions in interracial relations; they attempt to further undercut the power of the nation-state to exclude on the basis of race and to stratify labor by reworking the conventions of the genre most closely associated with that political body: the novel. Each writer theorizes exile as a structuring novelistic paradigm and as an alternative to the exclusions perpetrated on their group in the name of the American nation-state. The figure of the exile enables *Dark Princess* and *East Goes West* to make central those who have been pushed outside of normative political and cultural boundaries as well as to privilege the unique, global perspective that these figures bring to bear on narratives of American nationhood and citizenship. Both authors recognize that racialized labor exploitation acts as the bridge between a domestic program of political exclusion and the West's colonizing projects in Africa and Asia. Unmasking the racist imperatives of the nation and the nationalist imperatives of the novel allows each author to imagine the close political ties that bind Africans and Asians together.

Contemporary racial tensions inevitably serve as a backdrop to this project, and I end the book by thinking about the relationship between past, present and future. By juxtaposing Asian American and African American cultural productions, *Interracial Encounters* provides a historical context for an interracial relationship that has a more sustained and complicated past in the United States than commonly thought. What this study intends to show is that the oppositional, overlapping, and complementary relationships between these two groups have been necessary to the emergence of a certain fantasy of modern American identity. By examining what African Americans and Asians have written about each other, we can see how these writers coped with nationalist imperatives and imagined each other as being more than merely problems or perils.

The "Negro Problem" and the "Yellow Peril":
Early Twentieth-Century America's
Views on Blacks and Asians

In 1907, Howley, Haviland and Company released the sheet music for a
song titled "The Wedding of the Chinee and the Coon." The piece was
from the wildly popular musical comedy *A Trip to Coontown*, which
opened on Broadway in 1898 and ran for more than three years. The
cover image contains three figures. A Zip Coon, in flashy clothes and
wearing a broad smile, holds the hand of a Chinese woman with slanting
eyes; her costume is festooned with cherry blossoms, and her hair is held
in place by what look like chopsticks. Between them stands the black-
faced minister who is marrying them, holding a Bible in one hand and
the groom's forearm in the other. The background continues the generi-
cally oriental theme: it is colored a brilliant scarlet, and paper lanterns
with red symbols surround the connubial couple. The figures are straight
out of the minstrel or yellowface traditions, and the hilarity that they are
supposed to elicit from viewers is further emphasized by a lantern on the
cover bearing the words "Comic Song and Chorus." The comedic aspects
of this union can also be found in the lyrics to the song itself. The first
verse announces that there will be a "mighty jubilee / Way down in Chinatown tomorrow morning." The source of the celebration is the wedding of a "pretty Chinese girl" to a "coon," an event that is described as
"strange," a "surprise," and "the funniest thing that's happen'd for many
a moon." The second and third verses also focus on the humor of the
situation, counseling the guests against eating too much chop suey and
recounting the argument between the "joss-house priest" and "Parson
chickenfeather" as to who would officiate the ceremony.

Ridicule and denigration are the characteristics that we most often associate with minstrelsy, and yet, as Eric Lott has argued, the "racialist lampoon" that minstrelsy relies upon merely masks the "white obsession with black male bodies" (3), an obsession that continues to this day, albeit in different forms. In the case of "The Wedding of the Chinee and the Coon," we might extend Lott's argument to include the yellowface performance of the Chinese female character, but we must also take into account the fact that this comic scene of interracial desire and anxiety was produced by African Americans. In fact, *A Trip to Coontown* was the first Broadway musical to be produced, written, and performed by African Americans. Bob Cole, who wrote the music, and Billy Johnson, the lyricist, were both prominent African American showmen and impresarios. Cole was consistently praised by the African American press for his attempts to "elevate the Negro on the stage, by laying aside the stereotype style of Negro performances and opening up a new field for the more ambitious Negro on stage" (quoted in Abbott and Seroff, 70). Cole was also adamant that blacks be involved in all aspects of production: "We are going to have our own shows. We are going to write them ourselves, we are going to have our own stage manager, our own orchestra leader and our own manager out front to count up. No divided houses—our race must be seated from the boxes back" (quoted in Krasner, 318). Cole's insistence that African Americans control all aspects of production seems to be at odds with the politics usually associated with minstrelsy. David Krasner attempts to reconcile this contradiction by arguing that the songs in *A Trip to Coontown* challenge the minstrel tradition by "inver[ting], negat[ing], and revers[ing]" its preconceptions regarding racial stereotypes and by emphasizing the bitterness hidden in minstrelsy's humor (319). Krasner believes that the songs disguise their more critical approach to representing African American life by closely but not quite mimicking the familiar minstrel figure.

Krasner's claim constructs minstrelsy in a monolithic and authentic way that is at odds with its historical production, but I find his argument for the subversive potential in this musical compelling, although not for exactly the same reasons. I would argue that the presence of the Chinese bride, whose exoticism is both terrifying and desirable, and the song's depiction of the uproar that this marriage will cause signal the conflicted manner in which the Afro-Asian relationship was often conceived. The way the song and cover image waver between attraction and anxiety inevitably calls to mind Lott's theorization of minstrelsy as "an articulation of racial difference" that nonetheless represented an ambivalent fascination with, even desire for, black cultural practices (6).

The dynamic that Lott describes—the oscillation between revulsion and attraction—can be seen in this image and song as well. Certainly, part of what early twentieth-century audiences might have found amusing about this pairing was the notion that a black man and a Chinese woman could find each other physically desirable, let alone eligible for marriage. While the image on the cover plays into popular stereotypes about the physical and sexual deviancy of African Americans and Asians, it nevertheless slightly upends a familiar narrative that reserves marriage for middle-class whites. By focusing on an interracial love match in this manner, the image and song also acknowledge the larger possibility that an intimate Afro-Asian relationship could develop without the inclusion of a white participant, albeit never outside of racial attitudes, identities, and histories.

The tension in that cover image can also be found in the chorus, which again suggests that there might be more to this relationship than just laughs:

This strange amalgamation
Twixt these two funny nations
Gwine to cause an awful jumble soon.
Twill cause a great sensation
Over the whole creation
The wedding of the Chinese and the coon.

The use of the word "amalgamation" is unsurprising given the term's ubiquity in discussions circulating in the early twentieth century concerning the future of the races in the United States. For writers such as Charles Chesnutt, amalgamation, which he defined as the "fusion of all the various races now peopling this continent" ("The Future American," 131) represented a welcome and long-term solution to the problem of racial conflict.[1] Israel Zangwill, the turn-of-the-century intellectual, playwright, and Zionist, defended amalgamation, arguing that it "is not assimilation or simple surrender to the dominant type, as is popularly supposed, but an all-round give-and-take by which the final type may be enriched or impoverished" (203). The amalgamation that Chesnutt and Zangwill believe will ultimately be beneficial to the United States is presented in this song as less a cause for celebration than a cause for wonderment and anxiety. The image the song returns to throughout its chorus and three verses is that of "coons and Chinese all ming[ling] together." What is striking here is that the song spends no time on the bride and groom as individuals, nor does it delve in even a superficial or comedic manner into the nature of their romantic relationship. Instead, the focus is entirely on the social response within the African American and Chinese communities and the shockwaves that the wedding might cause outside of the confines of the ethnic ghetto. The anxiety about the world's reaction extends beyond the black and Chinese guests mingling with each other at the wedding to the specific Afro-Asian couple whose bodies will presumably be mingling with each other later that night. What will happen, in other words, when Afro-Asian babies are reproduced in the near future? Marriage—thought to be reserved for whites—makes this union "strange" and "funny," but the possibility that it might produce children is what will cause the "awful jumble" with implications for the "whole [of] creation." In the space of one verse, the union of two comical individuals has transformed into an issue of national and even global importance.

Thus, the song's slightly apocalyptic flourish (that all of creation will know about this union) seems to play into the sentiments of writers such as John Denison, who, in an article ominously titled "The Survival of the American Type" published in the *Atlantic Monthly* in 1895 argued that "negroes" and "foreigners" together could easily overwhelm white Anglo-Saxons and destroy the country: "Society will not cohere under such conditions. Intelligence cannot be ruled by ignorance. The higher force cannot be dominated by the lower. Nature will not tolerate it; she prefers disintegration and reorganization" (18). Denison's dire warnings about the proliferating presence of non-white people in the United States lurk under the hilarity that the song attempts to create around the idea of a "Coon" and a "Chinee" falling in love and marrying. The song and its image represent the real anxiety about what might happen if Africans and Asians mingled within the nation's borders. It also suggests that each group is made even less eligible for inclusion because of its association with the other. The case against Zip Coon's admittance into the national mythos is based in part on his relationship with the Chinee girl and vice versa.

The Afro-Asian encounter in this song is characterized by a series of complementary and competing characterizations of what that relationship may mean. "The Wedding of the Chinee and the Coon" provides a particularly rich example of how the figure of the Asian was vital in mediating the relationship between blackness and American national identity, and in turn how blackness was key in imagining Asian racial difference in relation to the nation. In this chapter, I explore the issues that "The Wedding" raises—the representation of the Afro-Asian relationship in its many permutations and the shifting signification of that relationship—in textual and visual productions that were meant to be consumed by a white audience. These cultural and political texts range from films (Cecil B. DeMille's *The Cheat* and D. W. Griffiths's *The Birth of a Nation*) to editorial cartoons from *Harper's Weekly*, opinion essays in widely circulating national journals and newspapers, and judicial cases (the Supreme Court cases *Takao Ozawa v. United States, United States v. Bhagat Singh Thind*, and *Plessy v. Ferguson*). *Plessy v. Ferguson* is a crucial text for this chapter and the book as a whole, and my reconstruction of the dissenting opinion into a drama of racial triangulation will serve as the bridge into the following chapters.

I begin with Anglo-America's representations of the Afro-Asian relationship because they provide a context for understanding what African American and Asian authors were working with or against when they crafted their own interracial representations. I understand that in starting with these racist portrayals I run the risk of recirculating the power of the center to define the margin and rendering "whiteness" a natural category that needs no explanation. However, because the significance that the nation attached to the Afro-Asian relationship so profoundly informed the interracial representations that African American and Asian authors imagined, I believe that an initial examination of the national framework in which they were enmeshed highlights aspects of the relationships between the groups that tend to be overlooked. The chapters that follow this one—indeed the vast majority of this book—can then track how African Americans and Asian American writers responded to their proximate relationship and the polyracial exclusionary models that were adapted to shut out the newly enfranchised black community and the recently arrived Asian population. One of the points I hope to make in this chapter is that the juxtaposition of African Americans and Asians was never stable or monolithic but played out in different media and a variety of disciplines. In the works I mentioned earlier, Asians and African Americans are imagined in a variety of relationships, ranging from hostile to romantic. This kind of flexible and relational positioning of the two groups reinforced the contingent place of both within the national polity and imaginary, thereby justifying the exclusion of both. Even if an author's ostensible purpose is to portray one or both of the communities sympathetically—as is the case in countless editorials, articles, and cultural products from this period—the juxtaposition of African American and Asian inevitably evokes contradictory or irreconcilable impulses regarding race. Understanding the numerous discursive fields working to uphold the myth of American identity is crucial in attempting to understand America's obsession with defining itself and its inhabitants. Although I situate my argument in this chapter within a particular history of race relations, my intent is not to provide an exhaustive history of Afro-Asian representations per se. Rather, my purpose in analyzing these disparate texts is to illustrate by example the multifaceted ways that the two groups were imagined in relation to each other and to provide a context for understanding the diversity of Asian and African American mutual representations. An analysis of how both groups were portrayed in a sampling of mainstream cultural productions will be helpful in understanding the politics behind their mutual representations, and I hope that the readings in this chapter will historicize and illuminate the incommensurability of the Afro-Asian representations that I focus on in the later chapters.

* * *

As I stated in chapter 1, throughout this book I explore the discursive space that African American and Asian figures shared in the nation's imagined community and pay attention to the specific and unique histories of each group. A comparative approach to Asian American and African American cultural histories reveals how a *multiplicity* of models for defining American identity was needed to justify the exclusion of both groups. A number of historians have already explored the interconnected nature of anti-black and anti-Asian racism in late nineteenth-century and early twentieth-century America. Indeed, American history is littered with examples of how the position of African Americans was only apprehended by comparing them to Asians or vice versa, particularly over the issue of labor. Gary Okihiro argues, "Before the Civil War, southern planters saw African slaves as a counter to immigration to their region. . . . After the war, the planters saw free blacks as a troublesome presence and sought to deport them outside the United States and to replace them with Europeans and Asians" (44). The problem with emancipated slaves in the Reconstruction era was that they could vote, whereas Chinese laborers could not. Moon-Ho Jung shifts the history of Chinese labor from the American West to the American South and the Caribbean, arguing that the figure of the coolie was "pivotal in the reconstruction of racial and national boundaries and hierarchies in the age of emancipation" (5). The slippage between coolie and slave, according to Jung, means that the passage of anti-Chinese legislation such as the Page Law (1875) and the Chinese Exclusion Act (1882) "marked the culmination of nineteenth-century slave-trade prohibitions" (6). Both Najia Aarim-Heriot and John Torok chronicle the ways that the Reconstruction debates in Congress also entailed discussing the question of whether or not the Chinese could become naturalized citizens. Blacks and Chinese themselves often used the legal advances or setbacks of the other to define their own position within the country. For example, Chinese laundrymen in San Francisco in the 1870s relied on the Fourteenth Amendment to challenge a series of city ordinances that were designed to target Chinese businesses even though the laws themselves contained no discriminatory language.[2]

The sense that Asian and African American populations posed a threat to the nation was no doubt exacerbated by economic and social uncertainties on the home front, along with developments in the international arena. The passage of the Thirteenth (1865), Fourteenth (1868), and Fifteenth (1870) Amendments (which supposedly secured equal political and legal protections for black men),[3] the arrival of floods of immigrants from southern and central Europe as well as labor from China, Korea, the Philippines, and Japan, the organization of the women's suffrage movement, and the burgeoning of American colonial and economic interests in the Philippines and China not only marked an important change in the way that Americanness came to be constructed, but also signaled the end of certain kinds of assumptions regarding national identity. The post–Civil War era witnessed a shift in the lines of exclusion that had formed the boundaries of an acceptable American identity and experience (white, male, propertied) since the start of the Republic. I should hasten to add that this kind of national redefinition happens continually, and I do not mean to suggest that this identity crisis is characteristic of only the early twentieth century. As Judith Shklar rightly notes, "The tension between an acknowledged ideology of equal political rights and a deep and common desire to exclude and reject large groups of human beings from citizenship has marked every stage of the history of American democracy" (28). However, I do want to suggest that, along with other demographic changes, the simultaneous "catastrophes" of African American emancipation and suffrage and increasing Asian migration threatened the inviolability of the link between whiteness and American identity in an unprecedented manner.[4] Newer and more diversified models for enforcing American identity had to be installed in order to stave off the millions of blacks and hundreds of thousands of Asians whose presence, physically if not socially or politically, could no longer be ignored. The steady evisceration of the Thirteenth, Fourteenth, and Fifteenth Amendments by the courts, the "one-drop" rule, Jim Crow laws, various anti-Chinese bills passed on the local and state level, and the increasing regulatory roles that disciplines such as anthropology and biology took on—all of these served to control the mobility of African Americans and Asians and to reserve the privileges of American identity exclusively for certain white Americans.[5]

Not only were the barriers for African Americans and Asians constantly shifting, but the very ideal to which they were being unfavorably compared was in a state of flux. It is important to note that the arrival of immigrants from all over Europe meant that whiteness as a category was undergoing a shift from the founding of the republic. As Matthew Frye Jacobson states, although "white privilege in various forms has been a constant in American political culture since colonial times . . . whiteness itself has been subject to all kinds of contests and has gone through a series of historical vicissitudes" (4). Jacobson argues that the conceptualization of whiteness changed from a "unified race of 'white persons' to a contest over [the] political 'fitness' [of] a now fragmented, hierarchically arranged series of distinct 'white races'" (42–43). Whiteness depends on a fantasy of ahistorical permanence in order to maintain its privilege. But the early twentieth century reveals how contingent and interconnected racial identities always are. Thus, the racist rhetoric directed toward the African American and Asian communities did not operate exclusively of each other or in a vacuum, but were linked structurally by broader ideas of race and racial difference. Anti-black racism and anti-Chinese sentiment developed in interconnected but not wholly parallel ways, meaning that even though both groups were often the targets of similar kinds of legislative prohibitions (e.g., the inadmissibility of Asian or African American testimony in courts of law and the prohibition against interracial marriages) different lines of racialized reasoning (some applicable to both groups, others applicable to only one) were used to justify that exclusion.

The supposed inability of African Americans and Asians to assimilate civilized American values because of their biological and cultural inadequacies formed powerful justifications for their political exclusion. These models not only provided a narrative for defining American identity; they also offered a way to manage American identity, ensuring that whatever legal gains might be made by African Americans and Asians, they could not be considered "truly" American. While some Asian groups and most Africans were thought to be savage, morally suspect, and sensual (e.g., Chinese men, like black men, were portrayed as being a sexual threat to white women), European American attitudes toward African Americans differed from their attitudes toward the Chinese because of perceived cultural and biological differences. It was widely believed that Africa was the "dark" continent, incapable of and inhospitable to civilized governance, yet most western Europeans and Americans acknowledged that the Chinese had once commanded a powerful and extensive empire. Teasing out the perceived differences between African Americans and Asians is as crucial as pointing out the common ground they shared.

Acknowledging that there were heterogeneous frameworks for exclusion based on the perceived cultural or biological differences attached to each racial group undercuts the logic behind racial binaries, a logic that implies that all minority groups are always only responding to a European American mainstream culture or that all minority groups are essentially interchangeable in their relation to white America. The discourse surrounding citizenship exemplifies how flexibly models of inclusion and exclusion could be when applied to African Americans and Asians. Citizenship has historically been one of the central ways to identify who belongs in the country and who does not, and as a subject position in antebellum America, it made wealth, whiteness, and masculinity coextensive with American identity. The political history of citizenship took a turn when it was extended to African Americans after the Civil War. As many historians have argued, with the suffrage of black men, the link between "whiteness" and "citizen" was broken, and citizenship became a less efficacious means of maintaining the exclusivity of American identity. In other words, as the term became more capacious and inclusive, it began to play less of a constitutive role in defining an American national subject. Walter Benn Michaels, for example, dismisses citizenship as a mode of interrogation in the early twentieth century because "[American] identity [had become] disconnected . . . from citizenship, which is to say, from the rights and obligations conferred upon the subject by his or her legal status as a citizen of the nation-state. Wops and kikes can participate in American elections, but being able to participate in American elections doesn't make them American" (15–16).[6] The granting of nominal citizenship rights to Africans and the increasing presence of non-Protestant southern and eastern European immigrants meant that citizenship was no longer the impressive barrier it had once been for defining an American identity. Michaels alludes to the fact that the admittance of "wops and kikes" into the national polity meant that citizenship as an identity marker had become empty of ideological meaning. Presumably, if even blacks, "wops, and kikes" can be called American citizens, then Americanness as a quality must be located somewhere else. The right to participate in the nation's politics did not necessarily grant one the right to participate in its national mythology, a disconnect that will be depressingly familiar to anyone living in post-9/11 America.

What Michaels fails to note, though, is that citizenship, with its rhetoric of inclusion and rights, was still an effective exclusionary tool in the early twentieth century against Asians and particularly the Chinese. The Chinese in fact were denied the right to naturalization by the Chinese Exclusion Act of 1882, an exclusion that prompted the creation of false personal histories and the appearance of "paper sons." Chinese Americans' anxiety surrounding their legal status would continue well past World War II, when the Chinese exclusion laws were finally repealed, but the question of Chinese inclusion, especially as figured on paper, is still an important trope in many Chinese American cultural texts, including canonical novels like Maxine Hong Kingston's China Men (1977) and Fae Ng's Bone (1993). My point is that the policing of American identity required more than one or two models of Americanness to maintain its lines of exclusion. Because citizenship alone could no longer reasonably serve as the legal gatekeeper of American identity for many groups of people, more numerous and differentiated models were needed to uphold and stem the rising tide of color. Along with citizenship, other models for imagining American identity were already in place by the early twentieth century to counter the political demands of African Americans and the troubling presence of Asians.

One discursive arena that gained in stature, even as the ability of citizenship to define, categorize, and exclude began to wane, was popular culture. The ostensible expansion of legal privileges to African Americans ironically had the effect of increasing the power of popular culture to define who an American could be. For example, in the early 1920s the Supreme Court decided to accept "common knowledge" as the means by which to categorize people into racial groups. In *United States v. Bhagat Singh Thind* an Indian man of "high caste" (Haney-Lopez, 221) argued that as a member of the Aryan or Caucasian race he should not be ruled ineligible for citizenship. Justice John Sutherland, writing for the majority, argued that the "words 'white person' were meant to indicate only a person of what is *popularly known as* the Caucasian race" (my emphasis).[7] Similarly, *Takao Ozawa v. United States* (1922) challenged the Naturalization Law of 1790, reserving naturalization for white men, by arguing that the statute originally was intended to exclude Africans and Native Americans from naturalization, and that Asians therefore should not be placed in the "nonwhite" category.[8] Furthermore, because the Japanese often had fairer skin than persons of European descent, Ozawa argued that he should be considered white. Justice Sutherland, again writing for the majority, countered that the statute does not exclude other racial groups but affirmatively includes "free white persons." He goes on to say that the "skin color" test, which Ozawa advocated, would "result in a confused overlapping of races and a gradual merging of one into the other without any particular line of separation" (quoted in Haney-Lopez, 200). The inability of the scientific disciplines to prove a biological basis for race translated into the Court's embrace of race as socially constructed and a discursive formation. By taking pressure off any one discipline to justify the discrimination against nonwhite racial groups, Sutherland made racial categorization that much more obscure and that much more difficult to resist.

If anything, these "prerequisite" cases demonstrate how the relationship between race and national identity emerges out of the interplay between social practices and institutional agendas, as Omi and Winant claim.[9] Literary and cultural productions were crucial in securing a conception of American identity for the general population; these images were then instrumental in setting legal precedent and government policy. Films, fiction, magazines, cartoons, and any number of other kinds of works not only reflect what the nation thought of itself; they also shape those attitudes. Lowe notes that the study of culture is relevant because culture stands as the "repository of memory, of history" (22); it is, in other words, a repository for those conflicts that politics cannot resolve. We need to look at cultural productions because it is in this realm that the myth of American identity reproduces itself. If cultural productions act as the primary vehicle for the dissemination of this American identity, then cultural productions should be the first place a critic looks in order to understand the impact of that construction.

The exclusionary discourses that proliferated during this period were tailored to suit each group's perceived deviances from whiteness.[10] In other words, neither Africans nor Asians could be real Americans, but the justifications for each group's exclusions were slightly different. For example, scientific discourses eager to imagine racial difference as progressive or hierarchical targeted African Americans by imagining their racial difference in terms of "blood,"; thus the proliferation of terms such as "quadroon" and "octoroon," a concept like "the one-drop rule," and aphorisms such as "Blood will out" and "Blood is thicker than water." While "blood" dates as far back as the eighteenth century as a metaphor for identity and black racial inferiority, in the early twentieth century those perceptions of blood merged into a discourse of natural history and the nascent discipline of anthropology. As I noted earlier, the reliance on science as a justification for racism and exclusion waned in the early twentieth century, mostly because of the inability of scientists to confirm that racial difference was in any way biological; that did not mean, however, that racist ideas stopped relying on a rhetoric of biology to prove their validity. Haney-Lopez notes the irony behind racism's use of biology as "proof" of inherent racial difference: "Science's inability to confirm through empirical evidence the popular racial beliefs that held Syrians and Asian Indians to be non-whites should have led the courts to question whether race was a natural phenomenon. So deeply held was this belief, however, that instead of re-examining the nature of race, the courts began to disparage science" (7). Even as the courts were dismissing the sciences because of their disconcerting *in*ability to prove racial difference on the biological or cellular level, a vast array of scientists kept pursuing that goal of essentializing racial difference into the body.

Nevertheless, in the late nineteenth century, the belief that blacks and whites were fundamentally different and incompatible reigned supreme. The Supreme Court's majority decision in *Plessy v. Ferguson* (1896), which I discuss in more detail later in this chapter, emblematized what had already been widely accepted in the United States since the end of Reconstruction: that social and political equality between blacks and whites could not be attained because of the impossible biological gulf between them. One need only look at the history of lynching in America to have an inkling of how profoundly white Americans constructed black difference.[11] Though most Americans did understand that blacks were too deeply integrated into the nation to be forcibly removed (as Chesnutt suggests in his speech that begins the introduction), many Americans were unwilling to imagine that blacks could be citizens. James Kimble Vardaman, a candidate for governor of Mississippi in 1900, expresses the biological logic of American identity when he states that a black person is a "lazy, lying, lusting animal which no conceivable amount of training can transform into a tolerable citizen" (quoted in Gossett, 271). Vardaman's diatribe, delivered in the midst of a gubernatorial campaign, indicates how African Americans were often portrayed in public arenas (both in the South and the North) as inherently and biologically inferior to whites. It also illustrates how blacks' supposedly animal nature precluded them from being "tolerable" citizens.

Unlike the Chinese, who were recognized as having once built a great empire, blacks were thought to have no inherent culture or history of civilization. In 1892, Thomas Nelson Page, a southern author of the plantation tradition and diplomat who went on to become ambassador to Italy under Woodrow Wilson, wrote in the *North American Review*, one of the most respected news and opinion magazines in the United States, that a black man does not "possess the faculties to raise himself above slavery. He has not yet exhibited the qualities of any race which has advanced civilization or shown capacity to be greatly advanced" (403).[12] Page's assessment of black-white relations is worth repeating here because the popularity and success he enjoyed throughout the United States as a writer and lecturer indicate the extent to which many Americans were willing to entertain such notions. According to Page's argument, blacks have not always been slaves, and they have lived everywhere in the world and been exposed to great civilizations. But overall, they are a race characterized by "mediocrity," and the examples of "black self-governance in Haiti and Liberia are enough to make even black sympathizers admit that blacks cannot rule themselves" (404). According to Page, blacks are incapable of understanding the difference between right and wrong, and to recognize blacks as equal to whites merely "inflames the ignorant Negro, who has grown up unregulated and undisciplined. The Negro does not generally believe in the virtue of women. It is beyond his experience. He does not generally believe in the existence of actual assault. It is beyond his comprehension. In the next place, his passion, always his controlling force, is now . . . for the white woman." [13] Page describes black men as criminals by nature, raping and killing the white women and children of the South. In his book *The Negro: The Southerner's Problem* (1904), Page argues that for black men social equality means "to enjoy, equally with white men, the privilege of cohabitating with white women" (quoted in Gossett, 273). For Page, African Americans were disqualified from being real Americans because of their innate violence toward and desire for white women.

Others chose to discuss black intellectual and physical inferiority as an explanation for why Africans were incapable of building a civilization and why blacks in the diaspora could not create cultural landmarks. Nathaniel Southgate Shaler, writing in the *Atlantic Monthly* in 1884, notes, "The armies of the Old World, the inheritances of medievalism in its governments, the chance evils of Ireland and Sicily, are all light burdens when compared with this load of African Negro blood that an evil past has imposed upon us. The European evils are indigenous; this African life is an exotic, and on that account infinitely hard to grapple with" (699). He goes on to explain that although black children are "sur-prisingly quick, . . . in the pure blacks, with the maturing of the body the animal nature generally settles down like a cloud on that promise" (700). The physical development of whites coincides with their increas-ing mental development, but as an African grows older he becomes "less intellectual than he was before; the passions cloud and do not irradiate his mind." Though Shaler does not say so explicitly, he clearly suggests that the undisciplined "passions" of the African body impinge upon its mental development. These qualities are *inherent* in all Africans; they cannot be avoided, and they are always passed down from parents to children: "The fundamental, or at least the most important, differences between them and our own race are in the proportions of the hereditary motives and the balance of native impulses within their minds" (700). African Americans lack the desire to cooperate and the power of "con-tinuous will." Just as Africans in Africa did not build empires or great nations, so too are African Americans incapable of working together in business, politics, or society. The combination of a "high development of the religious impulse with a very low morality" (702) means that those of African descent are incapable of creating a family unit, forging monoga-mous heterosexual ties, or perpetuating a domestic tranquility. Shaler states that the African inability to grasp these basic tenets of civilization "part the men who make states from those who cannot rise above sav-agery" (702).

The same discourse of biological difference was used to a certain extent as justification for the exclusion of Asians, but, in a show of how flexible these practices could be, the racial difference of Asians was constructed as cultural, especially at the end of the nineteenth century. Whereas the exclusionary tactics for blacks tended to rely on the argument that their primitive natures made them incapable of controlling their animalistic instincts, the arguments used against the Chinese tended to focus on the allegedly ancient and premodern quality of Chinese culture and bod-ies. Rather than being excluded because they were *like* blacks racially, the Chinese were excluded partly because they were perceived as being the exact *opposite* of blacks. Where no African people had ever attained the heights of civilization, most Americans understood that the Chinese, by common definition, had. Unlike Africans, who could never be in-cluded because they had never achieved anything as a race, the Chinese could never be included because they had already achieved everything they could as a race. The Chinese were incapable of becoming part of a modern, thriving, Western nation; indeed, they were often thought of as antithetical to the Western nation. David Li argues that the mid-1800s to the mid-1900s constitutes a time in U.S. history when the figure of the "oriental" was constructed as an "alien" (5–6).[14] An editorial in *Harper's Weekly* in 1892 that actually *opposed* the extension of the Chinese Exclusion Act that year nevertheless articulates the prevailing American attitude toward the Chinese: "There is no question that the Chinese are the most undesirable of immigrants, because, with all their useful qualities, they cannot assimilate socially or politically or morally with Americans" ("The Chinese Exclusion Bill," 362). In a similar vein, Charles Somerville, a police reporter and journalist, wrote an article for the popular magazine *Cosmopolitan* in September 1909 that promoted the idea of the absolute difference of Asians, stating that the United States is a "mighty crucible in the welding of a new people—Latin, Celt, Saxon, Hun, Slav, Scandinavian, Hebrew, and even Ethiopian and Mongolian—the Mongolian alone has been the absolutely insoluble element" (818). As an ancient but stagnant culture, the Chinese simply could not understand, much less participate in, the culture and politics of a nation that was so modern and so radically different from its predecessors in the civilized world.[15]

Cartoon images from the early twentieth century portraying the Chinese imply how far they have fallen in terms of civilization.[16] China's political, cultural, and economic power is firmly located in its past; in the narrative of historical progress that Americans constructed for themselves, the acme of Chinese civilization had occurred centuries earlier. Stuart Creighton Miller posits that China's great antiquity served as a pointed contrast to her supposedly depraved contemporary state. Chinese stagnation is unfavorably compared to American modernization. There is, in other words, something so new and fresh about American modernity that the Chinese are incapable of being a part of it. When Louis J. Beck, in his book on New York City's Chinatown, published in 1898, writes that the Chinese have "the most ancient form of any surviving nation on earth; ours [meaning America's] the most modern" (quoted in Lui, 6), he insinuates a progress narrative into his comparison between the two nations. Miller maintains that "China was viewed as singularly impervious to nineteenth century ideals of progress, liberty, and civilization to which an emergent modern America was committed" (vii). The age of the Chinese nation rendered it impotent, an infantilized old man who must be cared for by younger and more virile nations. On 25 September 1869, *Harper's Weekly* published a cartoon, "The Last Addition to the Family," that exemplifies this view of the Chinese in relation to the United States. The family in question is presumably the family of modern nations. A female incarnation of America (robed in appropriately patriotic gear, with an eagle perched on her head) is the matriarch of this global family; in her arms, she cuddles an infantilized Chinaman. America's pose and tender downward expression suggest maternal solicitude, but the grotesque figure of the Chinese baby holds the viewer's attention. The Chinaman's body resembles that of a baby, but his face is aged and wrinkled, his expression recognizably sinister. What provokes our disgust is the fact that the Chinaman acts like a child, even in the way he holds his thumb near his mouth as if he were about to suck on it. This bizarre image of the Chinese man and the duality that he literally embodies—at once infantile and aged—suggests how completely anachronistic and out of synch the Chinese and Chinese culture are with the modernity that America represents.[17]

The sense of China as an anachronism, helpless, and in need of American protection can be seen in a Thomas Nast cartoon titled "The Chinese Question" published in *Harper's Weekly* on 18 February 1871. Here Columbia, beautiful and proud, protects an exhausted Chinese man who is being pursued by an angry armed mob of white men. The cartoon is clearly sympathetic to the plight of the Chinaman, who rests submissively at the feet of the female and imposing Columbia. Anti-Chinese fliers are plastered on the wall behind him; the sign at the very top reads "Coolie, Slave, Pauper, Rat-Eater." The signs on the board behind him proclaim that the Chinese "are dishonest, vicious, immoral, heathenish," "rat-eater[s]," "barbarian[s]," and the "lowest and vilest of the human race." Almost undetectable in the background is a fire; a "Colored Orphanage" is ablaze. Empty nooses hang ominously from a tree nearby.[18] Despite its sympathetic stance toward the visibly emasculated Chinese and the invisibly pitiable blacks, what I find striking about this image is the way the Chinese and African Americans are linked—in this example, by their scapegoat status—in contrast to Columbia, who defines what makes America great (being female, just, and beautiful). The cartoon captures the interracial dynamics that I am describing: African Americans inform American responses to the Chinese and vice versa.[19]

Finally, a Nast cartoon titled "Every Dog Has Its Day" that appeared in *Harper's Weekly* on 8 February 1879 provides a compelling example of the way Negroes and Chinese were paired with each other (and with other racial groups) in order to imagine the limits of American identity. The cartoon shows a Native American man and a Chinese man surveying a wall filled with anti-Chinese propaganda. In the caption, the

Native American says to his Chinese companion, "Pale Face 'fraid you crowd him out, as he did me." In the background, relaxing on a bale of hay, sits a black man, who says, "My day is coming." The Indian and the Chinaman survey a wall of nativist slogans, and prominently displayed above their heads on that wall are two sketches. The first image, small but distinctly drawn, shows a Native American (identified by his feathers) being chased by a train. Underneath the train are the words "Go West!" Right below this is a very similar image: a Chinese man (identified by his long hair queue) chasing after a train that is heading in the direction opposite the one above. I will return to this cartoon in the next chapter, but what I wish to highlight here is the fact that both the Chinese man and the African American man are anachronisms in this picture of America, albeit for very different reasons. The Chinese man is pictorially linked to the Native American standing with him in the foreground. The point is unmistakable: the Native American has already been forcibly removed from the American landscape, and the Chinese is in the process of being removed. Despite the sympathy that this cartoon ostensibly shows toward the plight of the Chinese, it reinscribes the notion that the Chinese are beyond history and that their civilization, like that of the Indian's, has reached its apogee and is on a downward spiral. There are two ways to read the response of the African American man in the cartoon. One is that since blacks have never been able to build a "civilized" society on their own, as Thomas Nelson Page argued, they have not yet seen their "day"—presumably their time of cultural or political significance—although their promise to do so carries a vaguely hostile tone. Another is as a warning that the next group to be targeted will be his. Either way, the cartoon suggests that Chinese and Africans are linked by the fact that they are temporal anachronisms. Blacks will never rise above their position as slaves and servants to the white race because of their lack of intellectual development and cultural drive, whereas the Chinese and other Asian groups are a corrupted, infantilized, and emasculated relic of past glories that can never be reclaimed. Blacks and Asians occupy polar opposite positions in relation to civilization and time, but that radical difference serves to strengthen the notion that Europeans are the pinnacle of development. White American domination makes no sense unless it is sandwiched between African failures and Chinese decay. "Difficult Problems Solving Themselves," another cartoon, published in *Harper's* on 29 March 1879, makes a similar point. An African American man and a Chinese man stand back to back, heading in different directions, the worlds around them almost parallel and yet separated literally (a signpost bisects the image into two equal parts) and metaphorically by the historical and cultural gap between them.

Perhaps the most visible and compelling illustration of the racial dynamics that persistently linked and then differentiated black and yellow bodies can be seen in two films released in 1915, both of which were enormously popular: D. W. Griffiths's *Birth of a Nation* and Cecil B. DeMille's *The Cheat*.[20] The focus in these films is on black and yellow male bodies and their relation to gendered whiteness and narratives of nationhood. Griffiths's film has received a tremendous amount of attention, both for its filmic innovations and its racial politics. It depicts the formation of the Ku Klux Klan as a heroic response to the danger that rampaging former slaves posed to white womanhood and the social order in the aftermath of the Civil War. The film follows the intertwining stories of the Camerons, a plantation-owning family in the South, and the Stones, a politically active family in the North. For the purposes of my argument, I will focus only on those elements of the films that represent black male or Asian male desire for white women. In *Birth of Nation*, two scenes in particular come to mind, and they are possibly the two most dramatic in the film. In the first, Flora Cameron, the daughter of the southern family, throws herself off a cliff to avoid being raped by a former slave, Gus; in the second, Elsie Stone (played by DeMille's favorite actress, Lillian Gish), the daughter of the northern family, is nearly attacked by her father's scheming mulatto assistant (ironically named Lynch) and barely saved by her love, Ben Cameron, the head of the new Klan and Flora's brother. What is visually striking about both scenes is the glowing white skin that Flora Cameron and Elsie Stone possess; both women are so beautifully and expertly lit that they seem luminescent. In her analysis of the film Michelle Wallace argues that DeMille's use of black-and-white nitrate film, "perhaps the most lovely medium ever invented" (88), is the most compelling example of how he manipulated the technology of film to convey racial ideologies. The contrast between the whiteness of the women and the artificially darkened skin of their respective attackers renders in cinematic language the discourse of black male sexual predation. These scenes are all built around the premise that the one equality that black men coveted above all others was equal access to white women. Michael Rogin notes in his analysis of the scene in which Gus is lynched, "Stopping black men from penetrating white women gave birth to a redeemed nation instead. The nation was born, in Gus's castration, from the wound that signified the white man's power to stop the black seed" (176). Thus, the "birth" in the film's title refers to the birth of a new nation that the Ku Klux Klan will reclaim for white America and, by implication, the control that this newly masculinized white America will exert over the bodies of white women and black men.

DeMille's *The Cheat*, while less well-known, has aroused interest of late because its star, Sessue Hayakawa, was a minor sex symbol in the early days of the film industry and went on to have a productive stage and acting career in Hollywood and Japan. Hayakawa's popularity with white female audiences in the early stages of his American film career (in the 1910s) was not merely due to his handsome appearance; according to the film critic DeWitt Bodeen, Hayakawa aroused in American women an "urge to experience sex with a beautiful but savage man of another race" (quoted in Miyao, 3). Indeed, the actor that Hayakawa is most often compared to is Rudolph Valentino, the matinee idol who rose to superstardom in the 1920s and who "redefined the imagery of a masculine star" in ways that subverted and dissolved the binaries between masculine and feminine, whiteness and racial otherness (Miyao, 3).[21] Although Hayakawa is best remembered for playing villains, Miyao argues in his study of Hayakawa's career that his portrayals were often "surprisingly varied and ambivalent" (7). Susan Koshy, however, cites Hayakawa's Tori as a "prototype" of early twentieth-century cinema's image of the Asian man: villainous, morally corrupt, and pathologically desirous of white women (*Sexual Naturalization*, 66).[22] The plot evokes not only the nation's anxiety about Asian sexual predation but also its fears of economic domination. Hishuru Tori, the wealthy and socially connected anti-hero, gives the married socialite Edith Hardy a loan after she has embezzled money from the Red Cross to play the stock market in an attempt to finance her increasingly extravagant lifestyle.[23] Edith cannot repay him immediately because her husband's investments have not yet "come in." Tori, knowing that she will do anything to cover up her financial malfeasance and avoid a scandal, demands that Edith become his mistress, an idea that horrifies her. When she goes to his house to pay him back with funds that her husband has just earned on the stock market, he attempts to rape and brand her. (The first scene of the film shows Tori bent over his desk in his study, branding his initials into the pieces of art that he so lovingly collects.) In a scene that recalls Flora Cameron's decision to jump off a cliff rather than succumb to her black attackers in *Birth*, Edith frantically attempts to flee Tori's advances. She grabs a gun, shoots him in the arm, and runs out of the room, whereupon her husband, Richard, who has followed her out of curiosity, comes in, picks up the gun, and is immediately charged with attempted murder. Richard, of course, goes on trial to protect his wife, determined not to reveal what she went through at Tori's hands. In stark contrast to Richard's nobility, Tori falsely testifies in court in order to revenge himself on Edith. It is only when her husband seems on the verge of being found guilty that Edith rises and hysterically confesses the truth to a packed courthouse. Curiously and provocatively she proves the validity of her story by partially undressing, revealing the brand that Tori managed to sear upon her bare shoulder before she escaped his clutches. The crowd and the jury surge forward in an attempt to lynch Tori, who takes refuge behind the judge's bench, an act that obviously reinforces the benevolence and fairness of the American judiciary system. Somewhat incongruously, given what has just happened, the happy white couple stroll down the center aisle of the courthouse as if it is their wedding day, with crowds of people cheering their passage on either side, all thoughts of their marital troubles and financial misdeeds forgotten.

Birth of a Nation and *The Cheat* represent African American and Asian men, respectively, as depraved sexual predators, but in intriguingly different ways. The black men who terrorize the nation and lust for white women in *Birth* are savage and instinctive, but the actors who play the would-be black rapists are white men in blackface; even the mere representation of black male lust for white women must be further contained by the presence of a white actor's body. These former slaves are never shown in close-up, never humanized, and never represented as possessing any kind of human feeling or civilized inclinations. Tori, on the other hand, is portrayed as attractive, urbane, and cunning. Whereas *Birth* shows the audience that black men are dangerous because they can never achieve civilization, *The Cheat* suggests that Asian men are dangerous because they have. This calculating representation of Asian masculinity is as dangerous to white women as the cartoonishly violent black man. Tori's more humanized (if no less repugnant) representation on film is undoubtedly a result of the relatively powerful place that Japan occupied on the global political stage; indeed, Paramount Pictures took the Japanese consulate's complaints about the film seriously enough to change Tori's ethnicity to Burmese for the 1918 re-release of the film. Both films call upon a discourse that represented men of color as sexually deviant, but both also highlight how that shared characteristic can be represented in vastly divergent ways.

Despite the differences that separate the two films on a filmic and aesthetic level, both represent these racial threats as gaining potency because of the political and economic instability currently roiling the nation (World War I was in its second bloody year when both films were released). The threat of African American and Asian sexual assault, as differently manifest as they are, unifies the film's characters and its audience; unity in the face of a racialized sexual attacker thus distracts attention away from the economic, political, and geopolitical pressures that the nation faced. The collapse of the old order (figured as the antebellum south in *Birth* and a time before market capitalism in *The Cheat*) is imagined as the failure of white masculinity; at the first sign of weakness, both films suggest, the black and yellow man will attempt to make inroads politically, financially, and sexually. In particular, the attack on the nation's safety and economic stability is figured sexually, as an assault on white womanhood, the purity of heterosexual love, and the sanctity of marriage.[24] The post-Reconstruction period increasingly figured the United States "as the white female body: silent, helpless, in immediate need of protection from the black beast" (Gunning, 7). Ultimately, the African American and Asian villains in both films serve to reconstitute the heterosexual, patriarchal family, made stronger now because of its survival of the threat that the racialized male body represented.

I would stake, however, that the document that most dramatically reveals the ways that the figures of the Negro and the Asiatic were intertwined in this period is the Supreme Court case *Plessy v. Ferguson* (1896). The case itself began on 8 June 1892, when Homer Plessy performed what the historian Michael Ross has called "one of the most famous acts of civil disobedience in American history" (4): he boarded a train car in New Orleans reserved for white passengers and announced himself a "passenger of the colored race." Refusing to be removed into the Jim Crow car, Plessy was arrested and fined for breaking Louisiana's Separate Car Act. This statute had been passed two years previously and required separate and equal accommodations "for blacks and whites on all passenger railways other than streetcars" (Lofgren, *The Plessy Case*, 29).[25] Plessy's arrest was part of a legal challenge orchestrated by a New Orleans citizens group that brought in the famed civil rights attorney and author Albion Tourgée to act as legal counsel on Plessy's behalf as his case wound its way through the courts. Justice John Howard Ferguson presided over the case in district court and ruled that because Plessy was traveling on an *intrastate* train (and not on an *interstate* train), the state had the authority to pass such laws. In 1896, the case of *Plessy v. Ferguson* finally reached the Supreme Court, and a seven-to-one majority declared segregation constitutional, affirming for the next fifty years the constitutionality of de jure segregation in the United States.[26]

When people think of *Plessy v. Ferguson*, they think of it as a case that, perhaps above all others, exemplifies Jim Crow and the lengths the nation would go to justify black exclusion. This is the most familiar narrative surrounding the case, and it is amply justified given the fact that *Plessy* became the legal foundation for all kinds of discriminatory legislation against African Americans. But this seemingly straightforward narrative of white racism and black exclusion becomes more complicated when we realize that another racial group plays a prominent role in the *Plessy* saga. As far as the historical record shows, there was no Chinese man on the train at the time of Plessy's arrest. So why do the authors of *Plessy's* majority and dissenting opinions, Justices Henry Billings Brown and John Marshal Harlan, respectively, include extensive discussions of the Chinese in their judgments? In attempting to answer this question I will put forth an alternative narrative of *Plessy's* significance, one that highlights the persistent if unheralded presence of the Chinese within the history of race relations in this country. By recontextualizing *Plessy* within a history of Afro-Asian relations, an alternative narrative of segregation's foundational moment on the train emerges, one that emphasizes the multilateral nature of racial encounters and uncovers the ways that Asian Americans and African Americans often contest and disavow the ties that persistently bind them together.

When one looks at *Plessy v. Ferguson* through the lens of Afro-Asian relations, what becomes apparent is not so much that Harlan and Brown have different racial attitudes but rather how they both invoke the Chinese to justify their differing interpretations of the eligibility of blacks to call themselves Americans. In order to prove that the Louisiana state statute requiring separate train cars for blacks and whites did not impinge upon the freedoms of African Americans, Brown invokes the case of *Yick Wo v. Hopkins* (1886).[27] In that case, the Court ruled that the attempts of the San Francisco Board of Supervisors to control the proliferation of Chinese laundries in that city were unconstitutional because the legislation targeted Chinese-owned laundries and no others. As Brown notes, "[The San Francisco city ordinance on laundries] was held to be a covert attempt on the part of the municipality to make arbitrary and unjust discrimination against the Chinese race" (quoted in Thomas, *Plessy*, 50). A law that was used to target one particular group and rob them of their livelihood could not be called "reasonable." In finding the Louisiana statute "reasonable," Brown sets a standard for government action, arguing that governing bodies should be able to "act with reference to the established usages, customs and traditions of the people, and with a view to the promotion of their comfort, and the preservation of the public peace and good order" (50). Thus, while the Court considers the practice of using city ordinances to shut down Chinese laundries to be an "unreasonable" act on the part of government, requiring blacks and whites to sit separately while traveling strikes Brown as being well within the discretionary power of the state.

Brown invokes *Yick Wo* as a legitimate violation of the Fourteenth Amendment because it clearly targeted one group, the Chinese, for economic persecution;[28] on the other hand, Brown argues that the Jim Crow laws, of which the Louisiana statute was one example, are not a violation of the equal protection clause because they are applicable to both blacks and whites. In other words, because a white man could theoretically be arrested for sitting in a colored train car, just as Homer Plessy was arrested for sitting in a white train car, Jim Crow laws were constitutional.[29] Brown dismisses Plessy's assertion "that the enforced separation of the two races stamps the colored race with a badge of inferiority," going so far as to say that if black people do feel inferior because of their separate accommodations, "it is not by reason of anything found in the [Louisiana] act, but solely because the colored race chooses to put that construction upon it" (quoted in Thomas, *Plessy*, 50).

Brown makes clear that "racial" differences between blacks and whites are insuperable and innate. It is precisely because of this racial instinct that blacks and whites cannot comfortably socialize with each other; the deeply ingrained nature of this instinct explains why laws and the intervention of courts are powerless to overcome them: "Legislation is powerless to eradicate racial instincts, or to abolish distinctions based upon physical differences, and the attempt to do so can only result in accentuating the difficulties of the present situation. If the civil and political rights of both races be equal, one cannot be inferior to the other civilly [163 U.S. 537, 552] or politically. If one race be inferior to the other socially, the constitution of the United States cannot put them upon the same plane" (quoted in Thomas, *Plessy*, 51). Brown constructs racial difference here to be innate and visible on the body (note his emphasis on "physical differences"); what makes blacks unworthy of social equality with whites is simply the fact that they are black. Although he never states explicitly that *Plessy* will strip blacks of any notion of belonging in the United States, his meaning is obvious: inclusion in America depends upon an understanding of racial categories in which the divide between black and white reigns supreme.

Brown's allusion to a decision involving the Chinese (*Yick Wo* was one of the few cases brought before any high court in which the Chinese won) in a case that grapples with the limits of African American inclusion is no coincidence. His model for American identity, based on a biological construction of race, permits the Chinese a marginal position within America *only* in order to prove how undeserving African Americans are. For Brown, American race relations represent a zero-sum game in which the Chinese can be included but African Americans are excluded.

Justice Brown incorporates the Chinese by citing case law, but Justice Harlan stages a much more dramatic and imaginative scene of African American and Chinese conflict in his dissent. In his opinion, Harlan famously asserts, "Our constitution is color blind" and denounces the injustice of segregation and its utter incompatibility with the ideals that founded the nation.[30] He suggests that the "thin disguise of 'equal' accommodations for passengers in railroad coaches will not mislead any one, nor atone for the wrong this day done" (quoted in Thomas, *Plessy*, 59). As a contrast to the deserving and fully American Negro, he introduces the figure of the "Chinaman." Because of the centrality of this passage to my argument, I quote extensively from the opinion:

> There is a race so different from our own that we do not permit those belonging to it to become citizens of the United States. Persons belonging to it are, with few exceptions, absolutely excluded from our country. I allude to the Chinese race. But, by the statute in question, a Chinaman can ride in the same passenger coach with white citizens of the United States, while citizens of the black race in Louisiana, many of whom, perhaps, risked their lives for the preservation of the Union, who are entitled, by law, to participate in the political control of the state and nation, who are not excluded, by law or by reason of their race, from public stations of any kind, and who have all the legal rights that belong to white citizens, are yet declared to be criminals, liable to imprisonment, if they ride in a public coach occupied by citizens of the white race. (58)

The scene's power stems from its sentimentality: the black man, a defender of American liberty and nation during the Civil War, who "risked [his life] for the preservation of the Union," must ride in the inferior separate car or be hauled away as a criminal, while the "Chinaman," who is utterly unassimilable into the American nation, can safely ride in the whites-only car. The African American man, by virtue of his loyal service to the preservation of the Union, has earned that place on the train in a way that the late-arriving Chinese man has not. Harlan's sentimental narrative of African American faithfulness scorned and Christian American ideals betrayed echoes the themes in *Uncle Tom's Cabin,* but instead of a devoted Christian slave, the black man has become a devoted Christian citizen.

Harlan's plea for black inclusion is actually based on the same logic as the *Plessy* majority: that American identity is racially exclusive. He disagrees with the majority on where this line should be drawn, not on whether it should exist at all. Harlan does not question the fact of Chinese exclusion; in fact, he depends on the assumption of inherent Chinese difference to emphasize his point that Jim Crow policies are unjust to African Americans. For Harlan, Jim Crow laws do not recognize the truth of racial identity: that blacks are Americans, whereas the Chinese never can or should be. Introducing the figure of the Chinaman into his defense of black citizenship allows Harlan to defend the place of African Americans in the United States by pointing to another group that truly does not meet any of the criteria for American citizenship. With the Chinaman serving as straw man, Harlan strives to reveal the social and political history that black and white Americans actually share. His dissent, though passionate, believes in the integrity of racial categories of difference, especially as they relate to national subjects.

Thus, Harlan's objection to the statute resides in its irrational inclusion of the Chinese man at the expense of the African American man. The racial line drawn between black and white in the statute permits people who are even more alien, the Chinese, to slip through the legal cracks and enjoy the privileges of white comfort. The train in this scenario becomes the space where citizenship can be fully realized or denied. In attempting to redraw the line of exclusion to include African Americans, Harlan shifts from a racialized dualism of black and white as the model for conceiving American citizenship to a model that emphasizes national origin and participation in American history, with the train acting as the symbol of that historical relationship. Harlan rejects the majority opinion's defense of segregation as a reflection of "racial instincts" and pleads for an American identity based on the national history (and traumas) that whites and blacks share. To put it another way, Harlan does not consider blacks and whites to be on opposite sides of a racial binary but on the same historical national side. According to Harlan, the Chinese do not belong on the train because they have not participated in the history and struggle with which the nation defines itself.

"Race" and "American identity" were not fixed concepts in the early twentieth century; they were discursive systems that affected the writers of that time and were in turn affected by those writers. The very constitution of "American identity" and its shifting valences in various public discourses stemmed directly from fears about the African American and Asian presence in the United States. To see the power, the failure, and the ramifications of that discourse, one must look at the writings of African Americans and Asian Americans in conjunction with each other.

3 / Estrangement on a Train: Race and Narratives of American Identity in *The Marrow of Tradition* and *America through the Spectacles of an Oriental Diplomat*

The encounter between the Chinese and African Americans in *Plessy v. Ferguson* takes place on a train, a setting that I will suggest in this chapter is not irrelevant to the Afro-Asian encounter. Despite their differences in genre, politics, and intended audience, both Charles Chesnutt's novel *The Marrow of Tradition* (1901) and Wu Tingfang's memoir *America through the Spectacles of an Oriental Diplomat* (1914) contain a scene in which an African American man encounters a Chinese man on a segregated train; both imagine *Plessy v. Ferguson*'s scene of interracial conflict on the train otherwise. Chesnutt's and Wu's restaging of the *Plessy* incident as one between Chinese and African American indicates how seamlessly Justice Brown's and Justice Harlan's exegeses on the case had been incorporated into the historical memory surrounding that "originary" moment on a Louisiana train car. These texts make clear that the Chinese man had become as integral to the telling of the tale of exclusion and national identity as the African American man whose rights were violated and the train where the drama was set. By inserting the Chinese presence into one of the most notorious scenes of white injustice against blacks, these textual re-enactments remind us to look for the multiple narratives of interracial and multiracial relations boiling under the seemingly smooth surface of literary history. They reveal the presence of the Afro-Asian relationship, no matter how hidden.

In this chapter I foreground the Afro-Asian encounter embedded (and mostly ignored) in this moment in order to map out the spectrum of political responses that this relationship both emblematizes and arouses.

I argue that these textual iterations illustrate the ways the Afro-Asian encounter can rupture the institutionalized narratives and spaces of nation. That *Plessy*, *Marrow*, and *America* focus on the relationship between the African American and the Chinese man indicates how closely bound those two figures were with each other in marking the limits of a racially exclusive American identity in the early twentieth century. But into this racial equation we must also factor another variable: the setting of this racial drama on the train. These textual moments give an indication of the persistent association during the early twentieth century between the train and racial conflict.[1] The long historical and cultural association between the railroad and African American mobility and Chinese labor also forms a crucial backdrop to these textual representations. The importance of the train within these histories, combined with the apportionment of space by race, forces each character to consider the relationship between African Americans, the Chinese, and the laws that are meant to define their relationships to America.

Most critical debates about the train in the United States center on untangling its symbolic status within the nation's imaginary. Rather than thinking of the train as merely a symbol of the nation or as a blank screen on which the narratives of nation are affirmed or negated, I want to focus on the train as a *site*, a place and space where ideologies of race and nation collide with anxieties about the alienating effects of modernity on the individual. Even if train travel in the early twentieth century was a fairly ordinary occurrence, riding the train nevertheless alienated the individual from a stable sense of himself by disrupting time and displacing space; at the same time, within its walls the train car replicated the racial and social hierarchies that Americans imagined to be stable and based on nature. While my conceptualization of the train owes a great deal to Michel de Certeau's definitions of and distinction between *space* (which is characterized by motility) and *place* (which is characterized by stability), I am interested in investigating how the train constitutes both simultaneously; the situational *density* of train space makes it not only a felicitous backdrop for racial interaction, but also allows it to activate interrogations of race and hierarchy in the first place. The train is key in these texts precisely because it is both a social space and a motile space, a faithful rendering of social strata and political hierarchies that are imagined to be stable (an "instantaneous configuration of positions," to borrow a phrase from de Certeau [117]) and a fluid space defined by its mobility and intersectionality. The train operates as a site where assumptions about the relationship between races and national identity are made transparent and then disrupted. The train, in other words, estranges the characters and then the texts themselves from the familiar categories of identity, belonging, and nationhood.

This chapter then moves on to examine the Afro-Asian relationship in *The Marrow of Tradition* and *America through the Spectacles* as it plays out on the train. Chesnutt keeps the figure of the Chinaman and the setting of the train in his restaging of the *Plessy* moment, a crucial early scene in his novel. A fictionalized account of the race riots in Wilmington, North Carolina, in 1898, *The Marrow of Tradition* follows the intertwining histories of two prominent families: the Millers, who are black, and the Carterets, who are white. While returning from a business trip north Dr. Miller, one of the novel's protagonists, is ejected from a whites-only car upon entering the South and is forced to sit in a segregated car. At a later stop Miller sees through the window a Chinese laundryman and a black maid enter the whites-only car without complaint from the passengers or conductor. After witnessing this scene he meditates on the social and political injustices that African Americans must endure in their own nation. The Chinese man's presence on the whites-only car catalyzes Miller's thoughts about who should be included in a narrative of belonging in the United States. Although this scene seems to share with Harlan's dissent a palpable hostility to the "Chinaman," I suggest that the presence of the Chinese man on the train disrupts a certain kind of narrative that the novel is promulgating, one that reveals the injustice of racial prejudice against blacks by emphasizing the tight familial and communal bonds that bind black and white families together. In other words, the narrative of race that *The Marrow of Tradition* wants to tell is one that focuses on white-on-black oppression and violence. Miller's encounter on the train with the Chinese highlights the limits of that antiracist narrative—not just in terms of race (Miller and the Chinese man) but also in terms of class (Miller and the black maid). The entrainment of the Chinese man causes Miller (and the novel itself) to pause in its politicized agenda and confront the racial and class categories to which the novel itself subscribes and that the space of the train makes transparent.

I then move to Wu's *America*. A chapter titled "American Freedom and Equality" contains Wu's only description of racism in the United States: while waiting in a train station Wu cannot decide if he belongs in the segregated waiting room or in the white-only area. This is the only moment of hesitation in a narrative that is otherwise remarkably assured. Though he can give voice to a subject position that Harlan and Chesnutt illustrate as mute, Wu cannot make sense of or transform the racial dynamics in which he finds himself enmeshed. Unlike the imaginary and silent Chinamen in Harlan's and Chesnutt's narratives, Wu gives voice to his discomfort and hesitates over the choice presented to him of white or colored compartments. Eventually a porter informs Wu that he belongs in the white area; Wu complies with the porter's decision but notes uneasily that he does not seem to belong in either space. His confrontation with Jim Crow politics belies the portrait of American equality that he paints throughout the rest of his memoir. Wu hopes to play upon the nation's sense of fair play to extend protection to certain Chinese migrants, but this is a moment that throws him off that track. His perplexed attitude and lack of criticism of the racism he encounters, in a memoir that is brimming with confident commentary on the United States, signal how polarized and entrenched debates about black-white racial difference were. Wu's and Miller's experiences point to the fact that both African Americans and Chinese are powerless within a system that tells them where to sit and where not to sit on a train, who they are and who they can never be within the nation. The Afro-Asian encounter disrupts, unsettles, and estranges narratives, just as the train once did to passengers. The interracial representations in these two works signal the limits to their anti-racist agendas, showing us the blind spots of some anti-racist critiques.

Chesnutt and Wu rewrite one of the most notorious moments in the history of race relations into a narrative in which the African American and the Chinese are estranged from the familiar racial scripts of the nation because of the other's presence on the train. But, as I suggest above, what makes these scenes so fascinating is that they do *not* emblematize what else is happening in the texts in which they are embedded; rather, they complicate in messy and undesirable ways the narratives that Chesnutt and Wu create. For most of *Marrow* and *America* Chesnutt and Wu engage in a straightforward rebuttal of the racial stereotypes that affect their respective groups (blacks are unworthy, the Chinese are unassimilable, America is better than its racist past and present), but the setting of the train forces them to reconsider *everything* that they themselves assume about race and nation. The Afro-Chinese encounter that Wu and Chesnutt describe ruptures their texts. Dr. Miller in *Marrow* and Wu in *America* experience a moment of profound estrangement on the train, in which conventional narratives of American democracy and racial relationships cannot adequately explain the position in which they find themselves. In one moment Miller and Wu confront not only the injustice of racial segregation but also the total inadequacy of traditional constructions of race and national identity (as spatialized on the train) in accounting for Afro-Asian interracial experiences. In these cases it might be fair to say that the space of the train dictates the space of the novel. Ultimately, it is not just the characters who are forced to confront a situation for which their previous understanding of who can be an American has left them completely unprepared; the narratives themselves seem unable to incorporate the interracial drama they depict on the train into the wider tapestry of racial equality that they weave. Not unlike the train wrecks that occasionally jolted the nation, the collision of black and yellow bodies on the train brought to the surface the interlocking relationship between the two groups in defining national identity in ways that both undermined national narratives of racial difference and also escaped authorial control.

It is striking but perhaps not surprising that these texts focus their imaginative energies on the same particular moment on a train as emblematic of racial constructions in the United States. Given the train's importance to American economic, personal, social, and political life in the early twentieth century, I would argue that this kind of outsized drama around exclusion and inclusion *must* happen on a train. Trains have generated a tremendous amount of attention from scholars interested in the histories of law, transportation, labor, technology, or capital; theorists interested in space and time; and cultural critics interested in exploring the symbolic vocabulary and narratives of nation. My reading of Chesnutt and Wu makes visible the relationship between space and technology in the making and upsetting of racial categories. As I consider how the relationship between space and technology figures in the making and upsetting of racial categories I show that two distinctive railroad historiographies impact how Chesnutt and Wu represent that estranging moment of interracial encounter on the train. The first focuses on the train as a technology of modernity that forces passengers to confront and perhaps question definitions of selfhood because of the way railway travel disrupts temporality and spatiality. The train car becomes a space marked by instability and fluidity, in which the contrast between space and time "out there" is always emphasized against the space and time in the car itself. The second aspect of railroad travel that I want to explore is the elevation of the train to mythic status within the national imaginary. As a symbol of the country's idealistic progress or democratic failures, the train car itself is a microcosm of social and political hierarchies, a battleground on which certain national conflicts over race, class, and gender can be contested.

De Certeau's distinction between space (*espace*) and place (*lieu*) is useful in illuminating these two different approaches. The segregated train car is a place that is transformed into a space by Asian and African American bodies. By raising these two issues separately, I do not mean to create a strict divide between the kinds of spaces contained within railroad spaces; quite the contrary. I want to see how theoretical models relating to the train as a spatial experience intersect with the particular and unique place that the train has had in the American landscape, literally and figuratively. This kind of intersectional examination of the train will enrich my analysis of the links that Chesnutt and Wu make between the train, nation, and race.

As I suggested, Chesnutt's and Wu's interracial representations on the train, although minor, cause a kind of rupture in their respective texts. This fits in with ideas that theorists such as Wolfgang Schivelbusch, de Certeau, and Henri Lefebvre have described extensively: that train travel in and of itself can be an alienating experience. One of the most evocative aspects of Schivelbusch's influential study *The Railway Journey* is that he asks his reader to consider seriously what train travel must have been like for the railroad's first passengers, for whom hurtling forward at thirty-five miles an hour might constitute a mystifying and terrifying experience. According to Schivelbusch, riding the rails "annihilates" the passenger's sense of self by distorting his or her *perception* of time (a trip that had always taken days now took mere hours) and space (a place that had been unreachable and therefore unknowable could now be visited). Schivelbusch postulates that "what was experienced as being annihilated was the traditional space-time continuum which characterized the old transport technology. Organically embedded in nature as it was, that technology, in its mimetic relationship to the space traversed, permitted the traveler to perceive the space as a living entity" (36). Riding the rails, because it disrupts the passenger's sense of time and space, defamiliarizes the viewer from his surroundings, uncovers the constitutive practices that are masked in other, everyday spaces, and destabilizes the social relations and cultural assumptions that make up our lives (33). Schivelbusch's depiction of train travel as a radical defamiliarization based on location calls to mind Foucault's definition of a "heterotopia," which exists as a "counter-site, a kind of effectively enacted utopia in which the real sites, all the other real sites that can be found within the culture, are simultaneously represented, contested, and inverted" (23). Unlike utopias, which present an ideal society but are not actual or real places, heterotopias are places that actually do exist. Like a mirror, a heterotopia reflects back images of the world around it as a perfect representation, yet defamiliarizes the viewer from his or her surroundings. Heterotopias uncover the constitutive practices that are masked in other, everyday spaces; they destabilize the social relations and cultural assumptions that make up our lives. The train as a setting heightens the anxiety that this scene of interracial recognition causes precisely because riding the train can be an estranging experience. Thus, the train operates as a countersite to "regular space" and "real life," catalyzing a moment of crisis in each of these texts.

Although train travel in this country has diminished since the introduction of the automobile, its centrality in American life during the nineteenth and early twentieth centuries cannot be overemphasized. The train played a constitutive role in the nation's imagined community. Alan Trachtenberg notes that the train was the most vivid and dramatic sign of modernity in that period (quoted in Schivelbusch, iv). Eric Sundquist calls the train a "symbol of racial politics in American culture" and a "field of ritual drama" (439). Leo Marx, in his famous work *The Machine in the Garden*, notes that the train was "the embodiment of the age, an instrument of power, speed, noise, fire, iron, smoke—at once a testament to the will of man rising over natural obstacles, and yet, confined by its iron rails to a predetermined path" (191). The awe that God and the Church once inspired was transferred in the nineteenth century to the machine and technology, what David Nye and others have called the technological sublime. Nye owes an obvious debt to Benedict Anderson when he argues that what held the nation together after the fall of religion was the reverence of its citizens for the technological marvels that dotted the nation.

What makes the train such an effective *symbol* is the fact that no exegesis was required in order for ordinary Americans to understand its significance. Marx notes that the train's "meaning need not be attached to it by a poet; it is inherent in [the] physical attributes" (192) of strength and overwhelming power. Trains carry symbolic weight, cementing the nation's image of itself as a self-contained political entity and a rising industrial power. America's fundamental experiences of time and space— and of itself as a nation—were altered and influenced by the train. As Schivelbusch notes, "We have now clearly stated the two contradictory sides of the same process: on one hand, the railroad opened up new spaces that were not as easily accessible before; on the other, it did so by destroying space, namely the space between points" (37). The train destroyed and created time; in the same way it destroyed one image the nation had of itself, even as it created a new one. The popularity and convenience of train travel necessitated the invention of time tables and time zones; the train inducted the country into a coherent understanding of itself as a nation-state. The train and the technologies it necessitated structured the nation. It merged the geographic landscape of the country with a mythological narrative of nationhood. With the train concepts like "the coasts," "the Midwest," and even "manifest destiny" became conceivable, established spaces that allowed the construction of a whole and unified nation.

Its constitutive role in creating the nation explains why narratives surrounding the train are conflicted. Scholars from a variety of disciplines have commented extensively on the train's contradictory status in American iconography: on the one hand, it is a symbol of progress that allowed Americans to experience the individual freedoms that only this nation could offer; on the other hand, it is a symbol of the antidemocratic tendencies that increasing industrialization and corporatization were wreaking on America. And it is not just in the United States that the train is often imagined to be a symbol of both impending revolution and inexorable reaction. In his "Paralipomena to *On the Concept of History*," Walter Benjamin muses, "Marx says that revolutions are the locomotive of world history. But perhaps it is quite otherwise. Perhaps revolutions are an attempt by the passengers on this train—namely, the human race—to activate the emergency brake" (402). Benjamin's gentle upending of Marx's vision of history—the train and its unrelenting drive forward are not barreling us toward a proletariat revolution and state but are to be resisted and abandoned by workers before disaster strikes— suggests how entangled the railroad had become in the political struggles of the day, not just as an icon, but also as a literal vehicle for change or stagnation. If anything Benjamin's statement reminds us how much the signification of the train fluctuated depending on who was onboard.[2]

According to Leo Marx, for many Americans, "to see a powerful, efficient machine in the landscape [was] to know the superiority of the present to the past" (192).[3] The train's democratic propinquities were supposed to be evident even in the configuration of American train cars, which had an open seating configuration (as opposed to European compartments). Something of the romance associated with the railroad, especially as it relates to the frontier spirit, can be seen in Willa Cather's novel *A Lost Lady* (1923). The nation's pioneering spirit is embodied by the aging Captain Daniel Forrester, "a railroad man, a contractor, who had built hundreds of miles of road for the Burlington—over the sage brush and cattle country, and on up into the Black Hills" (4). The Captain tells Niel Herbert, the novel's worshipful protagonist, "All our great West has been developed from [our] dreams; the homesteader's and the prospector's and the [railroad] contractor's. We dreamed the railroads across the mountains" (45). The great men who built the West with the captain are all connected to the trains, and like these men and their past Niel romanticizes the railroad. According to Niel, the "morning freshness," "the spirit of freedom," and the "princely carelessness" that defined the Captain's taming of the West are rapidly dissipating under the "petty economies" of "shrewd young men" (90) who are only interested in profitability and self-advancement. Niel's platonic relationship with Marian Forrester, the Captain's much younger, spirited wife, is at the heart of this novella, and Marian's stubborn (in Niel's eyes) unwillingness to fit in to the elegiac narrative that Niel weaves is its central conflict. The train in this novel is a physical link to the nation's glorious past, one that tends to be overlooked and taken for granted but that nevertheless reflects the pioneering spirit that made the United States great.

Perhaps the most significant element in the romantic narrative intertwining the railroad with the nation is the transcontinental railroad. Like Captain Forrester's narrative of self-creation and nation building, the famous photograph of the completion of the transcontinental railroad creates a particularly romantic and hopeful image of the country's past and future. Nye describes the photograph as capturing "the climax to four years' frantic work . . . when the first transcontinental line was completed with the driving of the 'golden spike.' A. J. Russell's carefully composed photograph showed the meeting of a locomotive from the east and one from the west, with women and representatives from each line clasping hands in the center. Above the workers, posed on the cowcatchers of the two locomotives, one man stretched to pour Central Pacific champagne into a waiting Union Pacific glass" (72). Missing from this famous photograph and Captain Forrester's recital is the contribution of Chinese, Irish, Mexican, and African American laborers, who worked under dangerous and oppressive conditions to complete the track; it is this hidden history of the railroad that buttresses de Certeau's description of the train as a prison on wheels and contrasts sharply with Captain Forrester's construction of the train as a "liberating machine" (Nye, 46). De Certeau calls the train a "bubble of panoptic and classifying power, a module of imprisonment that makes possible the production of an order" (111). Train companies worked hard to include the social conventions and niceties of polite company in the train and train stations, so that train travel became no different from sitting in someone's parlor; this in turn ensured the reinscription of those hierarchies onto newly emerging spaces.[4] Railroad companies provided not only colored cars, but also ladies cars for unchaperoned women travelers and usually smoking cars for white men. The placement of these different cars speaks volumes about how gendered and racialized bodies were imagined in relation to technology: smoking cars were often placed directly behind the locomotive car, so that the gentlemen bore the brunt of the ash, smoke, and noise that emanated from the engine; colored cars might also be placed directly behind the engine.[5] Station platforms were often not long enough to span the length of the car, so the engineer would pull the train forward to allow the white passengers in the rear cars to safely alight onto the raised platform. If the Jim Crow car was near the front, black passengers had to make a dangerous leap to board or detrain because of the graded and rough ground that ran parallel to the tracks. Ladies cars were usually placed at the very end of the train, often thought to be the safest car on a train; if a train collided with a stationary object or with another train (as they often did), the devastating telescoping effect that characterized such collisions would be less likely to affect the final car in the chain. The division of space within a train and the differentiation of safety standards based on that space solidified class, race, and gender divisions. It also hierarchized the value of black and white bodies, male and female, the working class and the wealthy. In this regard the train was an attempt to reflect as accurately as possible the social order of the day. But it also naturalized those hierarchies by making the transition between social spaces outside to those inside the train effortless and seamless. The train thus was an apparatus for state control and an instrument for ideological categorization.

The stratified and segregated apportionment of space on a train (by race, by gender, and by class) reflected economic realities as much as it did social imperatives. Railroad companies were the first national corporations; they enriched their owners and investors and wielded an enormous amount of political and economic influence. The explosion of train travel and the corporatization of railroad companies privatized public spaces into the hands of a few and mapped existing racial hierarchies of American society onto these spaces. Corporations—not individuals— owned the railroads and the land on which they were built. The railroad system was the result of and in turn further spurred on the spatial categorization of people. Rather than having a democratizing effect, the reorganization of spaces served to underscore the categorical differences between groups of people: "For passengers, private space merged with public space, but the result was not a democracy of travel. Regulations set by increasingly distant corporations and then by state authority overrode individual choice" (Lofgren, "Training America," 279). As Barbara Welke notes, the organization of space within a train made clear the contradiction between America's rhetoric about individualism and its everyday treatment of nonwhite people and practice of racism. The train brought forward those contradictions into a modern, technologically driven age, when definitions of liberty, autonomy, and the government's role in managing its citizens were changing (Welke, 249).

The role that railroads played in establishing interracial relationships and racial identities in the American nation-state can be seen to great effect in two cartoons from *Harper's Weekly*, one of which I discussed briefly in chapter 1. These cartoons slightly predate the time span of my study (they are from the 1870s), but they show how enmeshed the question of American identity is with the image of the train, even in the late nineteenth century. In the first cartoon, "Every Dog Has His Day," an African American laborer is in the background while a Native American and a Chinese man survey a wall of nativist slogans. One slogan, "Go West!," is the caption to a sketch of a Native American being chased by a train. Another slogan, "Go East!," is the caption to a sketch of a Chinese man chasing a train. In the first image the Indian is being chased off his land by the encroaching presence of American settlers, but the meaning of the exhortation under the Chinaman is ambiguous. "Go East!" could be an order to go to the East Coast of the United States, where there was a smaller Chinese population, or it could be an order to return to *the* East, that is, China. Both interpretations imagine the train as a symbol of America's insatiable desire for progress as well as an instrument of its growing determination to control racial groups within its borders; in this cartoon the train forcibly moves populations of people because of their racial difference. Even in a cartoon that sympathizes with the plight of nonwhite populations in the United States (as this one seems to) the train symbolizes the ideological and technological power to move undesirable populations in the name of manifest destiny. Native peoples are literally chased off their land in order to make way for progress, and the Chinese are forced to relocate because of whites' fears that they are contaminating the American landscape with their alien and un-Christian ways and stealing jobs from "real" Americans.

Another cartoon from *Harper's Weekly*, "Difficult Problems Solving Themselves," published in March 1879, shows an African American man on the left, standing underneath a sign that reads "To the West," and a Chinese man on the right, standing underneath a sign that reads "To the East." The Chinese man leans on the sign and reads a newspaper bannered "The San Francisco Hoodlum," with the headline "Go East Young 'Man!'" The black man stands next to his family and holds a suitcase that reads "A. Freedman from Bull-Dozed State, U.S." The signpost bisects the cartoon, and one can see in the background a church spire, an American flag, and, on either side of both men, "Welcome" signs on store fronts. Although a train is not depicted in this image, it is safe to assume that the two men are standing at a train stop (many of which did not include a station house but were simply marked along the tracks); tellingly the black man is holding up his hat and flagging something to the left of the image. Presumably he is flagging down a train, a common practice for passengers wanting to board in the late nineteenth century. The "problems" in the cartoon are the African man and his family and the Chinese man. That individuals from both groups were seen as "problems" and not as "citizens" is emphasized by the quotation marks around the word "man" in the newspaper headline. Here the train is part of an unjust solution: the problems that African Americans and Chinese pose will disappear because they themselves will simply disappear to another part of the country. The train facilitates the unjust movement of these oppressed groups, enabling people to flee economic privation or physical violence but also ensuring the continuation of such violence as rejected populations move from place to place in search of work or safety. It was the forced migrations of African Americans and Chinese that allowed the United States to maintain a stable sense of itself as a nation in the face of modernization and industrialization.

The two historiographies that I delineated earlier—the train as a space characterized by movement that alienates a passenger from himself, and the train as a contested but stable microcosm of a nation's imagined community—are both in play in my readings of Chestnut and Wu. It is perhaps because the train is a space of contradiction—overdetermined and at the same time a blank slate, mobile and stable—that it can serve as the *ur*-space for early twentieth-century depictions of racial tension. A segregated train starkly reveals the fictive nature of "natural" racial divisions. Those who do not fit the imperatives of segregated space, who might, in other words, be able to deconstruct the link between space and race—a mulatto like Homer Plessy, a well-educated professional like Dr. Miller, or a Chinese like Wu Tingfang—must necessarily be crammed into one space or another if the structure of racial difference is to retain its coherence and integrity. This process of racialization collides with the technological innovations that the train symbolizes. In these texts these technological innovations, which African Americans and Chinese helped to create, actually helped enable and then further the process of racialization. Racialization itself emerged as a kind of technology at the same time and because of the railroad itself. The railroads mapped and maintained social orders (racial, gender, and class-based) onto the newly emerging spaces that technology was making possible.

The Marrow of Tradition and *America through the Spectacles of an Oriental Diplomat* go further than merely making the train a symbol of racial divisions. The estranging power of American train travel forces the characters to grapple with the inadequacy of the racial binary that orders how they view the nation, as well as each other. In these cases the space on the train is painfully antipodean to the inclusionary politics that both works profess, but it momentarily enables the characters to see and engage with the assumptions that the nation possessed about what kinds of racial difference could exclude one from national subjecthood.

Chesnutt's *The Marrow of Tradition* revisits the racial tableau imagined by Justice Harlan. On the train the injustice of black segregation is most pointed and poignant, perhaps because the railroad has historically played an enormous role in the cultural and economic lives of African Americans. As Barbara Welke observes in *Recasting American Liberty*, slaves in the antebellum South used the metaphor of the railroad to describe their journey to the North and freedom: "That those assisting blacks to escape from slavery used the railroad—complete with conductor, lines, stations, telegraph, and sophisticated organizational structure—as a metaphor for their enterprise is a dramatic testament to the symbolic power of the railroad in the nineteenth century" (280). For many blacks who had been tied to southern land, first by slavery and then by sharecropping, freedom meant freedom of movement, and the railroad became associated with the struggle for economic, educational, and social improvement. After Emancipation the railroad "was not an escape to freedom, but an expression of freedom" (281). Railroads took African American families north to Chicago and New York City. They enabled men and women to leave the land on which their ancestors had toiled to search for better economic opportunities in other parts of the country. The ability to ride somewhere—anywhere—was itself a symbol of freedom and hope, and it found constant expression in blues songs and other forms of African American cultural expression.[6] Dr. William Miller, one generation removed from slavery, has himself benefited from the mobility that the train offered to African Americans. In *The Marrow of Tradition* there is perhaps no greater symbol of Dr. William Miller's middle-class and professional status than the fact that he rides the trains to and from the North to work and transact business. That he does this straightforward act, associated with gentility and class aspirations, indicates how important the train could be in defining a middle-class black identity.

The railroad not only symbolized black economic progress; it also offered a pathway to middle-class status for many black men. In the postbellum era railroad companies hired black men as brakemen and firemen in large numbers, although they were not permitted to fill the more visible position of engineer. The Pullman Company was one of the largest employers of African Americans in the country, employing many men as porters, an occupation that embodied many of the contradictions associated with the train that I delineated earlier. The porter was a servant and at the same time ensured the safety of his passengers; he was entrusted with caring for the most intimate needs of his customers and yet had the worst-paying job on the train. In *The Story of the Pullman Car* (1917) George Pullman's biographer, Joseph Husband, acknowledges that "the porters occup[ied] a unique place in the great fields of opportunity." According to Husband, Pullman preferred having African Americans as porters because they had been "trained as a race by years of personal service in various capacities, and by nature adapted faithfully to perform their duties under circumstances which necessitate unfailing good nature, solicitude and faithfulness" (155). White passengers were reassured when they saw a black man as a porter: his innate desire to fulfill his duty to his masters meant that he would be unfailingly caring. The master now was not a plantation owner but the Pullman passenger. Pullman's drive to hire black men as porters on his train only partly explains why the position became so exclusively associated with that group. The economic privileges that being a porter offered made it particularly desirable. For African American men being a porter meant enjoying relative economic stability and prestige, and these considerations more likely explain why so many black men aspired to that occupation.

Black men did not occupy the more visible or prestigious position of conductor or engineer; it was thus inevitably a white man (the conductor) who bore the responsibility of policing the segregation laws of the various states through which a train traveled. Chesnutt changes the circumstances of his train scene from *Plessy* by making his protagonist visibly black and unwilling to challenge the rules of Jim Crow. Unlike the conductor in the actual *Plessy* case, who was part of the orchestrated challenge to the Louisiana statute, the conductor in *Marrow* insists upon Miller's removal to the colored car. The conductor's irritation in the scene mounts, not because Miller objects to being moved, but because Dr. Burns, Miller's white traveling companion and fellow surgeon, vociferously insists that Miller should be allowed to remain. When Burns demands to know why the conductor must move his friend, the conductor counters, "I'm sorry to part *friends*" (53). The emphasis signals the conductor's incredulity that a black man and a white man can be "friends." The fact that Miller is well-educated and a respected physician does not persuade the conductor that he has the right to ride in the first-class car; in fact the injustice of the scene is heightened by the text's suggestion that the conductor is not the social or educational equal of Miller. Impatiently explaining why Miller must move to the other car, the conductor obediently mimics the logic of the majority opinion in *Plessy*: "'I warn you, sir,' rejoined the conductor, hardening again, 'that the law will be enforced. The beauty of the system lies in its strict impartiality—it applies to both races alike'" (55). When Burns insists on moving to the colored car to stay with Miller, the conductor becomes "calmly conscious of his power" and is "scarcely [able to] restrain an amused smile" at Burns (55). Whites cannot ride in the colored cars, just as blacks cannot ride in the white cars; this is the logic that the majority opinion of *Plessy* appeals to in explaining why segregation does not breach the equal protection clause of the Fourteenth Amendment.[7] One of Albion Tourgée's attacks on segregation laws in the *Plessy* case centered on the fact that it put undue pressure on ordinary railroad conductors to make a snap decision about a passenger's racial affiliation; here Chesnutt portrays the conductor as enjoying the power the system affords him, separating "friends" of a higher social class than he because the law grants him the authority to do so. Rather than the conductor's feeling burdened by the responsibility of making racial identifications, the novel reveals how the exercise of this kind of power corrupts individuals and renders them more pliable to the ideology of racial hierarchies.

Here the train is not a symbol of freedom so much as a space that enables passengers and employees to accept passively the racial hierarchies of the day. Miller winds up calming Burns's outrage rather than feeling any on his own behalf: "'Never mind, doctor,' interrupted Miller, soothingly, 'it's only for a little while. I'll reach my destination just as surely in the other car, and we can't help it anyway'" (55–56). Although we should certainly read Miller's resignation to the situation as a result of his own sense of powerlessness before the state and individual whites, the novel also emphasizes how Miller deliberately detaches himself from considering the social and psychological consequences of segregation at the moment he confronts it. He lodges no complaint about his treatment to the conductor; if not for the complaints of Burns, Miller would have moved quietly and with little embarrassment. When Miller explains that separate train cars are "the law, and we are powerless to resist it" (55), he echoes the passivity of the conductor and the passivity of the *Plessy* majority. The conductor mimics the language and logic of *Plessy* as if no explanation were required, and Miller accepts the logic of racial difference without asking for much of a justification.

The train triggers Miller's (and the novel's) discomfort, but it can also assuage and soothe its riders into believing that everything is all right. The novel explicitly undercuts the notion of the train as a democratizing space by linking the locomotive with Captain George McBane. McBane, the son of poor southern whites, made his fortune in the postbellum era by leasing convict labor, and he is one of the three conspirators (along with Major Carteret and General Belmont) plotting to overthrow the political gains African Americans had made in post-Reconstruction Wellington, North Carolina, the fictional town where the novel's action is set. Described as "offensive," "aggressive" (57), slovenly, and gaudy, with several buttons on his vest undone and a "solitaire diamond blaz[ing] in his soiled shirt-front like the headlight of a locomotive" (53), McBane, who is riding the same train as Miller, deliberately enters the Jim Crow car in order to smoke. The comparison between McBane and a locomotive is provocative in light of the fact that Americans tended to extol the democratic nature of the railroad because it enabled people to move across the country.[8] The novel suggests that the train, as a newly emerging space made possible by technology, reflected and reinscribed the racial, gender, and class hierarchies of the day. McBane's appearance also makes a farce of the "separate but equal" doctrine that formed the heart of judicial arguments for Jim Crow (249). McBane, like the (segregated) locomotive, emblematizes a voracious expansionism that makes a mockery of the egalitarian rhetoric of the nation.

Once in the colored train car, however, Miller does spend time ruminating on the nature of the laws that force him—an intelligent, middle-class man who has lifted himself and his family out of the degradation of slavery after just one generation—to vacate a train car because of his black skin:

> The author of this piece of legislation [that mandated segregation on trains] had contrived, with an ingenuity worthy of a better cause, that not merely should the passengers be separated by the color line, but that the reason for this division should be kept constantly in mind. Lest a white man should forget that he was white,—not a very likely contingency,—these cards would keep him constantly admonished of the fact; should a colored person endeavor, for a moment, to lose sight of his disability, these staring signs would remind him continually that between him and the rest of mankind not of his own color, there was by law a great gulf fixed. (57)

Anticipating de Certeau's claim about the train as a space that policed and classified, Chesnutt's formulation deconstructs the supremacy of the difference between blacks and whites. The sign of segregation ("whites only") points to its failure as a system of natural signification. The signs marking segregation actually point to the failure of the rationale behind segregation: the allegedly "natural" instinct for racial separation. In the majority opinion for *Plessy* Justice Brown calls upon this assumption when he notes, "Legislation is powerless to eradicate racial instincts, or to abolish distinctions based upon physical differences, and the attempt to do so can only result in accentuating the difficulties of the present situation" (quoted in Thomas, *Plessy*, 51). And yet if these racial instincts are so ingrained in the human mind, why are the "staring" signs reminding people of their racial categorization so prevalent? The law, as the passage from *Marrow* explicitly points out, plays a crucial role in maintaining the gulf between blacks and whites; it creates and then reinforces racial difference. Later during the same trip the train stops to board a group of black laborers who emerge "from the conspicuously labeled colored waiting-room" (60). Chesnutt suggests that the gulf between blacks and whites, whether considered in biological or social terms, is created by the state itself. The gulf is not the result of a natural racial aversion but the result of constant propaganda by ingenious state legislation.

Miller's thoughts are arrested upon the entrance of a figure who troubles the idea that the gulf between blacks and whites is constructed, who indeed troubles the entire foundation upon which American identity has traditionally been contested:

> At the next station, a Chinaman, of the ordinary laundry type, boarded the train, and took his seat in the white car without objection. At another point a colored nurse found a place with her mistress.
> "White people," said Miller to himself, who had seen these passengers from the window, "do not object to the negro as a servant. As the traditional negro,—the servant—he is welcomed; as an equal, he is repudiated." (59)

Nobody—conductor, passenger, nor the Chinaman himself—objects to the Chinese laborer's place on the white car. In this passage, as in Harlan's dissent, the Chinaman is a type, not an individual but a collection of stereotypes so familiar and recognizable that no description or elaboration is needed. Chesnutt's description of the "Chinaman" goes against the grain of what his own novel embraces politically. Miller's thoughts seem to echo Harlan's dissent that it is unjust for a race as "alien" as the Chinese to be allowed entrance into a space of white privilege while blacks are not.

Let me be clear: I do not think this scene is important because in it we can find clues to Chesnutt's "true" attitudes toward other racial minorities or the novel's anti-Chinese bias. Rather, I think this scene is crucial because it shows us what the presence of the Chinaman in a segregated train space enables, as well as what it shuts down. The figure of the Chinese permits the novel an opportunity to represent, if not critique, the multiple levels of oppression that African Americans, the Chinese, and other racial groups face. Race is just one factor in determining social relations, and depending upon the social and physical situation its visibility might be heightened or diminished in relation to other identity markers, such as class and gender. The train is a relational space, not a categorical one, and the presence of the black maid makes that strikingly clear. Indeed the presence of the black maid and the Chinese laundryman distinguishes this passage from Harlan's vision of racial hierarchies. This scene in *Marrow* depicts several levels of categorization, of which race is one. Chesnutt points to the inconsistencies that riddle the majority decision of *Plessy* by having his protagonist observe that blacks are allowed to ride in the whites-only car if they are clearly there in the capacity of servant; it is not blacks themselves that white people seem to find objectionable, but specifically a black person who looks professional and has pretensions toward the middle class. The reason whites do not want to mingle with blacks is not because of a natural aversion between the races; rather whites only want to be around those blacks who occupy subservient positions and can thus reassure whites of their own superior niche within racial hierarchies. Miller's middle-class status affronts conventional hierarchies of race, and he is thrust into the colored car, despite his apparent affluence, to remind him of his place in the racial order. The maid's subservient position to her white mistress means that she already is aware of her place, both racially and socioeconomically. Forcing her into the colored car would thus be redundant and unnecessary; the train's usefulness as a space of social control is not required in this instance because the maid's class affiliation makes her inferior status clear.

Miller is not thrown out of the car because of his race alone; nor is the Chinese laundryman allowed to remain in the white car simply because of his race (as Harlan suggests in his opinion). Rather, these characters are placed in their respective spaces because of a combination of race and class. The racial and occupational statuses of the Chinese and the black maid reinforce how relational the entire system of racial identification is and lays bare the assumptions that maintain supposedly natural racial hierarchies. The insertion of racial difference in this story—the presence of the Chinaman—enables the reader to see how class overwhelms interpretations of that racial difference. In other words, it is the pairing of the Chinese laundryman *and* the black maid that levels the racialized logic of Harlan's decision, suggesting the possibility that African Americans and Chinese are victims of multiple kinds of oppression.

The complicated portrait of racial relations that emerges from this moment on the train is in stark contrast to Miller's decidedly elitist beliefs about class and privilege. At the same time that *Marrow* destabilizes racial hierarchies with the presence of the Chinaman and the black maid, Miller posits that his superiority, regardless of his race, should earn him a spot in the first-class cabin. He wonders why black servants *and* Chinese laundrymen (who are linked by the class they occupy) are permitted to ride in the whites-only car after he is thrown out of a first-class coach (even though he has paid for it) and forced to ride in a colored car. Miller believes he belongs in the white car because he has shown himself to be a productive and loyal citizen; his professional class, his superior education, and his elegant manners all give the lie to the racist belief that blacks are inferior to whites. Nor does he seem to believe that the black laborers riding in the colored car also belong in the whites-only car as he does. Miller is annoyed by the loudness and rough manners of the workers; he finds them to be physically repugnant and his intellectual inferiors. Although the laborers are portrayed as good-natured, and the novel gently chastises Miller for his inability to sympathize with the black workers around him, Miller perceives the educational and social gap between himself and his fellow travelers to be genuine and insuperable: "For the sake of the democratic ideal, which meant so much to his race, he might have endured the affliction. He could easily imagine that people of refinement, with the power in their hands, might be tempted to strain the democratic ideal in order to avoid such contact; but personally and apart from the mere matter of racial sympathy, these people were just as offensive to him as to the whites in the end of the train" (61).[9] Miller's categorization of these workers as "afflictions" echoes contemporary sentiments about race and infection that have been explored by other cultural critics.[10] It is difficult to see exactly what kind of "racial sympathy" Miller possesses at this moment. Perhaps most alarming, Miller goes on to suggest that rather than segregation based on race, segregation based on class might be more just: "Surely, if a classification of passengers on trains was at all desirable, it might be made upon some more logical and considerate basis than a mere arbitrary, tactless, and, by the very nature of things, brutal drawing of a color line" (61). This moment of class snobbery on Miller's part is in tension with the novel's own potentially radical tableau of racial conflict. Miller perceives class difference to be a less "arbitrary, tactless," and "brutal" foundation for segregation than the color line. The use of the adjective "tactless" to describe the effect of racial segregation speaks to his political passivity as well as the kind of class privilege that he effortlessly assumes; that he believes that segregation based on class would be less "brutal" or "arbitrary" indicates how narrow-minded he is on issues of social justice. The rest of *Marrow* chronicles Miller's move from passivity to political awareness, yet this moment effectively marks the novel's refusal to follow through on the implications of what Miller witnesses: that Chinese laundrymen and African American serving maids are twice victimized by an economic structure that exploits their labor and a racial caste system that renders them invisible, except as servants. The encounter between the Chinese man, the black man, and the black woman has deeply unsettled the novel and introduced another, alternative framework for understanding the black experience in America. Seeing these two people board the train and occupy a space explicitly reserved for whites makes transparent how arbitrary the entire system of racial classification is, and by extension the constitutive role that race plays in determining who can be an American.

The novel does not pursue this potential complementary and complicating narrative of racial difference and class alliances. Instead Chesnutt returns to more familiar if still vital territory by having Miller invoke a "democratic ideal," refocusing the novel on its project of reconciling the nation's rhetoric of egalitarianism with its practice of antiblack racism. Within a few paragraphs the novel has moved into a much more abstract register, and in the last few pages of the chapter the omniscient narration takes on a rambling quality. Calling Miller a "philosopher" (59), the narrative then chronicles his thoughts about whether or not white people value the rights of animals more than they do the rights of black citizens (60). After the black laborers get off the train the text describes Miller as having a "light heart" (61), which is buoyed in the end by the "consoling reflection" that nature had provided Africans with "a cheerfulness of spirit [that] enabled them to catch pleasure on the wing, and endure with equanimity the ills that seemed inevitable." Miller then finishes with the biblical quotation "Blessed are the meek, for they shall inherit the earth" (61–62). The haphazard nature of Miller's thoughts and his reliance on an old trope of black endurance in the face of oppression indicates how urgently Chesnutt is working to reground his novel in more recognizable racial terms. Having witnessed the Chinaman and the black maid boarding the whites-only car and been disturbed by its implications, Miller busies himself with reading his newspaper, and the novel does not pursue the political potentialities that the image stimulates. This turn to Miller's disjointed, philosophical thoughts signals the text's own discomfort with what it has depicted on the train car. Rather than exploring the new territory opened up by the space of the train, the novel returns to its historical milieu. The Chinese laundryman and the black maid are never mentioned again.

The novel's unwillingness to open up further the radical spaces that it has imagined might be a function of Chesnutt's own persistent inability to imagine the Chinese as Americans. As Brook Thomas notes, in the 1920s Chesnutt sympathized publicly with the Lums, a Chinese American family living in the South who wished to send their daughter to a white school. The Supreme Court decision *Gong Lum v. Rice* declared people of Chinese descent to be nonwhite, and the law legislating that students of Chinese descent attend nonwhite schools was found to be constitutional. In a speech on the topic Chesnutt recognized that the student, Martha Lum, and her family were American citizens. However,

Thomas argues that Chesnutt's assumptions about how Martha Lum's father gained his citizenship status reveal the limits of his own thinking about who can be Americans. Chesnutt assumes that the father, who is a citizen, has been naturalized, apparently unaware of the fact that various pieces of legislation and court cases had made naturalization impossible for the Chinese since 1882. Thomas points out that this assumption of naturalization on Chesnutt's part not only gestures to his ignorance about case law dealing with the Chinese but also suggests his inability to imagine a native-born Chinese population ("The Legal Argument", 331–32). In *Marrow* Chesnutt disrupts racialized national narratives with his description of Chinese and African American laborers occupying seemingly forbidden spaces, but ultimately the novel cannot push past the limits that it deems arbitrary and abusive. Chesnutt wrote, "There is practically but one race problem in the United States and that is the Negro problem" (quoted in Thomas "Legal," 332). *The Marrow of Tradition* belies the certainty of that remark.

While the Chinese man who appears in Harlan's dissent and Chesnutt's novel cannot be ignored, he also cannot be heard. Wu Tingfang's memoir fills that silence to an extent. Unlike Chesnutt's Chinese laundryman, Wu was neither laborer nor laundryman. He was born in 1842 in Singapore, a member of a well-known and wealthy Chinese family. He became the Chinese minister to the United States in 1897, a few years after the first extension of the Chinese Exclusion Act in 1892, and his tenure in that office ended in 1907. His chronicle of his life in the United States as a diplomat, *America through the Spectacles of an Oriental Diplomat*, was published in 1914, more than a decade after Chesnutt's *Marrow* was published and eighteen years after the *Plessy* decision. Drawn from Wu's experiences living, working, and traveling throughout the United States, *America* records his thoughts about what makes America and Americans unique. A colorful and popular figure on the Washington and New York social and lecture circuits, Wu worked tirelessly to protect Chinese interests in the United States and encourage dialogue and understanding between the two nations. His affection for the United States drew fire from his more conservative critics back home: in October 1901 the *New York Times* reported that it was very likely that Wu would be recalled from his post because "his popularity abroad is proof that [Wu] is not sufficiently loyal to the interests of China" ("Want Minister Wu Recalled").

The *New York Times* was certainly a fan of the minister; in the decade that he spent in the United States the *Times* carried more than a dozen

articles chronicling his activities, praising him for his wit, gracious-
ness, and good sense. In May 1901 the newspaper reported a speech he
made at the tomb of Ulysses S. Grant, in which he praised the former
president and Union general for his military acumen and his successful climb from humble origins to the presidency. The *Times* queries, "Is
it an unreasonable inference that a people whose representative freely
and with sincerity makes an address like this in praise of a great man of
the American Republic must have in their nature some capabilities for a
national life not alien to our own, and with [whom] we can hope in the
future to co-operate helpfully for both?" ("Wu Tingfang Pays Tribute").
While the *Times* points to the possible affinity that the Chinese, as embodied by Wu, might have for the political system of the United States,
the newspaper articles in general do not directly address the injustice of
Chinese exclusion; rather, they support the notion that the United States
should allow the migration of Chinese laborers into the country, because
the Chinese are not as frightening as popular opinion would have everyone believe.[11]

Wu uses his position as a foreigner and an outsider to philosophize on
the nature of Americans and their social and political institutions, using the travel genre to reveal to readers truths about their home country
that they themselves presumably could not reach as insiders. Although
the Chinese were reviled and seen as unutterably foreign in the United
States, most Americans understood that China had once been a world
power, culturally and militarily. That history, as well as his own rarefied
position as an educated diplomat and the popularity he enjoyed while
living in the United States, accorded Wu a level of respectability that
would have been difficult, if not impossible, for a Chinese laundryman
or laborer to call upon. Wu's socio-economic situation also meant that
he had the education to write his memoir in English, thereby reaching
the widest possible American audience, and the leisure time to pursue an
interest outside of his occupation. The fact that he was a Chinese diplomat with a career in the United States (and not a Chinese laborer working in the United States) makes his book palatable to his middle-class
readers by virtue of its association with an established literary tradition
and the author's respectable public and political position. Unlike Edith
Eaton, who wrote about the Chinese living in Chinatowns, Wu's position
as diplomat and minister prevented him from offering a snapshot into
Chinese life in the United States. He never mentions the plight of Chinese laborers in the United States or the political turmoil that his home
country was undergoing, preferring instead to focus almost exclusively

on America. Nevertheless, his experience of life in the United States as a Chinese man at a time when the Chinese were despised resonates with the situations of Chinese laborers. In other words, Wu must have been well aware of his alien status within the United States. Despite his constant efforts he was unable to lift the Chinese exclusion ban or influence American foreign policy in a manner favorable to China during his tenure as foreign minister.

What makes Wu's memoir so unique in Asian American letters is the fact that it focuses a critical eye on the United States itself. Although Wu includes brief descriptions of Chinese cultural practices that he must have known would interest an American reading audience, he is most interested in explaining America to Americans.[12] His observations about the inconsistencies and promise of American life and his status as a foreigner of high social standing inevitably position him in line with writers such as Alexis de Tocqueville (1831) and J. Hector St. John de Crevecoeur (1782); his outsider status, Wu implies, makes him the most accurate commentator on the United States. The curiosity that nations such as China and Japan piqued in the United States explains why such memoirs, which promised to describe the exotic customs, dress, and manners of the writer's home country, were often popular with the reading masses (Yin, 63).[13] To a certain extent Wu's memoir merges the exotic flavor of the oriental tale with the authoritative voice of the travel narrative. But what is striking about *America* is the extent to which America really is the object of his analytical gaze. With encyclopedic chapter titles like "American Government," "American Women," "American Business Methods," and "American Costumes," Wu sets himself up as an ethnographer and the United States his object of study. Ethnographic treatises of East Asian countries had been around for centuries, but Wu's assumption of the ethnographic mantle turns the table with a vengeance on what had become an American preoccupation.[14]

Wu's assumption of the ethnographer's mask may have been in response to the constant ethnographic gaze to which he himself was subject during his sojourn in the United States. Notices of his public appearances often included detailed descriptions of his dress. He is described wearing "silken robes of yellow and drab with a black cap of fez modestly jeweled" ("Southern Society Dinner"); "in his native costume of red and green silks was a picturesque figure in the row of black and white [tuxedos]" ("Silk Association Dines"); in a "gorgeous costume of yellow figured silk with small pink jacket" ("Minister Wu"); and in "a dark red jacket with peacock green sleeves" ("Farewell"). Despite this curiosity,

Americans naturally expected foreign writers and visitors to write about the United States positively, as well as in an entertaining manner. Unlike most ethnographers, who would not have expected their subjects to read their studies, Wu acknowledges his readers' expectations in his preface and apologizes to any he might offend with his depiction of the nation's "defects" (4). To justify his criticisms he invokes a "lady friend" who insists that he write about "our country" in an "impartial and candid way" (3). The use of the phrase "lady friend," with its connotations regarding class and gender, emphasizes Wu's own gentlemanly status and implies that the work is being done as a chivalrous favor. The contemporary iconography of Sino-American relations, which often represented China as an emasculated old man and the United States as his strong, motherly protector, is gently challenged in Wu's text.

From the start of *America* the United States receives Wu's praise for its egalitarian principles. While gently chastising the country for co-opting the terms "America" and "American," he also commends the nation as a "pleasing and unique example of the principle of democracy" (4). It is this courteous tone that he employs throughout the memoir that has led some to criticize Wu for not being a more vocal advocate for Chinese laborers in the United States. According to Xiao-Huang Yin:

> [The delicate position of the Chinese in America], in addition to genuine courtesy and tolerance derived from traditional Chinese philosophy and fear of displeasing their readers, often prevented them from speaking their ideas frankly. Although Wu declared that he would "make frank and unreserved comments on America," his criticisms in general were politely muted, tangential, and innocuous except in the case of racism. When he did make a criticism, he tried to put it in a humorous way and serve the dual purpose of showing that Chinese are both "cultivated" and [have] "good-will." (68)

Yin argues that Wu's critical comments about the United States are spoiled by his tentative tone and unwillingness to alienate his American readers. Yet in the review of the memoir in the *New York Times* Wu's critical tone is duly noted. The review, "Wu Tingfang Tells Us Just What He Thinks of Us," summarizes the more amusing moments of the memoir, mentioning specifically (although without comment) Wu's perplexing experience in the segregated railroad station, which I will examine below. The review notes, "Not for nothing has Mr. Wu devoted his life to diplomatic service. He has thoroughly mastered the art of presenting an unfavorable comment gently, courteously, and blandly. He starts a paragraph with a compliment and ends with another, but in between he sometimes expresses severe criticisms." As well, according to Yin, Wu hoped that his work might serve a dual purpose and that his descriptions of America might become a model for the modernization of China (65); in fact Wu writes that the customs of the American people could be "instructive to the Chinese" (3). Because China is in her infancy as a republic, a friendly relationship between the two countries would be beneficial to both, with the United States taking a leading role. Wu's advocacy of closer U.S.-Chinese ties takes for granted America's imperial efforts in Asia as well as its need for foreign markets to fuel its expanding economic reach. In this vein Wu writes benignly about American colonial interests in Asia: "It is well known that there are great potentialities for the expansion of trade in China, and as the Philippine Islands are close to our shores, and the completion of the Panama Canal will open a new avenue for the enlargement of trade from America, it will be to the interest of both nations to stretch out their hands across the Pacific in the clasp of good fellowship and brotherhood" (39). The logic of Wu's flattery and his acceptance of American expansion is shrewd: if the United States will not be swayed on ethical grounds to treat Chinese immigrants and laborers justly, perhaps gently reminding the United States of its burgeoning economic interests in China and Asia will force it to pay more attention to the Chinese government's complaints.

Wu saves his most pointed attacks on the United States for his discussion of the Chinese Exclusion Act: "The more substantial cause for dissatisfaction with the United States is, I grieve to say, her Chinese exclusion policy. As long as her discriminating laws against the Chinese remain in force a blot must remain on her otherwise good name, and her relations with China, though cordial, cannot be perfect" (22). He supplies a summary of the events leading up to the act, starting with the Burlingame Treaty of 1868 and blaming labor unions on the West Coast for the decision forbidding the entrance of Chinese laborers because of their fear of cheap Chinese labor. This "disagreeable difference" (26) between China and the United States is exacerbated by the fact that the "Chinese should be singled out for discrimination, while all other Asiatics such as Japanese, Siamese, and Malays are allowed to enter America and her colonies without restraint" (25).[15]

Although he campaigned endlessly for the repeal of the Exclusion Act, Wu's attitudes toward Chinese exclusion were not uniformly negative; they were complicated by economic and ethical considerations, as well as his ideas about the role of the nation-state in policing its boundaries. As a matter of course Wu concedes that the government has every right to screen out those "undesirable" immigrants who are criminals in their native country, "ignorant and illiterate" (10). However, he argues that welcoming hard-working and honest immigrants, regardless of nation of origin, should form the backbone of immigration law. He criticizes what he believes are unjust immigration policies, but his criticisms are based on drawing a distinction between the deserving immigrant and the undeserving immigrant. In other words, Wu does not challenge the government's right to exclude "undesirable" elements; he just wants the Chinese not to occupy that category. This position echoes Dr. Miller's own critique of Jim Crow in *Marrow*; he objects to a system of exclusion that labels him second-class, but he does not necessarily object to the notion of exclusion itself. Wu objects to the exclusion of Asians simply because they are Asians, and he objects as strongly to allowing any white person into the country simply because he or she is white: "So long as honest and steady workmen are excluded for no reason other than they are Asiatics while whites are indiscriminately admitted, I fear the prosperity of the country cannot be considered permanent" (11). In a speech to the New York Southern Society delivered over a decade earlier than the publication of *America* Wu warns that the Chinese exclusion laws "have kept out the better class of my countrymen" ("Southern Society Dinner").[16] He implies with this comment that Americans have been unable to form an accurate picture of the Chinese because stringent immigration laws have discouraged the "better classes" from coming.

While Wu's criticism of the United States is muted, to say the least, he does address the thorniest issue of the day, segregation, when he discusses America's distaste for social castes and elitism. According to Wu, trains, perhaps more than anything else, emblematize America's "dislike of distinction of classes, which arises from the principle of equality" (39). Wu makes this argument based on the fact that trains do not indicate the class of the train or how much the passenger might have paid for his fare: "The railroad cars are not marked first, second, or third as they are in Europe. It is true that there are Pullman cars, and palace cars, with superior and superb accommodation, and for which the occupant has to pay an extra fare, but the outside of the car simply bears the name 'Pullman' without indicating its class, and anyone who is willing to pay the fare may share its luxuries" (39). The irony, of course, is that although the cars are not *labeled* first or second class, those distinctions are maintained within the cars themselves, as Wu himself points out. Privilege in the United States is based on one's ability to pay, not on one's caste.

Ironically the cars that Wu labels democratic were built by exploiting the very Chinese laborers he tries to defend throughout the memoir. Contemporary Asian American literature has tapped into that history by making the railroad and the Chinese men who labored on and rode it central tropes in reclaiming a heroic and martial conception of Asian American masculinity. Writers such as Frank Chin and Maxine Hong Kingston have made the railroad an important landmark in chronicling and imagining the history of the Chinese in America, reminding readers that Chinese blood, sweat, and muscle built the transcontinental railroad for the United States in the late nineteenth century. Ironically one of the prime motivations for constructing a transcontinental railroad was to increase trade between Asia and the United States; a railroad spanning the American continent meant that goods could be transported more easily from the East Coast to the "Far East."

The contribution made by the Chinese to the building of the transcontinental railroad cannot be overstated. Chinese labor constituted almost 90 percent of the Central Pacific Railroad's workforce, and Chinese laborers tackled the dangerous task of laying down track through the treacherous Sierra Mountains (Takaki, 228–32). Yet despite their importance to the railroad, they were paid a fraction of what their white counterparts made. Like all railroad men, they worked long hours under extremely dangerous conditions. The lack of pay and the hazardous conditions led to strikes and violent countermeasures. In the spring of 1867 the Chinese railroad workers went on strike, demanding higher wages and a shorter work week. The Central Pacific broke the strike by cutting off supply lines to the Chinese camps, forcing the men to return to work or face starvation. As I mentioned earlier, despite the contribution of Chinese workers, not a single Chinese person was pictured in the famous photograph at Promontory Point in 1869. Chinese participation in one of the greatest technological feats in American history had been effectively erased.

This is an erasure that Wu never mentions in his memoir. Given his desire to present an image of the Chinese as civilized rather than as criminal laborers, perhaps Wu's omission is not surprising. The cozy insiderism that Wu cultivates changes, however, when he becomes a passenger on the train. His position as confident ethnographic investigator is shaken by his experience. In the very same paragraph in which he good-naturedly extols the virtues of American equality he makes the following brief observation, which the *Times* labels an "interesting personal incident" ("Wu Tingfang Tells Us Just What He Thinks of Us") and which constitutes the crucial scene in my analysis:

> I should mention that in some of the Southern states negroes are compelled to ride on separate cars. On one occasion, arriving at the railroad station in one of those states, I noticed there were two waiting rooms, one labeled "For the Whites," and the "For the Colored." The railway porter took my portmanteau to the room for the white, but my conscience soon whispered I had come to the wrong place, as neither of the two rooms was intended for people of my own complexion. (39)

This passage is notable for two reasons. First, there is no sense of injustice over the fact that segregation exists. Indeed, as in the previous passage, Wu seems content to point to the gap between what Americans claim versus what Americans do without offering an overt critique of the segregation he describes. The difference here is that Wu himself has become situated in that breach, an object to be placed as the porter commands. The moment suggests the extent to which a generalized American "dislike" of class distinction does not translate into the actual absence of distinctions. Second, this is perhaps the only passage in which the supremely confident Wu seems to lose his composure, even if for a moment. The choice he faces as to whether he belongs on the "white" or "colored" train causes anxiety; when the porter escorts him to the whites-only area, he feels that he is in the "wrong" place. Yet he cannot imagine himself fitting in comfortably in the colored area. He is thus left with the sense that there is no place for him in either space. He feels a sense of guilt and displacement, and although this does not translate into moral outrage, it is the reader's first indication that something is amiss in the way racial categories operate within the country.

Although Wu's confrontation with American segregation does not occur on a moving train (as it does in Harlan and Chesnutt), the feelings of anxiety and confusion that it arouses are very similar to what we see narrated in *The Marrow of Tradition* and in *Plessy v. Ferguson*. Like Miller in *Marrow*, Wu is told by a railroad employee where he belongs. A porter takes him to wait in the whites-only area of the train station, perhaps because of his position as a diplomat, perhaps because he understands "colored" to mean black only. Whatever the reason, Wu's position as diplomat has insulated him from the many economic, social, and political privations that Chinese laborers and miners faced, but his experiences in the station nevertheless place him in a position that he has scrupulously avoided throughout his memoir: that of racialized other. The position of privileged commentator that he has so assiduously cultivated comes crashing down as he finds himself an object in American racial politics; he transforms from an ethnographic observer to an ethnographic object in a moment. His response to this incident counters the charge made by Harlan, that the Chinese were taking advantage of antiblack prejudice to gain unscrupulously the benefits of citizenship for themselves. As Wu's anxiety indicates, riding in the whites-only car of a train was no more of a privilege for the Chinese than riding in a colored car was for African Americans.

The description of the incident in the train station, coming as it does in the middle of a chapter titled "American Freedom and Equality," upsets the otherwise controlled narrative Wu offers. This discomfiting incident cannot be reconciled with Wu's opinion of America as a land of "freedom and equality." As if to cover up his confusion and make up for his momentary loss of narrative control, he moves on immediately to another, seemingly safer topic, that of the streetcar. According to Wu, streetcars are even more democratic than railroad cars because in a streetcar a millionaire or a lady might ride next to a laborer or a "coolie": "There is no division of classes; all people, high or low sit in the same car without distinction of race, color, or sex. It is a common thing to see a workman, dressed in shabby clothes full of dirt, sitting next to a millionaire or a fashionable lady gorgeously clothed" (39). Wu praises the streetcar as a more appropriate mode of transportation for a republic because of its seemingly democratic apportionment of space. Rather than focusing on the space that seems to upset his easily managed image of America, he moves to a space that reestablishes his authoritative position. This quick textual leap onto another, safer topic echoes the move that *The Marrow of Tradition* makes after Miller's observation of the laundryman and the maid. Like Chesnutt, who goes on to a discussion of Miller as a "philosopher" in order to camouflage the far-reaching potential of the racial alliance that he has narrated, Wu moves on quickly to the supposedly safer streetcar without exploring the inequalities that his observations have brought to the light. He makes absolutely no attempt to reconcile the signs of segregation with the rhetoric of equality for which he praises the United States. Nor does he attempt to account for why a segregated train station should make him feel as if he were in the "wrong place." Wu's experience begs the question: If neither room was intended for people of his "complexion," then what space does a

Chinese person have in the United States? Wu never attempts to answer this question. His final thoughts in this chapter do not allude in any way to the racism or segregation that he witnessed; incredibly he concludes by stating, "America is one of the few nations which have fairly well approximated the high ideal of a well-governed country" (45). The memoir itself ends without a conclusion, and so the reader is left without any kind of explanation or rationalization for Wu's guilt-ridden moment in the train station.

There is no way to know if Wu knew anything about the *Plessy* decision or Chesnutt's novels, but that is hardly relevant. Having spent a decade in the United States playing the game of foreign diplomacy, he observed and learned enough about American customs to know how important the train was to the country, both ideologically and economically. He does not need to have read the Supreme Court case or *The Marrow of Tradition* to grasp the significance of the encounters he describes. His narrative reminds us that the Chinese person's presence must be accounted for in the early twentieth century if we are to understand the racial and political dynamics of the early twentieth century.

Indeed both Chesnutt's and Wu's inclusion of a Chinese figure in a scene on a Jim Crow car with whites and blacks indicates the extent to which the Chinese had become as firmly entrenched in this primordial scene of racial relations and national definition as the figure of the Negro himself. Wu is not the Chinaman that Harlan and Chesnutt imagine, and that is precisely the point: without Wu's adaptation of the "perfect train" story, the Chinese man would have remained a silent player in *Plessy*'s and *Marrow*'s calculations of racial and national identity. Although *America* is no more adept than the other texts at changing the landscape of racial difference (it seems in fact much more circumspect than the other works), Wu's memoir transforms the Chinese laborer, whom Harlan imagined riding comfortably in the whites-only car eighteen years previously, into a victim of the same racial oppression as the black man with whom Harlan sympathizes.

Although Homer Plessy's arrest in 1892 and subsequent challenge of the Louisiana statute mandating racial segregation on intrastate train travel aroused little interest in the national press, its impact can be seen in cultural productions that consistently associate the railway with racial tension. The contradictory symbolism that the train represents, as an icon of both American freedom and American racism, and that *Plessy v. Ferguson* brings into relief, reappears time and again in early twentieth-century American literature. Read as individual works or within their respective literary traditions, *The Marrow of Tradition* and *America through the Spectacles of an Oriental Diplomat* attempt to solve the dilemma of who can claim to be an American. But placing these works in relation to each other raises a whole host of issues that might not be immediately evident to those reading the texts exclusively within African American or Asian American discourses.

Both works expose the chasm between America's rhetoric of equality and inclusion and the reality of race-based exclusion, but they also betray their own unease over the possibility of presenting an alternative model for American subjecthood that can include *both* African Americans and the Chinese. While Chesnutt and Wu use the train to contest the racialization of American identity that the Supreme Court set up in its majority opinion of *Plessy*—a construction that would serve as the foundation for racial segregation for the next half-century—neither can overturn the comfortable if unjust systems of racial categorization already in place. If the train is a place where the inconsistencies between the realities of racial identities and the mythology of American inclusion can collide and be confronted, a location that renders starkly the inconsistencies and inequalities that lie dormant underneath the ideals of the United States as a nation, then it is also a space where such hypocrisies can be safely confined and left behind. In their re-enactment of Homer Plessy's arrest, neither of these texts imagine the way the incident *should* have gone; instead they depict the various ways that the incident can go wrong all over again. A former slave who loyally served the Union, riding like a criminal in a second-class car; a respected doctor, one-generation removed from slavery, forced to vacate a comfortable train seat for which he paid; the urbane and supremely confident Chinese diplomat, guiltily being led into a station waiting area reserved for whites—each text reimagines the scene from another perspective of injustice, but none of the works can conceive of a situation in which African Americans and the Chinese can ride trains in comfort while the democratic ideal to which they all claim to subscribe can be achieved. The train, which momentarily estranges the characters from received notions of American identity, does not lead to a more suitable or just alternative to the racial system already in place. Thus each work reverts to safer, more familiar master narratives about the power of the American democracy or myth of American class mobility. As quickly as the Chinese man and African American man collide in this constitutive space to destabilize the way that race and belonging have been conceived in the United States, the Chinese man vanishes again, leaving the black protagonist to go about the more familiar if no less important narrative of white-black violence. When the characters leave the train they leave behind the anxiety that the racial encounter on the train made possible and return to familiar narratives that ignore the unsettling possibilities that they just faced. The estrangement ends with the train ride.

4 / The Eaton Sisters Go to Jamaica

If Asian American literature were a family drama, the Eaton sisters would no doubt be its stars. The daughters of a penniless but aristocratic British artist and his English-educated Chinese wife, the Eaton sisters are widely considered to be the first authors of Asian American literature. There is also no doubt who would play the heroine and who would be cast as the villain in this family drama. In Asian American literary history, Edith Eaton is often represented as the "good" sister, while Winnifred, if she is mentioned at all, is relegated to the role of the "bad" sister (Hattori, 229).[1] The reason for this dichotomy is familiar to any student of Asian American literature. Edith is lionized as the resistant subject because she self-identified as Chinese at the height of anti-Chinese prejudice and wrote sympathetically about the Chinese in a series of journalistic pieces and short stories dating from the early twentieth century. Her younger sister is vilified as complicit in racist ideology for taking on a Japanese persona, claiming to be the daughter of a Japanese aristocrat, and penning numerous romantic novels and short stories set in Japan, about which she claimed to be an expert. While Edith toiled in Chinatowns, writing articles for local newspapers about the humanity of Chinese laborers, Winnifred wrote a number of bestsellers and was interviewed saying things like "I cannot forget that it was America who first set my mother's people [i.e., the Japanese] on the road they are traveling. Commodore Perry opened the door" (quoted in Birchall, 139). Edith died relatively young, in penury, and was buried in Montreal under a monument paid for by the local Chinese population with the inscription "The righteous one does not forget her country." Winnifred married a wealthy Canadian, worked and socialized in Hollywood for years as a screenwriter, cast off her Japanese identity during World War II, and lived comfortably to the ripe old age of seventy-nine.

The sisters are linked by the bonds of family and by their shared status as the first writers of Asian descent to write in English in North America, but they are clearly separated by the narrative I have just delineated, which has tended to celebrate the courageous Edith and marginalize the opportunistic Winnifred. According to Tomo Hattori's characterization, Asian American cultural critics have labeled Edith a "conscientious social critic," while Winnifred is often considered a "sellout and race traitor" (278). Shawn Wong, in his introductory note to Edith's short stories, exemplifies this bifurcation of critical appreciation when he asserts that both Edith and Winnifred had a "choice" (presumably about their authorial persona as well as the content of their fiction) and that readers are fortunate that "Edith made the choice to tell the truth" (65), suggesting, not so delicately, that Winnifred chose to lie. Game, set, match, Edith.

Edith's canonization in Asian American studies as literary fountainhead and Winnifred's relative absence from the field can be explained by the fact that critics trumpet Edith's resistance to American attitudes toward the Chinese and interpret Winnifred's self-promotion as a Japanese noblewoman as a form of racial hatred. This explains why Edith and her small body of prose have been the subject of numerous dissertations, conference papers, articles, and books, while Winnifred and her extensive oeuvre have remained relatively obscure. Much work has been done in the past decade to address this critical imbalance. Tomo Hattori, Sean McCann, Viet Nguyen, and Dominika Ferens have offered complex and important readings of both sisters from the perspective of Marxism, cultural studies, and ethnography. This recent scholarship reflects a trend in Asian American literary studies to read Edith in less hagiographic ways and to question the rhetoric of authenticity and betrayal that Winnifred's authorial persona and fiction has provoked.[2] In his article exploring model minority discourse, published in 1999, Hattori describes the fiction of both sisters as revealing the ways that racial subjectivity becomes interpellated and then commodified under systems of capital.[3] In *Race and Resistance* (2002) Nguyen uses the critical history behind the Eaton sisters as an example of how Asian American critics disavow their own commodification of race; through that disavowal writers like Edith and Winnifred are read in ideologically rigid ways.[4]

I agree that the literary critical history that lavished praise on Edith and punished Winnifred reveals more about the ideological allegiances of Asian American studies and offers a decidedly retrograde model, based on authenticity and identity politics, for thinking about Asian American identity. But I would not go so far as to say that critiquing Winnifred's and Edith's choices regarding self-identification (whether textually or not) is *always* motivated by a desire to present Asian American literary history in the most resistant manner possible. In my own analysis of the sisters, I find it impossible to dismiss the racial politics and material circumstances under which the texts were produced and marketed. Although I consider the recent critiques of Edith's texts to be thought-provoking and persuasive, I find the attempts to recuperate Winnifred's novels to be decidedly less compelling. Because I believe that the revisionist pendulum regarding Winnifred (although not Edith) has swung too far in the opposite direction, I do not attempt to recast her into an anti-racist crusader, nor do I read her texts as subversive revisions of racial hierarchies.

Although I argue that the racial politics behind Edith's and Winnifred's authorial personae and texts still matter, I agree with Nguyen and Hattori that the sisters have served as a kind of bellwether for the politics of Asian American studies generally. Given the fact that their work and lives enable critics to reflect on the state of the field, it is perhaps not surprising that the Eatons, whose work played an instrumental role in establishing an Asian *American* literary canon, are becoming central figures in the hemispheric approaches that are beginning to attract attention within Asian American studies. The Eatons are probably the first Asian American authors who can legitimately be called hemispheric in terms of their literary output and their lives. Both were born in Quebec, worked in the Caribbean, and lived their adult lives traveling throughout the United States and Canada; while the lion's share of Edith's work is set in western American Chinatowns and most of Winnifred's fiction takes place in Japan, the sisters also used Jamaica as the scene for both fiction and nonfiction. Despite the fact that the sisters each spent less than a year in Kingston (Winnifred lived there around 1895, and Edith came the following year), this chapter will put the spotlight on the fiction set in that location, positing that this location and the interracial encounters they depict there provide a key for understanding how they imagine their own subjectivities within a North American context. Their negotiation and representation of what it means to be Chinese within the nation-state are formed and re-formed by their encounters within a racially stratified colonial society. If the works of Edith and Winnifred are the cornerstones of an ethnic canon based on the nation, their Jamaican texts reveal the extent to which the struggles of Chinese in the United States cannot be separated from racial politics of colonialism abroad. Just as the Eaton sisters do not disavow the global in their construction of the national, for better or worse, they do not ignore the role that blackness has to play in the contingent and ambivalent articulation of their own identities as biracial Chinese women authors.

For the Eatons, then, the Afro-Asian encounter is not a moment of estrangement from national narratives, as it was for Charles Chesnutt and Wu Tingfang; it is instead an opportunity to apprehend and complicate their own subject positions as women of Chinese descent. In their memoirs they grapple with the ways that their identity as Chinese women are bound up in their attempts to situate themselves as women authors. For Edith and Winnifred, being a biracial Chinese woman writer means defining oneself against the trope of middle-class white womanhood; this in turn necessitates grappling with the pervasive fear surrounding black male sexual predation. Although both Edith and Winnifred depict interactions with the black people who inhabit Jamaica, each employs the Afro-Asian encounter in her fiction and memoirs for radically different purposes. The chapter starts by examining the relationship between gendered and racialized authorship and representations of blackness in Winnifred Eaton's memoir *Me: A Remembrance* (published in 1915). Although she had become famous as the half-Japanese novelist Onoto Watanna, Winnifred's anxiety about her biraciality and whether it impacted her legitimacy as an author, heroine, and "lady" pervade her depiction of herself as "Nora Ascough."[5] In her attempt to claim for herself the historically precarious position of professional woman writer, Winnifred turns to representing the black male rapist. In writing about her experiences in Jamaica, particularly with Afro-Jamaican men, she thus calls upon a long-standing cultural fantasy of the white woman in distress and black male rapist in order to define her own racial, gendered, and class status. Winnifred's memoir puts into action the supposition that if white womanhood in the early twentieth century is partly defined by the instinctive and uncontrollable desires of black men, then in order to be considered a white woman and obtain the privileges associated with that position one must be coveted and frightened by black men. The black figures do not merely solidify her claim to white womanhood; they also legitimate her claim to the privileges of authorship—a claim that has historically been rendered tenuous by her gender and her biracial status.

Feminist scholarship of the past three decades has shown us how difficult it was for women writers of the nineteenth century and early twentieth to claim the status of authorship. Nina Baym writes that the "myth of America" promised any individual "complete self-definition" in a land "untrammeled by history and social accident" (11); the problem with this vision, according to Baym, is that the society to be cast aside and the landscape to be conquered are "depicted in unmistakably feminine terms" (12). In a discourse that equates Great American Literature with tales of critique and that simultaneously represents women as the symbol of the society that must be resisted, it is no wonder that the woman writer becomes, not merely an anachronism, but "the enemy" (9). Nora's horrified reactions to the romantic advances of the Afro-Jamaican men displace some of the static surrounding her racial otherness; the fact that her response is intuitive and unthinking, thus trading upon an essentialized vision of white womanhood, strengthens her claim to the position of author and heroine. Afro-Jamaicans become the stock figures that prove her status as a white woman, a lady, and a protagonist, even though her story depicts her as a working girl, without family, and of "foreign" blood. The stain of racial otherness is wiped clean with the Afro-Asian encounter.

Edith Eaton, known by the pen name Sui Sin Far, was never as popular an author as her sister.[6] Her representation of the interactions she had with blacks contrasts with Winnifred's. My examination of this relationship, which is central to her short memoir, "Leaves from the Mental Portfolio of an Eurasian" (published in 1909) and developed further in her short stories about the Spring Fragrances, "Mrs. Spring Fragrance" (published in January 1910 in *Hampton's Magazine*) and "The Inferior Woman" (published in May 1910 in *Hampton's Magazine*), makes up the rest of this chapter. Rather than shoring up her sense of entitlement as a white woman, Edith's interactions with Afro-Jamaicans in "Leaves" do the opposite; they remind her of how contingent and imperfect her own mimicry of white womanhood is. These encounters with the island's African population, which ironically make it easier for Winnifred to pass as a white woman, make it impossible for Edith to do the same, and she ends up outing her racial identity to the colonial establishment.

Edith's inability to perform white femininity in the face of white racism and black oppression while in Jamaica manifests itself in the short fiction that she sets in the United States, "Mrs. Spring Fragrance" and its sequel, "The Inferior Woman." Unlike "Leaves," neither story has black characters; nevertheless, both are engaged in the broader questions of racial exclusion that "Leaves" raises. Although Edith's purpose undoubtedly was to write fiction that depicted the Chinese in a sympathetic light, the language of these short works compellingly reveals the interconnections between Chinese exclusion and other types of racism; both make their intervention by focusing on the rhetoric of racial difference that national narratives use in order to exclude minority groups. "Mrs. Spring Fragrance" and "The Inferior Woman" critique two kinds of narratives that were central to the articulation of an American identity: first, that American identity is universally available, exceptional, and invested in principles of equality and individuality, and second, that races of people can be placed into hierarchies based on physiological and cultural differences. My reading strategy takes into account the contemporary discourse that linked racial difference and national identity; this comparative approach enables one to see how Edith's defense of the Chinese implicitly critiques systemic racial practices that oppressed African Americans as well.

Winnifred's choice of a Japanese identity reflects the ethnic distinctions within American orientalism. Diana Birchall posits that Winnifred's selection of a Japanese pen name and persona reflected the fact that she was "always a good canny judge of what was popular" (35). Dominika Ferens points out that "the turn of the century was a perfect moment to become a 'Japanese' novelist" (117). To quote the organizer of the St. Louis World's Fair of 1904, "The interest of the world is centered on Japan" (quoted in Christ, 675). Although stories about Japan and China were probably equally popular with the American reading public, the Japanese were thought to be more modern than their Chinese neighbors, a distinction that the Japanese government encouraged. Carol Ann Christ notes that "Japanese actions during the St. Louis fair . . . portrayed China as needing Japanese protection and cultural conservation" (683). While "the Western press abas[ed] China as a vulnerable, unwieldy conglomerate ripe for exploitation," reporters lionized and admired Japan's ascent to "modern nation" status in the span of a few decades (683). Winnifred's decision to adopt an aristocratic persona also probably influenced her decision to pass as Japanese, since the Japanese were thought to be more refined and cultured than any other nationality in Asia. Of course, this "canny" ability to position herself in the most marketable way possible came back to haunt her during World War II, when the Japanese became a hated and feared enemy,[7] and it was this decision to try to attain widespread popularity by pretending to be Japanese that doomed her to decades of dismissal by Asian American literary scholars.

Although Edith is widely regarded as the first figure in the Asian

American literary canon, it is actually Winnifred who was the first Asian American writer, since her novel *Miss Numé of Japan* was published in 1899. By 1915, the year of *Me*'s publication, Winnifred's career as a successful popular novelist was on the wane, although she was still well-known. The memoir was originally published anonymously, but it did not take critics long to uncover the true identity of "Nora Ascough," the memoir's narrator and subject.[8] The question of *Me*'s genre is a vexing one and worth lingering over for a few moments. The introduction, written by Winnifred's friend and fellow author Jean Webster, declares the "main outline of everything" in the work to be true, "though the names of people and places have necessarily been changed in order to hide their identity" (1). Nora, the text's heroine, confesses at one point that her "success [as an older woman] was founded upon a cheap and popular device" (153).[9] Here Winnifred seems to be acknowledging her pose as a Japanese woman, a curious admission given the fact that she continued to publish and grant interviews under the name Onoto Watanna and did not publicly renounce that persona until World War II. In a sensitive and astute afterword to the work, Linda Trinh Moser writes, "The textual silence regarding Eaton's Chinese ancestry makes it difficult to read *Me* as an autobiography, let alone an ethnic one, but it is not impossible. Despite fictional elements, *Me* draws parallels between the lives of Nora and Eaton" (358). Katherine Hyunmi Lee argues that *Me* should be read as a work of autobiography not only because it is a "narrative befitting its chameleonic author," but because doing so sheds light on the assumptions that underpin Asian American subjectivity, issues that are also present in later Asian American works such as Maxine Hong Kingston's *The Woman Warrior*, another text that blurs the line between fiction and nonfiction (182).

Relatively little is known about Winnifred's young adult years (the time span that *Me* covers), so it is impossible to confirm how much of the memoir is based on actual events in her life. Moser describes the lengths that the narrative goes to render itself as true to life as possible, and in broad terms, there is a tremendous overlap between Winnifred's experiences and Nora's.[10] Like Nora, Winnifred moved away from her large family in Montreal to try her hand at journalism in Kingston, Jamaica; like Nora, Winnifred left Jamaica after less than a year to move to the United States. Although *Me* covers only a few years of Nora's young life, she makes reference at various points to her future success as a playwright and writer, the kind of success that Winnifred enjoyed throughout her professional life.

The question of genre is undoubtedly an important one, but I would argue that it is another version of the authenticity debate that has long plagued Asian American studies (and Winnifred Eaton), and its lingering presence on the critical scene has obscured the genre and narrative issues that the book raises repeatedly. By focusing on whether the memoir is fiction or nonfiction, critics have overlooked what is the most striking aspect of the text: the excessive and persistent manner with which Nora reassures the reader of her own attractiveness, pluckiness, and innate good breeding. This is the aspect of the text that draws the most initial comment, but no critic has attempted to theorize the purpose that such nausea-inducing self-promotion might have. Certainly there is nothing subtle about Nora's portrait of herself as a young woman, and at times her hyperbolic self-congratulation verges on the ridiculous. She describes herself as having "strains of genius somewhere in me": "I had always lived in a little dream world of my own, wherein, beautiful and courted, I moved among the elect of the earth. Now I had given vivid proof of some unusual power!" (4). She also insists, "[I have] the most acute, inquiring, and eager mind of any girl of my age in the world" (6). Speaking of an older, wealthy romantic rival, she scornfully asserts that if this woman were stripped of her expensive clothing "she would [be] transformed into a common thing": "But I? If you put *me* over a washtub, I tell you *I* would have woven a romance, aye, from the very suds. God had planted in *me* the fairy germs" (349–50). The relentless vanity that Nora displays prompts Birchall to ask bemusedly, "Was 1915 a time of such unselfconscious individualism that a woman could so openly and naively express her admiration for her own uniqueness? Other literary heroines . . . were praised for their singularity, but Winnifred's brand of self-congratulation was at times almost breath-taking" (28).

In the postmodern age it is easy to interpret such passages as expressions of textual irony or satire. Nora's embrace of romance certainly calls to our attention the conventions of the genre, including its class, sexuality, and racial erasures. But her heightened desire to fit the mold of the romantic heroine does not necessarily indicate an attempt to deconstruct those conventions, as postmodern critique often does. Nora assumes that the values she enthusiastically espouses are the values of her reading audience. I would argue that there is nothing ironic or tongue-in-cheek about her, and that the narrative presents her and her version of events exactly as she sees them. *Me* works extremely hard to prove that Nora is the most unique and desirable young woman to have ever lived and therefore deserves to be the center of the narrative. Her narrative must be constructed in this way—with the fairy-tale references and the language of romance—in order to account for the fact that she is, as she says, the daughter of a woman from an unnamed and exotic land. Nora's defensive posturing about her own exceptionalism is symptomatic of other anxieties within the text, surrounding her racial identity, to which she only obliquely refers, her class affiliation, and her status as a woman trying to earn a living as a professional writer. Nora herself does not directly reveal the "far-distant land" from which her mother hails, although she mentions that her father in his youth lived in India, China, and Japan (3) and that she herself is "foreign-looking," like her mother (6).

These moments of pleasurable self-mythologizing are the most visible signs of Nora's attempts to authenticate her own experience as a legitimate heroine, which is tied to Winnifred's attempt to solidify her status as author. Winnifred's donning of the mantle of authorship is legitimated by this text's emphasis on its own adherence to the storytelling conventions of romance and fairy tales. Anxieties about authorship are shot through Winnifred's oeuvre. Her novel *The Heart of Hyacinth* (1903) tells the story of Hyacinth Lorrimer, a white woman who has grown up believing that she is half-Japanese. This novel contains many of the same plot elements as Winnifred's other Japanese romances: a quaint Japanese setting, interracial love, cultural clashes, and a child-like, much-adored heroine. Hyacinth learns of her monoracial background when her biological father, who believed that she was dead, comes to claim her from her Japanese foster mother, Madame Aoi, and her foster brother, Koma, who is himself half-British and the son of a British nobleman. Even after learning the truth of her birth and parentage Hyacinth defiantly insists that she is Japanese and resists returning to her father and stepmother. Early in the novel Koma, who has just returned to the village after being educated in England, resolves that Hyacinth must learn to think of herself as a "Westerner," as he has. He holds a mirror up to Hyacinth's face, and she, "possessed by an uncanny fear," declares passionately, "That's not me. No! That's [a] lie. I am here—here! That's not me" (81). Hyacinth's shock stems from the fact that the mirror does not reveal the Japanese subject she believes herself to be. Koma, who blends perfectly the West and the East, is determined to show Hyacinth that she has been passing and that she needs to reconcile her American appearance with her Japanese upbringing. Although her reflection initially upsets her, she eventually learns to find the image she sees in the mirror attractive: "She had discovered the secret of the mirror, and somehow it had lost all terror for her—nay, it held her with a strange delight and fascination" (81).

The parallel between this moment—a young woman attempting to prove her Japanese subjectivity even as she is confronted with evidence to the contrary—and Winnifred's status as author should be clear. Hyacinth's terror speaks to an anxiety in the novel and throughout Winnifred's works that one cannot construct oneself through words or history alone. Hyacinth does not learn to love or accept the reflection but regards it with a "strange delight"; in fact she looks at the mirror only when no one else is around. Her reconciliation with the image in the mirror represents an attempt to mask the anxieties surrounding race and authorship that the text betrays, but that reconciliation has its limits, as it is portrayed as furtive and somewhat ambivalent.

The anxieties that are merely suggested in *The Heart of Hyacinth* appear much more clearly in *Me*. Winnifred-Nora's self-aggrandizement signals an uncertainty about the legitimacy of her position as the protagonist and author of her own story. Nora's outsized insistence on her physical desirability and her ultimate refinement coupled with her silence on the subject of her mother's origins represent an attempt to shore up the precariousness of her privileged position as a middle-class, white woman author. It is only her proximity to whiteness that makes her a reliable, appealing, and sympathetic heroine for the reader; therefore, the text makes every effort to associate her with white womanhood. This is where the black Jamaican population serves its purpose. Sandra Gunning, in her compelling study of the intersections between lynching, sexual violence, and race, argues that the black male rapist "proved particularly useful for white Americans seeking to come to terms with post–Civil War anxieties over national unity, black emancipation, altered gender roles, growing labor unrest, European immigration, and the continued evolution of the United States into an increasingly multiethnic nation" (6). According to Gunning, this stereotype actually expressed white male anxiety over the political consequences that black male enfranchisement might have. Martha Hode argues in *White Women, Black Men: Illicit Sex in the Nineteenth Century South* (1997) that interracial sexual relations did occur with some regularity in the antebellum South, and though they often elicited responses of shame or averted glances, they rarely caused the kind of violence that would occur in the era following Emancipation. By the 1870s, the fear of the black male rapist had been translated into the language of social rape, with the nation acting the part of the white female victim, "silent, helpless, in immediate need of protection from the black beast" (7).

In the case of *Me* the black population in Jamaica—and Nora's decidedly horrified reaction to it—usefully fortifies her position as a white woman. It is particularly Nora's *instinctive* response that solidifies her class and racial status. Winnifred calls upon the specter of the black male rapist in order to more decisively link Nora's "othered" body with the white body of the nation.

From the moment Nora's boat arrives in Jamaica, she is overwhelmed and alarmed by the sight of so many black inhabitants. Ferens describes this moment as straight out of the "classic island ethnographies of Louis de Bougainville, Raymond Firth, and Bronislaw Malinowski" (116):

> A crowd seemed to be swarming on the wharves, awaiting our boat. As we came nearer, I was amazed to find that this crowd was made up almost entirely of negroes. We have few negroes in Canada, and I had seen only one in all my life. I remember an older sister had shown him to me in church—he was pure black—and told me he was the "Bogy man," and that he'd probably come around to see me that night. I was six. I never took my eyes once from his face during the service, and I have never forgotten his face. (*Me*, 19)

Nora's memory of her first encounter with blackness recalls Frantz Fanon's description of the psychological drama that erupts when a child points to him and says, "Look, a Negro!"—only Nora is playing the part of the white interlocutor. This moment in which the child names the "Negro" is constitutive of the black man's experience as a colonized subject. In the colonial context, Fanon argues, the black man must not only be black, but "he must be black in relation to the white man" (110). While Fanon rejects the suggestion that the converse is true—that white men are white in relation to black men because white men can ignore the fact of blackness or ignore its gaze in a way that black men cannot—I would argue that in this scene of interracial colonial encounter narrated by Nora, there *is* a kind of a complementary move across racial and gender lines. This scene not only establishes the "Bogy man's" blackness, shame, and guilt, it serves the equally important purpose of implying Nora's whiteness, innocence, and privilege. Nora not only sees the "Bogy man" and the black Jamaicans as "object[s] in the midst of other objects" (Fanon, 109), she simultaneously sets herself as the subject with the power to name them as objects and gaze at them with impunity. Although her gaze is not a masculine one, it does nevertheless carry the weight of racial categories and colonizing power with it. Winnifred's move here to name the colonized subjects strategically substantiates her status as an author and silently disavows her own racialized status.

If the initial descriptions of Jamaica read as if they were straight out of an anthropological text, Nora's assumption of the mantle of ethnographer only highlights the space that she places between herself and the other island inhabitants: "It was, therefore, with a genuine thrill of excitement and fear that I looked down upon that vast sea of upturned black and brown faces. Never will I forget that first impression of Jamaica. Everywhere I looked were negroes—men and women and children, some half naked, some with bright handkerchiefs knotted about their heads, some gaudily attired, some dressed in immaculate white duck, just like the people on the boat" (20). Her "discovery" of Jamaica (with the blacks positioned as natives) calls upon colonial discourse and rhetoric to strengthen her claim to whiteness and, through whiteness, authorship. Though Nora herself is from a colonial backwater, she deflects the colonial gaze that might be trained upon her by the elites of the island by focusing exclusively on the exotic otherness of the Afro-Jamaicans. Her own response to the island, the "thrill of excitement and fear," contains loathing mixed in equal measure with desire. She also invokes the language of colonial conquest when she calls Jamaica "this new land I had discovered" (21). Her enchantment with this "new land," which commingles her "loathing and appetite for blackness" and a "fascination with and a fear of racial mixing" (Gunning, 20), feminizes the island and its colonized inhabitants, placing her squarely in the position of a colonizing power and masculinizing her own gaze.

While Nora seems enthralled by the half-naked bodies and gaudy display of clothing in front of her, the moment any of these bodies attempts to approach her, or place themselves in proximity to her, she unthinkingly and naïvely reacts with terror: "I started up screaming when I felt a hand on my shoulder, and looking up in the steadily deepening twilight, I saw a smiling face approach my own, and the face was black! I fled toward the boat, crying out wildly" (21). Nora's overreaction is not presented as such by the text; in fact the ship's officer toward whom she flees offers her sanctuary and promises to "skin the hide off [the] damned black baboon" who had presumed to touch her. The captain's power and privilege are strengthened in this scene, but so are Nora's; only a white, middle-class woman could expect to be so shocked by the approach of a black man, and so her response of cold-blooded fear and the active ministrations of the ship's crew to her distress once again implicitly cement this image of her.

Nora's time in Jamaica seems one long attempt to fight off the advances of black men. Again and again, when confronted with black men, she reacts with "sudden panic" or a fear that is repeatedly characterized as "instinctive" (40). This idea that her fear, loathing, and fascination are all intuitive and socially unconstructed is crucial to Nora's positioning of herself as a white, middle-class woman. This trope of "instinct" bolsters her claim to white womanhood and the protections and privileges it afford her. It also, perhaps surprisingly, distances her from the racialized identity to which she alludes at various moments. In describing "my mother's land," Nora asserts that she has an "instinctive feeling about that country": "A blind man can find his way over paths that he intuitively feels. And with me. I feel as if I knew everything about that land, and when I sit down to write—why, things just come pouring to me, and I can write *anything* then" (176). As she freely admits, her knowledge does not stem from her having lived in or visited her mother's land, but rather from something within herself, something that is not particularized to race but does seem to rely on the popular conception of a female intuition. Her position as an expert on "that land" is not to be questioned or held to any kind of rational or logical standard; it is simply a part of her.

The text works very hard here to establish Nora's insider status, and the life she leads in Jamaica does that even further. Upon her arrival she sets out to introduce herself to Mr. Burbank, a local businessman involved in politics who is counted one of the island's wealthiest bachelors. She is shocked to discover that Mr. Burbank is a black man, with an "ingratiating" face and manner; upon meeting him she refuses to shake his hand, not out of malice or outrage—reactions that might be construed as socially constructed—but simply because she is afraid to touch him. Mr. Burbank is a racial phantasm, conjured to validate Nora's desirability as a white woman and then transformed into a rapist and monster in order to prove her genteel sensibilities. While alone with her one day in the statehouse, where Nora works as a journalist for the local newspaper, Mr. Burbank proposes marriage ("'God! how I love you!'" he blurts out without any kind of preamble [54]), even though the two have never exchanged a greeting or even a word, and then attempts to kiss her. Burbank's blunt proposal and physical treatment once again shock Nora, who had always dreamed of her "first proposal" as a "golden beam" or a "lovely moment" in the "dreaming days of [her] young girlhood," populated by a "beautiful throng of imaginary suitors" (54). This imagery of romantic, chivalric love, a staple of middle-class womanhood, once again highlights Nora's suitability as writer and protagonist, and her response to Burbank's physical touch cements this position:

Had I been older, perhaps I might have managed that situation in some way. I might even have spoken gently to him; he believe he was honoring me. But youth revolts like some whipped thing before stings like this, and I—I was so hurt, so terribly wounded, that I remember I gasped out a single sob of rage. . . . Suddenly, I felt myself seized in a pair of powerful arms. A face came against my own, and lips were pressed hard upon mine.

I screamed like one gone mad. I fought for my freedom from his arms like a possessed person. (55)

There is a curious passive-aggressive quality to this passage. Nora's suggestion that it is her lack of experience and her youth that explain her distress is not really believable; this is exactly how a white woman *should* act when accosted by a black man. Flora Cameron, when physically assaulted by a former slave in *The Birth of a Nation*, responds by throwing herself off a cliff, a tragedy that triggers the formation of the Ku Klux Klan. Nora's disingenuous attempt to excuse her dramatics by referencing her youth therefore rings false in a text that revels in the character's theatricality. For her contemporary reader there would have been nothing undignified about Nora's reactions to such an attack; Roger Hamilton, Nora's mysterious benefactor, probably echoes the sentiments of many readers when he declares, "Down South we lynch a nigger for less than that" (75). He punctuates this menacing statement by clenching his fist on the table in front of him. The fact that the attack on Nora would have resulted in a lynching reinforces her status as a white woman, with all of its racial and class categories, sweeping aside the uneasiness with which she has presented herself. The interracial encounter in *Me* triangulates the subjectivity of Nora; calling upon the discourse of black sexuality that roiled the country in the aftermath of Reconstruction, *Me* marks Nora as white by making her the object of the desirous black male gaze.

Although she was the younger sister by over a decade, Winnifred arranged for Edith to come to Jamaica to replace her sometime in 1896 (Ferens, 68). In her memoir, "Leaves from the Mental Portfolio of an Eurasian," Edith recounts her various experiences with racial prejudice in Canada, Jamaica, and the United States. At times, especially when is focusing on her early childhood and family life, she relies on essentialist constructions of race and identity. By doing so, she seems to participate in discourses that were used to defend African American inferiority and Chinese exclusion. Indeed when her collection of short stories was first published reviewers praised them as outstanding examples of ethnography, assuming that she was scrutinizing life in Chinatown from an anthropological perspective.[11] Describing a fight in which a racist bully attacks her older brother and her, Edith explains that "the white blood in our veins [fought] valiantly for the Chinese half of us" (219). For Edith that "white blood" symbolizes a willingness to defend herself against attack; it also symbolizes that aspect of herself that wants to contest injustice and defend the helpless, in this case the Chinese half of herself. Edith's use of "white blood" here is jarring because it seems to imply a disjunction between her internal subjectivity and her outward appearance, thereby reinforcing the notion that certain races have certain character traits. In other words, she and her brother may *look* Chinese, but in spirit they are decidedly white.

While moments like these may be expressive of Edith's "defiant" spirit, they also serve as a corrective to the hagiographic tone that often accompanies critical assessments of her work. Edith's attitudes toward race and racial difference are fluid, contradictory, and contextual. But I would argue that they are at their most radical and ethically bound when she is contemplating her relationship to black Jamaicans. What is striking about "Leaves from the Mental Portfolio of an Eurasian" is the number of times the memoir explicitly links the Chinese and the Afro-Jamaicans. In her representation of the Afro-Jamaicans, however, Edith underscores the imbricated and conflicted nature of the relationship she imagines between herself and this group. She understands that the constant positioning of blacks and Asians in relation to each other solidifies white privilege to name, organize, and control that relationship. Over dinner at her boardinghouse in Kingston, Edith is subjected to a racist conversation in which the boarders debate whether the Chinese or the blacks are more repellant physically and spiritually:

> "I cannot reconcile myself to the thought that the Chinese are humans like ourselves. They may have immortal souls but their faces seem to be so utterly devoid of expression that I cannot help but doubt."
>
> "Souls," echoes the town clerk. "Their bodies are enough for me. A Chinaman is, in my eyes, more repulsive than a nigger."
>
> "They always give me such a creepy feeling," puts in the young girl with a laugh.
>
> "I wouldn't have one in my house," declares my landlady. (224)

These repellant opinions, stated as if based on verifiable fact, speak to a racial economy in which Chinese and Africans exist only in order to be compared with each other in terms of their relative degradation. Edith's landlady concludes the conversation by declaring that she wouldn't have a Chinaman in her house. (Ironically, of course, the landlady does have one in her house.) Edith's declaration to the gathered assembly that she is Chinese not only directly refutes their racism (which is all the more insidious because of its small-talk, dinner-conversation nature) but is a worrisome reminder that the physiological or phenotypical traits that undergird the logic of racial identities are tendentious at best. The constant attempts to compare the deprivation of one racial group with that of another serve the purpose of strengthening the power of a monolithic colonial white authority. Even thousands of miles away from the seat of colonial power such a discussion serves to cement the colonizer's control over the island and its inhabitants. It is important to note that it isn't a conversation about the degraded conditions of the Chinese alone that elicits Edith's coming out, but one in which the participants argue about the comparative degradation of Africans and Chinese. Later, a naval officer propositions her, assuming that because she is Chinese she must be a prostitute. In both instances Chinese racial difference is made comparable to African American racial difference: the Chinese are thought to be sexually immoral, physically debased, lacking human feeling, and no better than the Africans that populate Jamaica.

Edith's representation of Afro-Jamaicans is informed by her colonial environment and her own position in relation to the Africans and Europeans as a woman, a person of Chinese descent, and a laborer striving to maintain her middle-class status. Her editor at the newspaper where she works is initially unaware that she is of Chinese descent and considers her "one of us." Edith rejects this position of being "not quite/not white" (Bhabha, 92). Upon her arrival in Jamaica she finds herself

> surrounded by a race of people, the reputed descendants of Ham, the son of Noah, whose offspring, it was prophesied, should be the servants of the sons of Shem and Japheth.[12] As I am a descendant, according to the Bible, of both Shem and Japheth, I have a perfect right to set my heel upon the Ham people; but tho I see others around me following out the Bible's suggestion, it is not in my nature to be arrogant to any but those who seek to impress me with their superiority, which the poor black maid who has been assigned to me by the hotel, certainly does not. My employer's wife takes me to task for this.

"It is unnecessary," she says, "to thank a black person for service." (225)

Edith's use of this biblical story—promulgated in various forms prior to the nineteenth century to explain racial difference and justify racism against Africans—is far from untroubled. In this passage she seems to accept the notion that Africans are the "sons of Ham"; their degraded condition relative to whites is therefore a result of the collective guilt they bear for the sins of their supposed ancestor. The wife's admonishment that maids should not be thanked arises from a belief that black people are born to serve white people and should not be commended for doing what comes naturally to them. Although she distinguishes her treatment of the servants from her treatment by her employer's wife, Edith nevertheless speaks of her "perfect right" as a descendent of both Shem and Japheth to look down upon Africans. Perhaps more than anything, her rejection of this racist script at the same moment she invokes it as her "right" signals the conflicted common ground that she feels she shares with these "sons of Ham"; it also emblematizes the extent to which Afro-Asian representations can oscillate between antagonism and alliance, sometimes within the span of a few sentences. Within this passage we see Edith attempting to establish her identity by subscribing to traditional notions of difference that the Ham, Shem, and Japheth story emblematizes, but we also see her drawn to the African maid because of their shared racial and class marginalization, even though those around her admonish her to ignore that connection. Although Edith does not elaborate on this incident, the text suggests that because she herself is a working woman (she went to Jamaica to be a journalist) she must acknowledge the labor of the maid who cleans her room, even if it is only to thank her. In Jamaica Edith plays an uncomfortable part in the colonial apparatus, and she suggests here that it is a role that she cannot play very well.

The Afro-Jamaican characters make appreciable Edith's racialized status and her alienation from the European colonial authority. In a culture that values whiteness above all else her partial self-identification with the Jamaicans clashes with her ability to pass as a white woman. She describes her acceptance by whites because of her light complexion and non-Asiatic features: "Occasionally, an Englishman will warn me against the 'brown boys' of the island, little dreaming that I too am one of the 'brown people' of the earth" (225). Allying herself with the "brown people of the earth" flies in the face of the religiously inflected schema that she had articulated earlier. Her refusal here to draw a distinction between herself and the "brown people" suggests that she does not accept the racial hierarchy that would separate Africans and Asians from whites. Her claim to "brownness" reveals the most basic assumption of racial hierarchies: that Africans and Asians, no matter where they are in relation to each other, can never be white. Thus it doesn't matter if she is "yellow" or "brown" or "black"; the fact that she is "not-white" is enough. But Edith's ability to imagine a political solidarity between the Chinese and the Jamaicans is circumscribed by the absence textually of black characters. Those who do appear serve to highlight her consciousness rather than reveal any of their own. The presence of Afro-Jamaicans profoundly influences how she views herself as a woman of Chinese descent and the relationship between herself and the other racial communities on the island. Neither woman of leisure nor laborer, neither black nor white, neither wife nor mother, neither servant nor master, she struggles to understand her place in this colonial setting. And that struggle is defined by the relationship that she and others imagine between herself and the Africans who inhabit the island. Edith's halting attempts to express a sense of solidarity with the black laboring classes in Jamaica represent a problematic if earnest desire to understand what kind of interracial alliance can be formed based on mutual marginalization.

Edith's ambivalence toward blacks in "Leaves" can also be found in her fictional works, even though no black characters appear in them at all. Indeed, instances of explicit cross-racial representation are exceptions rather than rules in Edith's fiction. Nevertheless, her link to the Afro-Jamaicans and her defense of the Chinese cannot be understood outside of the discursive racial politics and representations of the day that consistently intertwined "Asiatics" with "Negroes."[13] Her radical potential in terms of her representations of racial hierarchies is arguably most fully realized in stories that do not seem overtly to deal with race, whether Asian or African, at all. A more characteristic example of her representation of racial difference can be found in two of her most famous short stories, "Mrs. Spring Fragrance" and "The Inferior Woman." Both recount the attempts of Mrs. Spring Fragrance, the wife of a Chinese merchant living in Seattle, to bring together a young couple that has been kept apart by disapproving parents; in "Mrs. Spring Fragrance" the lovers are Chinese, and in "The Inferior Woman" they are white. In the first story Mrs. Spring Fragrance's matchmaking and her attempts to thwart the arranged marriage of her Chinese neighbor lead to a conflict within her own happy marriage. A misunderstanding arises, leading Mr.

Spring Fragrance to worry that his wife does not love him, since they themselves had an arranged marriage. In the second story the plot revolves around Mrs. Spring Fragrance's effort to convince her stubborn friend Mrs. Carman that her son Will is better off marrying the working-class Alice Winthrop (the titular heroine) and not the socially prominent Ethel Evebrook. Alice initially rejects Will's offer of marriage because she will not marry into a family that thinks she is not good enough for their son. In both stories misunderstandings are cleared, prejudices are overcome, and true love blesses all.

Although Edith's purpose undoubtedly was to write fiction that depicted the Chinese in a sympathetic light, the language of these short works compellingly reveals the interconnections between Chinese exclusion and other types of racism. My reading strategy takes into account the contemporary discourse of racial difference and national identity, which enables one to see how Edith's defense of the Chinese implicitly critiques systemic racial practices that oppressed African Americans as well. So when Edith's stories condemn racism against the Chinese, they are not just condemning the Chinese Exclusion Act or stereotyped images of the Chinese; they are also condemning the entire process by which racialized groups are excluded.

Edith's short stories counter two popularly held assumptions about the inclusive nature of American identity. The first is that American identity is universally desirable, progressive, and available to any individual who can appreciate its exceptional status among nations. Because the Chinese and Africans are not as highly developed culturally or intellectually as whites, both are incapable of understanding, let alone experiencing, the transformative wonder of being a "real" American. We can see this most clearly in the short story "Mrs. Spring Fragrance." Mrs. Spring Fragrance undercuts arguments for African American and Asian exclusion by directly exposing the racist underpinnings behind the powerful narrative of transformative American identity and citizenship. In a critique coded in a language of romance and love, "Mrs. Spring Fragrance" contests the notion that American identity is somehow transformative or the natural result of an individual's embrace of liberty and freedom. These transformative narratives claim to reflect an essential truth about what it means to be an American, but "Mrs. Spring Fragrance" exposes the racialization at the core of these narratives. Africans and Asians can never participate in such a narrative because both groups exist to substantiate the exclusion of racialized groups.

Edith deconstructs an understanding of American identity that privileges the transformative potential of simply being and becoming American. The belief in this transformative potential was widespread, and its rhetoric should be familiar to Americans today since it still serves as the basis by which most Americans define themselves. For a succinct articulation of this ideal, we can turn to the writings of Theodore Roosevelt, who advocates the equality of all "good" Americans, presumably regardless of their race. Roosevelt states that the two "demands upon the spirit of Americanism" are, first, to "tolerate no kind of divided allegiance in this country," and second, to "treat every good American . . . as on a full and exact equality with every other good American, and set our faces like flint against the creatures who seek to discriminate against such an American. . . . To discriminate in any way . . . is a base infamy from the personal standpoint, and . . . utterly un-American and profoundly unpatriotic" (60). Roosevelt's use of a rhetoric of equality is undermined by his insistence on a monolithic vision of who an American is. He has no room in his definition for any kind of American that does not fit into his patriotic paradigm of pure Americanness. This inflexibility emblematizes how the rhetoric of a "good American" can be used to justify the exclusion of undesirable populations. Africans and Asiatics could never be "good" Americans because they were not even starting from a position that acknowledged them as civilized or even fully human. Roosevelt demands that every immigrant reject the "abhorrent" idea of being a "hyphenated American" and exhorts all of us to "be Americans, pure and simple! . . . Either a man is an American and nothing else, or he is not an American at all" (60–61). According to Roosevelt's logic, to be American is "pure and simple" and to be a "hyphenated American" is unnatural and deviant. There is no middle-ground, no flexibility in the definition of the two; they are separate and distinct, and being American means abandoning one (inferior) identity position in favor of another (superior) one.

Appropriately the way that Roosevelt is described by his own biographers and historians exemplifies this idealization of American identity as one that defies easy explanation. In a hagiographic collection of Roosevelt's speeches and essays (from which the passage above is quoted), the editor, Hermann Hagedorn, proudly points to a cartoon printed in the *New York Times* after Roosevelt's death in which the figure of History stands before a plaque, at the top of which is emblazoned "Theodore Roosevelt." Below the name appears a list of labels ("President," "Soldier," "Statesman," and so on), each of which has been crossed out by History. At the bottom of the plaque, in large letters that would have made John Hancock proud, History has written "American." Hagedorn writes, "Nothing this man did . . . means so much as what he was. And what he was, was . . . above all, an American" (70). Hagedorn's stylistic gyrations in that last sentence capture, or rather *fail* to capture Roosevelt's American identity. The tortured wording emblematizes in grammatical terms the transformative and exceptionalist language that surrounds the notion of "American." Indeed the sentence's overheated tone and convoluted syntax contribute to the notion that Americanness as such cannot be spoken of in a "pure and simple" way, despite protestations to the contrary. The quality that best defines Americanness cannot be contained in language; as a process, Hagedorn suggests, it defies linguistic capture. The mythic, exceptional, and transformative quality of American identity means that our everyday language fails to describe it adequately.

At times Asians living in the United States co-opted this logic of transformation in their attempts to gain American citizenship. They willingly made themselves participants in the kinds of nationalist fantasies in which Roosevelt's speech participates. An example of this can be seen in the landmark Supreme Court case *Ozawa v. United States* (1922), which I discussed in chapter 2. As I have already stated, although the *Ozawa* case initially seems to challenge citizenship as the exclusive property of white Americans, the plaintiff's argument actually ends up strengthening the notion that American citizenship is the exclusive domain of white bodies; Ozawa simply wants to expand the definition of whiteness rather than challenge the exclusionary construction of American citizenship.[14] Ozawa argued for the constitutionality of his citizenship status by pointing to his embrace of middle-class white values and domesticity: he was educated in the United States, a native speaker of English, and married to a white woman. He also contended that being of Japanese descent, his skin was as white as any European's. In their zeal to win naturalization rights for Asians, Ozawa and his legal team reified the romantic notion that America really is in the heart (to borrow a phrase from Carlos Bulosan) and not in one's face or (presumably) on one's skin. In his essay on cosmopolitanism and Younghill Kang, Stephen Knadler performs an incisive reading of the assumptions behind assimilationist narratives and the ways that Asians seeking American citizenship in the early twentieth century reinscribed the link between whiteness and American identity. Knadler calls the view of America as a transformative space within the subject a "transpositional affective state." Although this kind of construction of national identity initially seems to be liberatory and not race-based, it reinforces the idea that one must be or idealize a certain caste or color in order to belong. American identity can be achieved by anyone as long as he or she truly embraces the middle-class, white values that supposedly make up the backbone of the nation. Americanization or naturalization is about conforming to those values, not challenging them. I would only add to Knadler's "logic of naturalization" that the process by which the immigrant or racial other arrives at that affective state is as important as the state itself.[15]

The Mrs. Spring Fragrance stories anticipate the flaw in *Ozawa* that Knadler discusses, a full ten years before the case codified it, and critique the "pure and simple" logic of American identity that the Roosevelt speech exemplifies. With its opening description of the "Americanized" Mrs. Spring Fragrance and her merchant husband, the story immediately situates itself within a particularly loaded discourse of American identity. Presumably Mrs. Spring Fragrance's American status stems from her fluency in English and her ease with American ways and people.[16] Mr. Spring Fragrance, the story emphasizes, is "called by the Westerners 'Americanized,'" and Mrs. Spring Fragrance is considered "even more 'Americanized'" (17) than her husband. The appearance of "Americanized" in quotation marks emphasizes the arbitrary and shifting meaning of the term. Edith's use of the passive voice also signals the ways in which the Spring Fragrance stories contest the prevailing mythology that shrouds the process of Americanization. People do not Americanize; they are Americanized (or not) by others. According to the rhetoric here, the Spring Fragrances' successful Americanization is contingent upon their ability to meet certain requirements that have been imposed upon them by "Westerners." They are not the subjects of a transformative and natural process but rather bemused objects within a culturally inscribed system of exhibiting American identity.

A conversation between Mrs. Spring Fragrance and her neighbor Laura encapsulates the contingent nature of American identity. To comfort Laura as she confronts the possibility of entering into a loveless marriage, Mrs. Spring Fragrance quotes to her a "beautiful American poem written by a noble American named Tennyson":

Tis better to have loved and lost,
Than never to have loved at all. (18)[17]

Mrs. Spring Fragrance's tone throughout the story wavers between gentle irony and sincere solemnity, making her thoroughly likable to her white neighbors and to us readers. Clearly she has misstated the facts

surrounding the poem: the poem may be beautiful, but it is not American, and neither is the poet. But this repetition of "American" is more
than just another example of Mrs. Spring Fragrance's "quaintness," a
characterization her neighbors use to describe her repeatedly. The text's
insistence upon her misidentification indicates that her Americanization
seems to be less successful and complete than the story initially suggests.
More than that, the repetition of her error (an "*American* poem written
by an *American*" poet) registers an anxiety about what the term "American" means. Mrs. Spring Fragrance's insistence upon the Americanness
of the most identifiably British poet in literature makes us question how
successful her Americanization process is, and what the terms for defining that success might be.

Mrs. Spring Fragrance's characterization of the poet as "noble" seems
another ironic misstep; by calling a supposed American "noble," she suggests a link between the United States and nobility, which runs counter to one of the foundational tenets of what makes American identity
exceptional: that all Americans are equal and do not rely on blood or
titles to describe who they are. Rather than being another example of her
"quaintness," however, this seeming misstep is crucial to my reading of
the story, for it is proof of her radical success in interpreting, and thus
critiquing, the nation: Mrs. Spring Fragrance actually assesses perfectly
the gap between the nation's mythology of equality and inclusion and its
history of African American and Asian exclusion and articulates certain
words that the nation would rather keep hidden or deny. She insists upon
nobility not because she has incorrectly absorbed America's attitudes toward its citizens but precisely because she grasps the reality behind the
rhetoric so perfectly. Her errors, rather than undermining the perfection
of her Americanization, actually reinforce her perfect understanding of
the America that she and her husband experience.

The conversation between Young Will Carman, the Spring Fragrances' neighbor, and Mr. Spring Fragrance over the meaning of this particular line of poetry emblematizes the ways in which the Spring Fragrance
stories demythologize narratives of American identity. Will informs Mr.
Spring Fragrance that the poem means "it is a good thing to love anyway—even if we can't get what we love, or as the poet tells us, lose what
we love. Of course, one needs experience to feel the truth of this teaching" (19). To love someone is a "good thing," a culturally and individually
valued experience, no matter how that experience turns out in the end.
The power of Tennyson's phrase stems from the fact that it privileges
the romantic and the unknown over the practical and the everyday.

However, the fact that Will, a young, liberal, white man, says this to a Chinese man whose brother sits imprisoned on Angel Island and who can never become a citizen of the land where he lives and works indicates another register of interpretation besides the one of "love" that serves as the ostensible focus of the conversation between the two men. The vocabulary that Will uses to describe love is similar to the terms used to talk about American identity. Indeed the story makes clear that the discourse of Americanization during this period was all-encompassing and was frequently couched in a mystical language not dissimilar from what Will describes as "love." Will, and the society for which he serves as spokesman, privileges love as a natural state that does not need to be explained. Love becomes a transformative event that defies any kind of explanation, an affective state that only those who have experienced it can understand. Like American identity, love is a romantic mythology to which it is better to subscribe than not to believe at all.

When Mr. Spring Fragrance expresses skepticism about Will's notion of love, Will retorts that matters such as love depend on "temperament" (19). If the language of love is a subtext for the language of American identity, then the implications of Will's use of this word becomes clear: only those possessing a certain temperament have the ability to experience that state of love. Temperament dictates the limits of a person's experience; without a certain temperament, one cannot fall in love in the proper way and therefore have the appropriate feelings for love itself and the object of one's love. Will's innocent statement reveals the violence behind the benign language of "temperament" and "experience": they can be used as tools to enforce the limits of acceptable American identity. Only those who are white have the choice of becoming American, just as only those who have the correct temperament can experience the joy of falling in love. The Chinese and African Americans can never experience citizenship because the experience of American identity is one that is, by definition, not applicable to them. American identity—which, like love, is thought to be transformative and a symbol of universal truths—masks the exclusion at the heart of its discursive construction.

Mr. Spring Fragrance responds to Will's "sad but wise" smile over love that "it is disobedient to reason," an ironic statement that runs counter to the assumption expressed in Will's homily by aligning love with reason and (presumably) duty with passion. Mr. Spring Fragrance counters the notion that love results from a desire to reason or intellectualize issues. Distressed by Will's remarks, he adds that it is "better to have what you do not love than to love what you do not have" (19), expressing an idea

that is more reasonable than passionate. He resists Will's easy investment of experience with authenticity and authority. Loving America
isn't the same thing as belonging to it; or, to put it another way, if Mr.
Spring Fragrance cannot have America, then he will choose not to love
it. Squashing Will's romanticization, Mrs. Spring Fragrance implies
that being a citizen and having the rights and privileges associated with
citizenship is preferable to loving America and not being a citizen. The
language of Americanization, which like the language of love is thought
to be "authentic" and a signal of universal truths, masks citizenship's
exclusive nature. Mr. Spring Fragrance's vehement rejection of the "experience of love" and his identification of Will's supposedly spontaneous
and universal romantic ideas with something that is more akin to logic
and reason parallel the story's own attempt to expose the racialization
and alienation behind such terms. The story suggests that American
exclusionary policies are not "spontaneous" acts based on universal or
natural human instincts, as Justice Brown suggests in *Plessy*, but efficient
mechanisms for politically marginalizing many racial groups.

The second assumption that Edith's stories counteract is that races of
people can be placed into hierarchies based on physiological and cultural
differences. "The Inferior Woman" takes on the ways the nation relied
on a biology of racial difference to support racist social and political
policies. The story signals its critique with its shifting definitions of the
words "superior" and "inferior." Edith gestures to the possible similarities between those communities labeled as racially inferior in order to
encourage readers to think about racialization as a process that connects
various marginalized groups, despite the differences in their histories.
This gesture, though only hinted at, seeks to redress the isolation and
alienation of each group within the United States.

"The Inferior Woman" recounts the attempts of Mrs. Spring Fragrance to bring together a young couple that have been kept apart by
disapproving parents. Will Carman loves Alice, a working-class office
girl, who by working hard has become the assistant to an important
businessman. Will's mother disapproves of the match and wants Will to
marry the socially prominent and politically active Ethel. Because she is
proud, Alice refuses to marry Will without Mrs. Carman's blessing. Mrs.
Spring Fragrance, we are told at the story's start, is writing a book for a
Chinese audience about the strange ways of her American friends. With
her child-like candor, she eventually manages to convince Mrs. Carman
that Alice is indeed the best choice for her son, and the two eventually
marry. The title of the story is the name that Mrs. Spring Fragrance

assigns to Alice, presumably because of Alice's inferior social standing but also because she can detect Mrs. Carman's belief that Alice would make an inferior wife. For the same reason, Mrs. Spring Fragrance calls Ethel "the Superior Woman" and refers to both women by these rather odd and bulky monikers throughout the story.

On the surface this appears to be a story in which race does not play a role. Instead the story seems to be a morality tale about how "true love" should be the final arbiter of a couple's destiny. Unlike other stories by Edith that deal more directly with anti-Chinese prejudice, "The Inferior Woman" props up the notion of America as a land of opportunity, especially in its lionization of Alice, the working-class wonder and the eponymous heroine. The story suggests that Mrs. Carman's assessments of Ethel and Alice based on their class is completely arbitrary and inaccurate. While Alice seems to be a modern woman, what she really prizes is her femininity; unlike Ethel, who has far more radical ideas about gender, Alice merely wants to serve the men in her firm as wisely and kindly as she would a husband and children in her home. Despite the trappings of modernity that surround her, she is in her heart a very old-fashioned girl.

I would argue that this is a story about race masquerading as an acceptable heterosexual romance. The story encodes its agenda into the language of romance itself, revealing its concern with race at a moment when Alice is pondering why she refused Will's proposal. Alice concludes, "When a gulf of prejudice lies between the wife and mother of a man, that man's life is not what it should be. . . . Prejudices are prejudices. They are like diseases" (40). The notion that prejudices are "like diseases" uncovers the story's buried text of race and national identity. It alludes to a popular model for explaining the influence on white America of nonwhite populations and immigrants. Priscilla Wald notes that the quarantines instituted to control outbreaks of cholera and typhus in 1892 exemplified how "fear of infection legitimated legal and spatial responses to cultural concern" (654). As early as the mid-nineteenth century Bayard Taylor had argued for the exclusion of the Chinese based on their bizarre sexual practices, claiming, "Their touch is pollution. . . . Justice to our own race demands that they not settle on our soil" (quoted in Gossett, 290). Immigrants and nonwhite people were seen as contagions, spreading a metaphorical disease into the heart of a healthy America. Alice's statement that prejudices are diseases touches upon the story's key critique of these racial discourses.

The language of disease is important because it points to the story's critique of the "science" behind race. Although Edith has been read in relation to various political movements of her period (Chinese rights, women's suffrage, progressivism), few have examined the impact that racialized biology and science might have had on her work, especially in a story like "The Inferior Woman."[18] I want to examine that story in connection with this science that was so instrumental in justifying African American and Chinese exclusion. I focus on Edith's use of the language of inferiority and superiority because it explicitly conjures up the discourse of racial biologism and positions the story as a critique of the way the sciences of biology and anthropology were categorizing racial groups into hierarchies of culture and development. According to Lee D. Baker, until the mid-nineteenth century most American scientists explained racial inferiority in theological terms: Africans had fallen from God's grace, which explained their physical, mental, and spiritual debasement relative to whites. The theory of polygenesis was seriously advocated by the natural historian Louis Agassiz (the founder of American anthropology) and his students Samuel Morton and Josiah Nott as a way of explaining black intellectual and social inferiority.[19]

The rise of the sciences, the emergence of the social sciences, and the acceptance of Darwin's theories on evolution in the nineteenth century signaled a profound shift in the conceptualization of racial difference. As Thomas Gossett points out, "The nineteenth century was a period of exhaustive and—as it turned out—futile search for criteria to define and describe racial difference" (69).[20] While blood as a signifier for black racial inferiority dates as far back as the eighteenth century, in the early twentieth century that construction of blood merged into the discourse of natural history and the nascent discipline of anthropology, both of which took into account Darwin's theory of evolution and other scientific discoveries in legitimating racial difference. Apologists for racial segregation increasingly attempted to define racial difference using scientific techniques to point to quantifiable biological differences between races. According to these new theories, which relied on misconceptions of Darwin's theory of evolution, white people constituted the pinnacle of evolutionary history, the most advanced form of life on the planet, while blacks and other people of color represented earlier stages in that history or lower forms of evolution. The Supreme Court's decision in *Plessy v. Ferguson* confirmed what had already been widely accepted in the United States since the end of Reconstruction: that social and political equality between blacks and whites could not be attained because of the biological gulf between the two groups. As Gossett notes, "By 1900, the idea was widely accepted that both intelligence and traits of character tend to be inherited, and one of the proofs of this contention was believed to be found in race" (158).

African Americans were not the only targets of this new form of racialized science. Americans accepted the idea that Chinese culture was inferior to their own to justify Chinese exclusion; as Stuart Creighton Miller points out, "China was viewed as singularly impervious to nineteenth century ideals of progress, liberty, and civilization to which an emergent modern America was fervently committed" (vii). Miller points to the images of the Chinese as infantile (both physically and culturally) and servile, while African Americans were thought to occupy an earlier fetal stage in human development (158).[21] Indeed the supposed evolutionary and cultural infancy of these nonwhite groups became a powerful justification for European and American imperialism in Asia and Africa. Civilized nations had a responsibility—the white man's burden, in the words of Rudyard Kipling—to "raise" their little brown brothers (to quote William Howard Taft). Those with nonwhite skin were seen as incapable of possessing the intelligence or the capacity to be civilized, and no amount of improvement in their social, economic, or educational position could make them the equal of whites.

Edith's story questions science as a privileged discourse for describing people, suggesting that it is contingent and riddled with ideological assumptions. "The Inferior Woman" seizes upon the racial hierarchy that this discourse of racialized science props up with its unrelenting emphasis on the words "inferior" and "superior" to describe the two women. In Edith's story the rationality and methodology that such terms rely on as proof of their accuracy are rendered meaningless. Edith deconstructs the terms "inferior" and "superior," a vocabulary that was inextricably linked to such scientific endeavors. By focusing on the *rhetoric* and *language* of such racist discourses, she is able to assess critically the laws and hierarchies that keep both African Americans and Chinese out of America. The story's insistence on this kind of language strikes a dissonant chord in an otherwise harmonious love story.

Based on our own understanding of what constitutes American success stories, we as readers believe from the beginning that Mrs. Spring Fragrance has *misnamed* the two women. The story's "superior" woman (Ethel) is actually inferior, while the story's "inferior" woman (Alice) is superior and the better wife for Will. Our assumption that these sobriquets are ironically used is reinforced when we hear Alice's story: she was orphaned as a young girl and climbed to a successful position of assistant through her own hard work. Ethel herself acknowledges Alice's superiority when she states that women such as Alice have "graduated from the university of life with honor": "Women such as I, who are called the Superior Women of America are after all nothing but schoolgirls in comparison. . . . [Alice's] heart and mind are better developed. She has been out in the world all her life; I only a few months" (36). In other words, Alice has been out practicing what Ethel has only theorized; Alice, then, is the better example of a modern American woman.

But the story's finale throws that interpretation into turmoil. Mrs. Spring Fragrance has finally convinced Mrs. Carman of the error of her ways, and Will and Alice's love story is happily resolved. When Mrs. Spring Fragrance expresses her satisfaction that Will and Alice will finally be wed with his mother's blessing, Mr. Spring Fragrance queries, "What about the Superior Woman?" Mrs. Spring Fragrance responds surprisingly that although she "loves" the Inferior Woman, she wants her own daughter to "walk in the groove of the Superior Woman" (41).

Mrs. Spring Fragrance's decision to choose Ethel over Alice as a model for her own unborn daughter—even though the whole logic of the story dictates that Alice must be the model—undercuts the story's ostensible message of democratic individualism. The reader initially believes that this is another example of Mrs. Spring Fragrance's "quaintness." Given the way Alice has been praised during the course of the story, even by her rival in love, Mrs. Spring Fragrance's response to her husband's question is surprising. Having spent the entire story trying to get Mrs. Carman to see the superiority of Alice, why does Mrs. Spring Fragrance want her daughter to "walk in the groove of the Superior Woman"?

I would argue that Mrs. Spring Fragrance's surprising answer is not really surprising at all. In fact she has gotten it exactly right. Her selection of Ethel reveals how well she understands the ideological work behind the nation's *seeming* valorization of Alice. America wants to believe that the "inferior" are actually the "superior," but the reality is of course that the inferior are just that, inferior, and must stay that way. Mrs. Spring Fragrance's praise for Ethel is not couched in the language of democratic individualism, but is steeped in a language of hierarchy and entitlement: Ethel is "radiantly beautiful and *gifted* with the *divine* right of learning" (41; my emphasis). Mrs. Spring Fragrance wants these "gifts" and "divine rights" for her own daughter because these are what she perceives as valuable in the United States. Though she loves the inferior woman, she wants superiority for her own daughter because she understands that superiority based on wealth and class (to which Ethel has access) is desirable, despite all the lip service otherwise, even in a democratic nation. Her supposed error is highly indicative of the story's own critique of the material inequities hidden behind the rhetoric of American equality.

Our own confusion and surprise over the story's end and Mrs. Spring Fragrance's final announcement is in fact a gentle indictment of how completely we readers have absorbed the myth of the self-made American. We expect Mrs. Spring Fragrance to announce that she wants her daughter to walk in the groove of the Inferior Woman, to emphasize the story's seeming point that hard work, genteel femininity, and individual character are worth more than good birth and a privileged upbringing. The irony of Mrs. Spring Fragrance's choice lies in the fact that her daughter, although she will be an American citizen, will never be thought of as a superior woman because she is a person of Chinese descent.

That it is Mrs. Spring Fragrance who first names these two women inferior and superior is only part of the irony. Her constant revision of the terms "inferior" and "superior" suggests that their meanings are not fixed but contextual; the reader's confusion over what "inferiority" and "superiority" mean at the end of the story also intimate that these words, loaded as they are with racialized connotations, do not transparently reflect some kind of reality. Rather than reaffirming the received meaning of these words or using them as accurate descriptions of real-life differences, the story upsets how we consider the words in relation to each other and how we use them to describe people.

If American identity, as it was popularly and scientifically understood, was riddled with racial ideologies, then what possible model for national belonging did Edith Eaton have for people such as herself? In order to answer that question, I want to return briefly to the concluding images in "Leaves from the Mental Portfolio of an Eurasian" as well as to another of Edith's short stories, "The Story of One White Woman Who Married a Chinese." The characters who inhabit these stories (and indeed most of the stories in the collection) are not well-off, and their unhappy fates compared to the well-to-do Spring Fragrances seems to suggest that a higher social class and money might palliate the experiences of Chinese living in the United States. But in these other stories the success of the Spring Fragrances depends upon one's perspective and seems highly contingent. In the incident in "Leaves" in which she is told not to thank the Jamaican servant girl for her housework, Edith feels compelled to express her appreciation to the maid, not only because the maid, like Edith, is "colored," but also because Edith herself hovers between the line dividing the working class from the leisure class. The Jamaican maid and Edith share not only a racial position in white culture, but also a class affiliation.

Edith's own life, as she recounts it in "Leaves," suggests a more ominous alternative to the assimilationist and biologically racialist narratives that she has dismantled in the Spring Fragrance stories. She tells of growing up in England and Canada, the second child of Edward Eaton, the younger son in a wealthy British merchant family, and Grace Eaton, who was ethnically Chinese but raised and educated in England as a missionary (her parents and all other family members remain unnamed in the memoir). Edith describes how she and her siblings dealt with the racism and ostracism they encountered while living in England, Canada, and then the United States.[22] After leaving Jamaica she relocated to the United States and from 1898 to 1910 lived and traveled throughout the American West writing about the Chinese in short stories and essays, all the while supporting herself with stenography and typing jobs. Suffering from poor health, Edith finally returned to Montreal, where she died in 1914.

At the end of the story, Edith imagines her body traveling endlessly back and forth within the nation and then straddling the divide between China and white America: "So I roam backward and forward across the [American] continent. When I am East, my heart is West. When I am West, my heart is East. . . . After all I have no nationality and am not anxious to claim any. Individuality is more than nationality. 'You are you and I am I,' says Confucius. I give my right hand to the Occidentals and my left to the Orientals, hoping that between them they will not utterly destroy the insignificant 'connecting link.' And that's all" (230). Edith refuses to claim the nationality that Roosevelt thunderously demands all "true" Americans must take. Instead she moves from coast to coast, accepting the fact that she has no nationality because she knows that such narratives of "true" national identity exist only to exclude. "The Story of One White Woman Who Married a Chinese" ends with a similar image, a mother worrying about the future of her biracial son caught between the white and Chinese worlds: "Only when the son of Liu Kanghi lays his little head upon my bosom do I question whether I have done wisely. For my boy, the son of the Chinese man, is possessed of a childish wisdom which brings tears to my eyes; and as he stands between his father and myself, like us and yet unlike us both, so will he stand in after years between his father's and his mother's people. And if there is no kindliness nor understanding between them, what will my boy's fate be?" (77).

This image of a divided racialized body straddling worlds is an ominous alternative to the racially exclusive narratives of American identity that Edith has already dismantled in the Spring Fragrance stories. To be the "connecting link" means running the risk of being torn apart; it is a position of instability and potential violence; the terse finality of the last sentence in "Leaves" ("And that's all"), absent of any sentiment, emphasizes that point. Theodore Roosevelt articulates the anger that can be directed toward someone in Edith's position when he states menacingly, "We can have no 'fifty-fifty' allegiance in this country. Either a man is an American and nothing else, or he is not an American at all" (61). Perhaps Roosevelt's dramatic pronouncement provides an answer to the worried mother of "The Story of One White Woman" who queries what will happen to her boy if mutual understanding between racial groups cannot be achieved: her son can never be the American that Roosevelt—and the nation—idealizes.

The "connecting link" also serves as a metaphor for understanding how Edith's fiction can connect different racial communities. To be the connecting link is to be rejected, but it is also to *connect*. This particularly potent image of connection points to the possibilities of multiple kinds of cross-racial dynamics. If critics want to read Edith as an important landmark in the narrative of Asian American studies, then it might also be fruitful to contextualize her work as a landmark in the history of multiracial and cross-racial affiliations. At various moments in the twentieth century, African Americans and Asians have sometimes been forced to see and sometimes have voluntarily seen how American racial discursive practices have marked them as outsiders to the nation, unworthy of citizenship, and enemies of each other. If Edith is concerned with counteracting pathological images of Chinese masculinity in circulation in the early twentieth century (in stories such as "Her Chinese Husband," for example), then it stands to reason that she is contextualizing that construction of masculinity in relation to "normal" white male masculinity *as well as* criminalized black male masculinity.

American literary studies has tended in the past to analyze a minority writer within the particular tradition to which he or she belonged racially without considering how the work might be commenting subtly upon the interaction between several racial communities. By focusing on the interplay between Asian American and European American or African American and European American literary traditions, we forget that African Americans and Asian Americans were also responding to each other's fraught presence on the American landscape. As my reading of Edith's and Winnifred's works proposes, when Asian American authors undertake an evaluation of the politics behind American inclusion in their works, they are also implicitly questioning the place of African Americans in narratives of citizenship and inclusion.

5 / *Quicksand* and the Racial Aesthetics of Chinoiserie

Helga Crane sat alone in her room, which at that hour, eight in the evening, was in soft gloom. Only a single reading lamp, dimmed by a great black and red shade, made a pool of light on the blue Chinese carpet, on the bright covers of the books which she had taken down from their long shelves, on the white pages of the opened one selected, on the shining brass bowl crowded with many-colored nasturtiums beside her on the low table, and on the oriental silk which covered the stool at her slim feet.

The very first paragraph of Nella Larsen's *Quicksand* describes the novel's biracial protagonist, Helga Crane, surrounded by objects from China and the Orient.[1] This initial description of Helga sitting amid oriental finery, unhappy with her life at a technical school for African American children, establishes a motif that recurs with surprising frequency throughout the novel: the constant textual linkage between oriental objects and Helga Crane. Oriental knickknacks adorn Helga's homes; Asian-inspired objects arouse her admiration and appreciation for beauty; Chinese silks embrace her body and upholster her furniture. Yet this particular trope has not aroused much interest from Larsen's numerous critics. Given the tremendous amount of valuable and insightful critical commentary that *Quicksand* has generated over the past three decades, this oversight asks for an explanation.[2] Perhaps the urgency of this trope is overshadowed by the novel's dramatic depiction of the psychological damage that racism and sexism wreak on its African American heroine;

in fact most of the critical output on *Quicksand* has concentrated fruit-fully on the novel's depiction of the oppressions endured by middle-class African American and mixed-race women in the face of white racism and idealized notions of femininity.

Or perhaps the lack of critical engagement with this trope suggests a tendency in American literary studies to situate a minority writer within the particular tradition to which she belongs racially, without considering how her works might also comment on the interaction between several racial communities. As I alluded to in my introduction, this silence also manifests itself in the ways literary scholarship sometimes assumes a bi-nary, black-white structure for understanding how racial identities circu-lated in the early twentieth century in general and *Quicksand* in particular, a binary structure to which, I would argue, the novel itself does not wholly subscribe. This exclusive focus on an understanding of race as a binary be-tween black and white in early twentieth-century American literary stud-ies explains in part the absence of detailed critical consideration of why Larsen would so consistently associate Helga with oriental objects.[3] This chapter attempts to address that absence by arguing that oriental objects and the discourse in which they are enmeshed play a pivotal role in under-standing the novel's representation of Helga's subject position as an Afri-can American woman. As my reading of the Eaton sisters proposed, when Asian American authors undertake an evaluation of the politics behind inclusion or exclusion in their works, they are also implicitly questioning the place of African Americans in narratives of citizenship and inclusion. In other words, Asian American works that grapple with questions of in-clusion and exclusion emerged out of a historical moment in which images of Africans and Asians were imbricated. In this chapter, I suggest that the reciprocal is also true too, that African American writers, even when they do not represent Asian figures directly in their works, are situating Asians, as well as themselves, within a discourse of race, citizenship, and inclusion. I therefore offer another lens through which to read Larsen's first novel, one that takes into account the ways that the signification of Asia has in-tersected with the discursive history of blackness.

In this chapter, I examine the impact of Larsen's striking deployment of chinoiserie on the novel's critique of racial politics. It would seem at first glance that these images recirculate the exoticizing conceptions of the Far East that pervade the United States. Deborah McDowell sug-gests in the footnotes of the edition of *Quicksand* published by Rutgers University Press that Larsen invokes orientalism to add a dash of ex-otic color to her storytelling. I think, however, that to level the charge of orientalism against *Quicksand* and Larsen and dismiss its depiction of oriental objects as symptoms of a racist project is too easy and simplistic a reaction to a novel that defies most kinds of racial expectations. Rather, this textual obsession with chinoiserie serves two purposes. The first, and the one I spend the most space exploring, is that *Quicksand* identifies Helga with chinoiserie to dramatize her desire to flee the repressive discursive systems that categorize African American womanhood. The oriental objects that encircle her and that Americans love to display have been wrenched from their cultural contexts into an environment in which their only purpose, no matter what their original function, is decorative and aesthetic. Europeans and Americans were alternately captivated and repulsed by the Orient as a place and Orientals as people, but objects purporting to be oriental in design or origin were fascinating and desirable. This image of an Orient ineffable and immutable gave oriental objects a "theatrical existence not subject to the usual workings of Nature and History" (Guy, 66). Helga's ambivalent relationship to chinoiserie stands in distinct contrast to several other characters, whose attitudes toward Helga, and by extension chinoiserie and other exotic objects, reveal how chinoiserie can animate, mobilize, or strengthen their privileged position as consumers and arbiters of art. Whereas these other characters—notably Anne Grey, Aunt Katrina, and Axel Olsen—conceptualize objects from the East and Africa as a means to cement their own social mobility, position of privilege as cultural arbiters, and sense of themselves as modern consumers, Helga imagines herself *as* chinoiserie, erasing the line between self and other precisely because she perceives the other to be empty of any kind of historical signification.

My characterization of oriental objects relies heavily on the groundbreaking formulation of orientalism first put forward by Edward Said. Although Said focused his field of inquiry on Europe's orientalizing of the Middle East, many of the arguments he makes about the nature of orientalism can be applied to American attitudes toward East Asia. Said writes, "The Orient at large . . . vacillates between the West's contempt for what is familiar and its shivers of delight in—or fear of—novelty" (59). In my reading of Helga's orientalism in *Quicksand*, I depart from Said's notion that "the relationship between Occident and Orient is a relationship of power, of domination, of varying degrees of a complex hegemony" (5). The hegemony that he insists characterizes orientalism, although self-evidently present in Helga's relationship to oriental objects, is not, I would argue, what is central to or most interesting about her orientalism. Rather, Helga's orientalism reveals the flexible and strategic ways in which orientalism can be used to understand and construct racial identity and difference. She performs the same kind of aestheticization upon herself to avoid grappling with a historical discourse of African American womanhood that demonizes and hypersexualizes her. Her self-orientalizing impulses are not presented unsympathetically throughout the novel; that she must perform this kind of self-effacing move indicates how very limited the subjective options are for African American women. Although several women in the novel combat those prevailing representations, Helga finds their solutions to be as limiting and unappealing as the stereotypes themselves. The other characters' attitudes toward the oriental objects that Helga arrays around her range from hostile (in the case of the southern teachers who work at Naxos) to acquisitive (in the case of Helga's friend Anne). Chinoiserie offers a potential model for selfhood that forgoes the need for explanation or contextualization; the novel suggests that Helga finds chinoiserie alluring precisely because she perceives—to her cost—that these objects exist outside the realm of historical signification.

Helga's investment in chinoiserie shifts slightly once she leaves the United States to live in Denmark. Her orientalized position reinforces the novel's placement of her in an international economy of race and sex rather than in a strictly domestic one. A substantial portion of the novel's action is set outside of the United States, not only to make the point that racist and sexist representations of African American womanhood do not stop at national borders, but also to emphasize that the interlocking nature of discourses on the African "savage" and the Asian "Oriental" is one that is truly transnational in its scope and dissemination. The Danes urge Helga to become her "true self" by unleashing the savage they believe lurks within every African American person, but, as we shall see, objects from Asia still have an unsettling if implicit role in that transformation. *Quicksand* not only attacks America's racist attitudes toward African Americans but also points to the parallels between Western modernism's construction of the African savage and its contemporaneous fetishization of the Orient. The novel links these two discursive practices by portraying how the Oriental and the savage become "things"—commodities that enable Western consumerism and at the same time enable the disavowal of the capitalist roots of that consumerism because they are connected to the aesthetic. Helga's transformation into an African savage while in Denmark marks the culmination of the self-aestheticization project that she began in the United States. This achievement, ironically and poignantly, reveals to Helga the failure of her project and the impossibility of leaving behind a history of black oppression. Her ultimate abandonment of this model of subject identity reinforces the reader's sympathetic reaction to her personal travails, despite her seeming self-involvement. She has assumed that chinoiserie escapes the realm of historical and racial signification because it has been decontextualized; by the novel's end she realizes that this process of decontextualization itself constitutes a kind of racial project. Her trip to Denmark forces her to recognize that to be an object of art is to be racially marked.

I end this chapter with a brief reading of the final allusion to China in *Quicksand*. This critical focus calls attention to the fact that, despite its seeming recirculation of the discourse surrounding chinoiserie, *Quicksand* gestures toward the possibility of an alliance between African Americans and Asians based on their shared experience of racialization. On the one hand, the novel employs chinoiserie to signal Helga's desire to flee the field of racial signification; on the other hand, it also makes use of oriental objects to emphasize that African Americans and the Chinese share a history of oppression in the United States. At the same time that the novel plays upon orientalism's evacuation of meaning to illustrate Helga's historically overdetermined position in America, it depicts oriental objects to forge a connection between African American and Asian communities based on a shared history of exclusion and objectification. Helga's orientalism, the novel suggests, is born of necessity; it exists even as *Quicksand* suggests a possible connection between Asians and African Americans. The novel's conflation of African savage and chinoiserie in the body of Helga reflects the complementarity between the racialization process that African Americans and the Chinese undergo. The racial oppression that African Americans and Asians endure "belts the world," to borrow Du Bois's formulation, not just the United States.[4]

Larsen cements this connection by calling on the supposed incompatibility of the Chinese with the American social and political body. African Americans are no more acceptable to white Americans than are the Chinese, and in fact are as strange, exotic, and undesirable as the Chinese. The novel's constant depiction of oriental objects and use of orientalizing language to describe Helga's body and clothing reinforce her literal and metaphorical exclusion from the American nation because those things associated with China could not be more un-American. While other writers and critics of the period imagine black inclusion by excluding the Chinese, Larsen in *Quicksand* suggests that African Americans, *like* the Chinese, are denied access to an American identity, which is reserved for white bodies. *Quicksand* suggests how closely coupled the cultural and political conditions of African Americans and the Chinese are in both the United States and western Europe. In its strategic use of oriental language and imagery, the novel reveals how tightly the exclusion and objectification of blacks pivots on the exclusion and objectification of Asians and vice versa; it also points to a possible common ground for a future political alliance between the two groups based on that shared experience of alienation.

America had been uneasy about Chinese immigration to the United States since the mid-nineteenth century, but that hostility did not become a matter of national policy until 1882, with the passage of the first Chinese Exclusion Act. Although Larsen wrote her novels decades after that initial moment of xenophobic and nationalist hysteria, the question of Chinese inclusion in American public life was still being debated in the 1920s. The passage of the Alien Land Laws in California in 1920 made Asian ownership or leasing of land illegal, and the National Origins Act of 1924 (also called the Albert Johnson Immigration Act) essentially ended all immigration from Asia as well as southern and eastern Europe. As I pointed out earlier, two important Supreme Court cases, *Ozawa v. United States* in 1922 and *United States v. Bhagat Singh Thind* in 1923, declared all East and South Asians ineligible for naturalized citizenship. Larsen wrote her novels only a few years after this string of judicial decisions and legislative actions declared Asians unworthy of calling themselves Americans.

And yet despite the overwhelming and broad support for such anti-Asian legislation, the popularity of commodities that invoked China continued unabated into the twentieth century.[5] Starting in the eighteenth century in England, the chinoiserie craze stemmed from an "aesthetic of the ineluctably foreign, a glamorization of the unknown and unknowable for its own sake" (Porter, 28). The English built pagodas in their gardens, drank tea out of porcelain cups, spoke of the beauty and utility of Chinese pictographs, and read voraciously accounts of Chinese life and customs. A young American nation, eager to show itself to be as civilized as any country in Europe, conscientiously copied this taste for chinoiserie as proof of its cultural sophistication.[6]

The popularity of chinoiserie stemmed in part from the perception that such strange and beautiful objects were used by the Chinese in their everyday lives and that they captured in miniature the essential differences between Western nations and the East. An item's status as Chinese made it a work of art and wonder. The American belief that the chinoiserie pieces that they collected were genuine representations of

China had at its heart the assumption that Chinese culture and people could be reduced to an object: small, containable, and displayable. Ironically the history of chinoiserie effectively dismantles the notion of cultural authenticity that Westerners relied upon in order to distinguish themselves from China and Asia. The reality was that Chinese artisans and manufacturers fashioned their "authentic" Chinese wares in order to cater more effectively to English and American tastes. P. J. Marshall and Glyndwr Williams note that the Chinese were well aware that they were peddling to the Europeans what the Europeans themselves thought China was:

> Much of what Europeans believed to be typically Chinese in the form, colouring or decoration of objects they bought was in fact due to the skill of the Chinese in providing what was expected of them. Even early in the seventeenth century, patterns of "Chinese" motifs were being sent eastwards from Europe to be imitated. If eighteenth-century Englishmen envisaged China as a willow-pattern world of quaint figures crossing little bridges, they were envisaging what was essentially a construct of Europeans' own imagination. (86–87)

The manufacture and production of chinoiserie by Chinese exporters undercut any notion of chinoiserie's authenticity. According to David Porter, the fetishization of Chinese objects by the West transforms "symbols of awe-inspiring cultural achievement into a motley collection of exotic ornamental motifs," which serve "merely [as an] aesthetic arena for the surface play of signs" (29–30). Critics of the chinoiserie crazes that swept England and the United States at various times claimed that the public's fascination with these oriental symbols signals a sense of confusion over their own culture and, by extension, their national identity. This distrust of chinoiserie can be traced back to such figures as Samuel Johnson and Oliver Goldsmith. These critics of chinoiserie complained about its theatrical existence in the Western imagination; they worried that because chinoiserie (like China itself) was so utterly foreign and wholly different from the West it was not subject to the usual workings of signification and meaning making that could be applied to other areas of aesthetics and culture.

Despite the opposition to Chinese immigrants, Chinese objects were often prized and desired by the middle class. Robert Lee notes, "At the end of the nineteenth century, commodities associated with the Orient became a central trope of the feminized consumer culture, through the consumption of Oriental decorative arts and domestic products produced in the 'Oriental style. . . . . Both Chinoiserie and Japonisme became popular motifs in women's clothing styles and in household design" (124). According to Thomas Kim, oriental objects signaled the owner's cosmopolitan taste and appreciation for art. The Orient was not merely a symbol of exoticism but also a crucial way for the twentieth-century consumer to understand his or her place in the market and in modern society. The Orient is thus not outside of modernity but constitutive of modernity itself (383, 385).

And yet the favor that Chinese objects found in American society did not necessarily contradict Americans' implacable hostility to Chinese people in general and Chinese migrants in particular. The association between chinoiserie, japonisme, and femininity domesticated the potential threat that Asian countries posed to the United States politically and economically. By aligning such products with the feminine body or the domestic sphere, American companies alleviated the menace that these nations (and their inhabitants) represented politically, economically, and socially. Rachel Lee examines popular representations of Asians in the early twentieth century to illustrate America's simultaneous fear of and attraction to the Orient, arguing that "although editorial prose condemned Asians as probably sites of infection, at the same time, advertisements capitalized on the allure of the Orient to sell products" (253). According to Lee, fear of the "yellow peril" actually led to the increased sales of oriental products as a way of exercising symbolic control over a population that threatened the nation's understanding of itself. The commodification of the Orient enabled its consumers to control it.

A love of commodities certainly characterizes Helga Crane.[7] *Quicksand* follows a restless and acquisitive Helga as she searches for love and fulfillment. Wherever she goes her initial enthusiasm for each city and group of friends she encounters is eventually replaced with feelings of disgust and dissatisfaction. Helga starts at Naxos, a Tuskegee-like institution in the Deep South, but quits because she cannot bear the school's prudish social strictures and narrow political agenda.[8] The bourgeois black community in Harlem initially dazzles her, but she eventually learns to despise the hypocrisy and smugness of the "talented tenth," who seem so disconnected from and contemptuous of other black people. Alarmed by her growing feelings for Dr. Robert Anderson, a leader in the community and the former head of Naxos, Helga flees to Copenhagen and joins her mother's family. Initially she allows her aunt Katrina and uncle Poul to transform her into an exotic objet d'art, but she eventually rebels and finds herself missing the United States. Back in New York she is rejected by Anderson but seduced by the religious (and sexual) ecstasy offered by a southern minister, whom she immediately marries. Helga's realization several years later that her life has sunk into a morass of unending domestic duties comes too late to save her; constant pregnancies have robbed her body of its strength and beauty, and the emotional tug of motherhood forces her to give up any dream of starting her life over.

Critical inquiry into *Quicksand* has overwhelmingly focused on the issue of how Helga constitutes her subjectivity in the face of the political and social oppression that she bears. Black feminist readings of the novel have tended to examine how issues of race, sexuality, and gender intersect in Helga.[9] This debate often takes the form of an interrogation into the novel's gender and racial politics, whether or not the novel resists the racialization of black women or somehow recirculates denigrating images of black women.[10] Poststructuralists have used the novel to deconstruct notions of subjectivity, focusing particularly on Helga's alienation and her futile search for a sense of herself that will fit into the society around her.[11] This critical dialogue serves as the background for my own investigation of Helga's sense of herself as a black woman. I contend that oriental objects vitally inform her own conception of her subjectivity; the epigraph that starts this chapter dramatizes that relationship. *Quicksand* begins with a framed image of Helga in order to comment on the historical representation of black women in the United States. As the objects of a discourse that simultaneously dehumanizes, racializes, and sexualizes them, African American women have no control over the nature and dissemination of their own representations. Helga feels that her experiences and actions are necessarily defined and interpreted by the historical, cultural, sexual, and racial matrices that work so diligently to define black womanhood in the most degraded terms.

Helga finds herself in a discourse of sexualized black femininity that had been in circulation since before the Civil War. Female slaves were blamed for seducing their white masters into interracial liaisons. After Emancipation, in an age when women were seen as the moral guardians of the family and the race, even the myth of the rapacious black man was blamed on black women; presumably because African American women were so sexually voracious, black men had been forced to develop a more aggressive attitude to match their partners (Giddings, 31). Such notions reveal how tightly gender conventions were enmeshed with racial scripts. Black women were thought to have "low and animalist urges" (82) without any of the virtues that characterized white womanhood.

In *When and Where I Enter: The Impact of Black Women on Race and Sex in America* (1984), Paula Giddings cites several sources that compare black women unfavorably to white women: "black women had the brains of a child, the passions of a woman," and, unlike white women, were "steeped in centuries of ignorance and savagery, and wrapped about with immoral vices." In this era, the idea of a moral black woman was incredible: "I sometimes hear of a virtuous Negro woman," wrote a commentator for *The Independent* in 1902, "but the idea is absolutely inconceivable to me. . . . I cannot imagine such a creature as a virtuous Negro woman" (quoted in Giddings, 82).

The pervasiveness of the notion that African American women were morally suspect cannot be underestimated, and it finds its ways into the most academic and seemingly objective tracts of the day. E. Franklin Frazier, in his landmark study *The Negro Family in the United States* (1938), notes almost casually that "promiscuous sex relations and constant changing of spouses became the rule with the demoralized elements in the freed Negro population" (79–80). The black families that made a successful transition from slavery to freedom were the ones in which the "authority of the father was firmly established and the woman in the role of mother and wife was fitted into the pattern of a patriarchal household" (88). Although Frazier acknowledges that economic and sociological factors influenced black attitudes toward sex, he begins from the premise that the "well-organized" family has an authoritative male at its head. His chapter "Unfettered Motherhood" focuses exclusively on the seemingly permissive attitude that black women have toward sex and illegitimate childbirth, arguing in the case of several women that they were "seemingly unconscious of the moral significance of motherhood outside of marriage" (93). Motherhood outside of marriage is "significant" because it indicates a failure of the innate morals that Frazier assumes all mothers should have. The lack of horror on the part of black single mothers toward their unmarried status signals their essential sexual depravity and moral degradation.

Helga wishes to leave behind this history of repression that orders her life as a black woman and escape into a space that completely evacuates her body and experiences of anything other than beauty, that drastically dehistoricizes her until she is an object of art. She wants, in other words, to become a piece of chinoiserie, beautiful and radically dehistoricized.[12] I would also argue that Helga is not interested in finding a subject position that enables her to create a self-sustaining identity, as other critics have claimed.[13] Rather, her solution is to escape into an identity that transforms her completely into an aesthetic object.[14] She assumes that decontextualizing her own body is the only way to preserve a self that cannot be annihilated by racist discourses or forced into conformity by counterdiscourses.

The particular nature of the relationship between Helga and oriental objects is set up in the first scene of the novel. The reader first meets Helga at dusk, as she relaxes in her room at Naxos after a long day of teaching. This first page reveals her self-containment within a space that she has arranged so that she might be its artistic center. She attempts to resist the sexualization and racism that she as a black woman must face by turning herself into chinoiserie, the most objectified aesthetic object imaginable. Larsen writes, "Only a single reading lamp, dimmed by a great black and red shade, made a pool of light on the blue Chinese carpet . . . and on the oriental silk which covered the stool at [Helga's] slim feet" (1). From the beginning the novel associates Helga with China; she is surrounded by luxury goods that are meant to evoke the mystery associated with the Far East. Her clothing emphasizes the image of a woman more orientalized than Americanized: she is dressed in a "vivid green and gold negligee and glistening brocaded mules, deep sunk in the big high-backed chair, against whose dark tapestry her sharply cut face, with skin like yellow silk, was distinctly outlined" (2).[15] The emphasis on the heavy fabrics and deep colors of Helga's clothing create an atmosphere of exoticism around her body. The mention of "yellow silk," a product closely associated with China, explicitly invokes that nation. The fact that the skin on Helga's "sharply cut face" is "like yellow silk" (2) transforms her own body into an oriental object.[16]

The tropes of framing and chinoiserie are further intertwined in the initial detailed descriptions of Helga's clothes. Her exotic trimmings and Chinese-looking apparel are described at the novel's start, as she nurses her grudge against her stultifying life at Naxos. Her attraction to things oriental is just one quality among many that make her feel unwelcome at Naxos. Her interest in Chinese objects (whether they really are from China or not) is similar in spirit to her love of color and baroque clothing; both are manifestations of her "indefinite, queer," and "disturbing" ways (7). Her search for beauty is linked to her love of oriental objects and fabrics; her admiration for oriental objects stems from the same desire to escape the social and political repression that the Naxos administration seems to believe is the only way to counter white racism. Helga wants to escape this frame of libidinous sexuality that is the conventional way of understanding black women, but not into one that makes her a moral paragon. Writing in March 1925 of the marginalized and precarious position that black women occupy, Elsie Johnson McDougald proudly and defiantly presents an image of the African American woman who "is courageously standing erect, developing within herself the moral strength to rise above and conquer false attitudes. She is maintaining her natural beauty and charm and improving her mind and opportunity. She is measuring up to the needs and demands of her family, community and race, and radiating from Harlem a hope that is cherished by her sisters in less propitious circumstances throughout the land" (quoted in Lerner, 171). The nobility of the statement is undercut by the impossible standards that it sets; it is these very standards against which Helga rebels. The women who work at Naxos offer a solution to the dilemma that Frazier's report describes, that is, to deny the existence of any kind of sexual impulse and to repress those around them. The matrons and teachers at Naxos despise how Helga dresses herself. They particularly object to her "trimmings," those items that finish off her outfits: "Old laces, strange embroideries, dim brocades. Her faultless, slim shoes made them uncomfortable and her small plain hats seemed to them positively indecent" because they highlight Helga's body (18). The discomfort that these items, which essentially frame a woman's body, provoke in the women of Naxos emphasizes Helga's incompatibility with the frame offered by bourgeois black southern life; the clothes that literally enclose her seem to make her too conspicuous in the frame of existence offered by Naxos. The alternative offered by Naxos is as stifling as the stereotype that Frazier's study articulates.

Helga's sense of alienation from Naxos stems in part from the fact that she has no history—that she is the product of a seemingly sordid relationship between Danish and West Indian immigrants. The uneasy relationship between her and the matrons of Naxos does not necessarily stem from her biracial heritage so much as it does from the fact that her parents were "nobodies"—in both the black and white worlds. It is this marginalized status within both the European and African American communities that partially motivates Helga's attraction to chinoiserie; these objects, like her, do not fit into the categories-of-being already in circulation in the United States. Her biracial status is not given much attention in the novel itself; unlike Clare and Irene, the protagonists of Larsen's novel *Passing*, Helga never attempts to pass, and even when living in Denmark she remains identifiably black. As a biracial woman Helga occupies a symbolic netherworld, just as Asians did in the American racial economy of the early twentieth century. The presence of Helga and oriental objects points to the fragility of the supposedly natural and insuperable binary between black and white. *Quicksand* suggests that Helga's mixed racial heritage allies her to the Chinese objects she admires because, like those objects, her presence cannot be accounted for within prevailing racial ideologies of black and white.

Helga's desire to escape Naxos arises from the disgust she feels toward the school's zeal to whitewash itself in an attempt to undo stereotypes about black inferiority and promiscuity. Fleeing Naxos and traveling to a place where people will appreciate her as a chinoiserie-like object of beauty offers her the illusion that she can flee the black community's struggle to define itself against a racist discourse. It is this search for a different, dehistoricized frame in which to place herself as well as her desire to forget the intertwined history of sexism and racism against black women that sets Helga apart from the others. In her eyes, Naxos's insistence on propriety, particularly in women's dress and behavior, turns its African American students and teachers into automatons who are so afraid of resembling the stereotypes of black identity then in circulation that they have, in a sense, re-enslaved themselves. In their attempts to counter the prevailing stereotypes associated with black men and women, Larsen argues, the people of Naxos—and Helga herself—are still shaped by their responses to those conventions. Helga wants to wrench herself away from this influence.

Helga's sense of alienation is captured briefly early in the novel. Contemplating her unhappy life at Naxos she sits with a copy of Marmaduke Pickthall's *Saïd the Fisherman*. Pickthall (1875–1936) was an English novelist whose fame stemmed from his tales about the Orient. In her editorial footnote on Pickthall, McDowell conjectures that Larsen includes the peculiar choice of an orientalist novel in order to provide "eastern color, movement and sharp authenticity. Perhaps Larsen intends an ironic contrast to the dull sobriety and sterility of Naxos" (243). If the insertion of Pickthall were the only moment when the text invoked orientalism, then McDowell's analysis might make sense; however, Pickthall is only one among many examples in which the novel makes reference to the Orient in relation to Helga Crane. Although *Saïd the Fisherman* explicitly refers to a romance about the Middle East (and not China), Helga's unthinking choice of this particular novel at this particular moment, when she feels most alienated and out of touch with the world around her, is a telling indicator of how she imagines her identity as a black woman. She picks up *Saïd the Fisherman* at a moment when "she want[s] forgetfulness, complete mental relaxation, rest from thought of any kind" (2). It is in fact at those moments when Helga feels most alienated and longs for some kind of mental escape from her troubles that objects associated with the Orient are most explicitly described in the novel. As she resolves with energy to leave Naxos in the most dramatic way possible, she "automatically" plays with "the Chinese-looking pillows on the low couch that served for her bed" (15). The unthinking and "automatic" nature of Helga's actions and the way that *Quicksand* narratively links her to the Orient when it is describing her alienation suggest that she occupies the same kind of alienated position within a domestic economy of sex and race that the Orient does. In other words, Helga wants to be like an oriental object because it is dehistoricized, but the novel suggests that she *already* is like an oriental object because she occupies a similar, highly historicized, and almost overdetermined position within the American imaginary.

East Asian objects and chinoiserie continue to encircle Helga as she moves to Harlem. She is initially excited by the vibrant cosmopolitan life she sees around her, especially as it is embodied by her friend and eventual roommate, Anne Grey. Anne's relationship to the chinoiserie and oriental art that she owns operates in a different way than Helga's. The novel describes a display of oriental items in Anne's house in order to accentuate her inability to read, much less criticize, American racial scripts. Race work is the cornerstone of Anne's life, and yet Helga is unsettled by the racist attitudes that Anne displays toward those African Americans who do not fit her middle-class milieu. Anne believes completely in racial uplift and states, "The most wretched Negro prostitute that walks One Hundred and Thirty-fifth Street is worth more than any president of these United States, not excepting Abraham Lincoln" (48). Despite the nobility of and passion behind Anne's support for racial uplift, Helga feels increasingly uneasy as she comes to realize the limits of Anne's sympathy for black people. Most troubling is the way Anne copies the attitudes and culture of white European American society: "While proclaiming loudly the undiluted good of all things Negro, [Anne] yet disliked the songs, the dances, and the softly blurred speech of the race. Toward these things she showed only a disdainful contempt, tinged sometimes with faint amusement" (48). Despite her enthusiasm for "race work," Anne finds distasteful anything associated with black folk culture. Her contempt stems from her implicit assumption of superiority over the less cultured and educated African Americans, who love folks songs and dance.

Quicksand exposes Anne's hypocrisy in its description of her perfectly decorated home, in which various items—Chinese chests, Japanese prints, Eastern rugs, jade-green settees—improbably exist in harmony with each other. When Helga first arrives at Anne's house in Harlem she notes with approval that it "was in complete accord with what she designated as her 'aesthetic sense.' . . . Historic things mingled harmoniously and comfortably with brass-bound Chinese tea-chests, luxurious deep chairs and davenports, tiny tables of gay color, a lacquered jade-green settee with gleaming black satin cushions, lustrous Eastern rugs, ancient copper, Japanese prints, some fine etchings, a profusion of bric-a-brac, and endless shelves filled with books" (44). The "historic things" are explicitly distinguished from the Asian objects; that they mingle "harmoniously and comfortably" with the Asian art is worthy of mention. These objects of the East (the Chinese tea chest, the lacquered jade-green settee, the Eastern rugs, and the Japanese prints) signal Anne's good taste and material comfort. She fills her house with such objects with little sense of what they might mean; they signal her conviction that such objects are interchangeable and mysterious symbols of an essentialized East. *Quicksand* links Anne's uncritical consumption of chinoiserie with her hypocritical and racist stance toward working-class and rural blacks, but the novel takes a much more forgiving stance toward the orientalism that Helga embraces. Helga wants to become chinoiserie to escape the racist and sexist discourse of black womanhood, but in wanting to do so she implicitly recognizes that chinoiserie is culturally decontextualized by Americans; she understands, in other words, that the disavowal of history that is essential to chinoiserie's operation only emphasizes that chinoiserie is racialized. Anne, on the other hand, cannot see how her enjoyment of chinoiserie is in itself racist, just as she cannot see how her dismissal of working-class African Americans completely undermines her stated desire for racial uplift. She perpetuates an essentialized notion of Asian racial difference, even as she rails against the racism that blacks endure. Her blindness to her own racist attitudes toward working-class blacks manifests in her unquestioning acceptance of chinoiserie's place in a middle-class home. The chinoiserie and japonisme that decorate her home illustrate the duplicity of Anne's race work; the novel implies that her sense of herself as an African American woman and her devotion to the idea of race work rely upon imposing her own middle-class standards of art, taste, and behavior onto those whom she deems beneath her socially and economically.

Helga is particularly perturbed by her sexual attraction to Robert Anderson, which reemerges when she meets him while living with Anne in New York. Sharing a ride home with Anderson in a cab one evening, she feels "a strange ill-defined emotion, a vague yearning rising within her" (50). When Anderson fixes her with a "steady gaze" and says, "You're still seeking for something," she is overcome by another "vague feeling of yearning" (50). Flustered by her own reaction, Helga then feels "a sharp stinging sensation and a recurrence of that anger and defiant desire to hurt which had so seared her on that past morning at Naxos" (50). Afterward she treats Anderson coolly, even rudely. Her unease stems from her anxiety that acknowledging her attraction might somehow legitimize the racist accounts of black female sexuality still in circulation; her feelings for Anderson might in fact force her to negotiate her own relationship to the prevailing representation of black femininity. Her constant suppression of these feelings stems from the historical precariousness of the notion of a black "lady." Helga flees New York because she fears her own sexual attraction to Anderson will mean that white society's view of black womanhood will be validated. In attempting to counter racist images of black women as sexually promiscuous, she rejects any expression of sexuality that might be construed as another example of black moral inferiority.[17]

As at Naxos, Helga fixes on Chinese objects when she feels the unsettling arms of racial expectation and history closing in upon her. The objects enable her to defer serious thought about her racialized position in the United States, but they also signify her desire for a subjectivity unmarked by historical constructions of black women. It is exactly at the moment when Helga decides to leave New York to visit her Danish relatives and to escape her disconcerting interest in Robert that Anne's Chinese objects reappear:

> [Helga] busied herself with some absurdly expensive roses which she had ordered sent in, spending an interminable time in their arrangement. At last she was satisfied with their appropriateness in some blue Chinese jars of great age. Anne *did* have such lovely things, she thought, as she began conscientiously to prepare for her return. . . . Helga dusted the tops of the books, placed the magazines in ordered carelessness, redressed Anne's bed in fresh-smelling sheets of cool linen, and laid out her best pale-yellow pajamas of *crepe de Chine*. (56)

In the first passage describing Anne's house, the objects are mingled with bric-a-brac in a confusing profusion. In this passage, Helga regards much more deliberately the Chinese objects around her. She can appreciate the beauty of the expensive roses only when they are placed in a

Chinese jar; she can be a conscientious friend to Anne only when she lays out the yellow crepe de chine pajamas. Helga's obsessive interest in finding the appropriate place for things resounds with her own desire to find an appropriate place for herself, where she can be admired for her beauty. As she is about to cross the ocean to meet strangers and a new nation, these objects of China strangely offer her a sense of comfort and appropriateness, as well as allay her buried resentment toward Anne and the guilt she feels over leaving her for Denmark.

Once Helga arrives in Denmark she is no longer merely surrounded by chinoiserie; she herself *becomes* chinoiserie. She is immediately confronted with her aunt Katrina's overwhelming interest in how she dresses, looks, and presents herself. The Dahls wish to enter Copenhagen's high society, and they see Helga as their ticket into that world. They are clearly wealthy and only need Helga as a fashionable, exotic icon in order to accomplish their entrance into the social elite. Katrina tells Helga, "You must have bright things to set off the color of your lovely brown skin. Striking things, exotic things" (68). She is greatly disappointed in the tameness of Helga's daily wardrobe; when she looks through Helga's clothes she finds only one article acceptable: "'Now that,' [Katrina] said, pointing to the Chinese red dressing-gown in which Helga had wrapped herself when at last the fitting was over, 'suits you'" (68). Helga must prove her authentic "exotic" self by dressing the part that Katrina has envisioned for her. The Chinese dressing gown "suits" Helga because it further emphasizes the very kind of aesthetic decontextualization that Helga has tried to achieve. In Denmark, though, rather than going through this process alone Helga now has an entire city encouraging her. On a shopping spree she allows her aunt to purchase for her dresses with plunging necklines, feathers, "primitive" jewelry, high-heeled shoes, and a "black Manila shawl strewn with great scarlet and lemon flowers" (74). The text here conflates the Orient with the exotic savage, revealing the two images to be built along similar and mutually buttressing lines of objectification. Katrina encourages Helga to pursue her project of decontextualization because the more Helga becomes like a piece of chinoiserie, the more she also can be molded into the European notion of an African savage.

Helga describes herself in three terse statements as "a decoration. A curio. A peacock" (73). The absence of verbs and the fact that she identifies herself with objects signal her complete transformation from subject to object, a transformation that the novel makes clear is aided by Helga herself. After she overcomes her initial discomfort at being the object of such curious stares, she gives "herself up wholly to the fascinating business of being seen, gaped at, desired" (73). She enjoys the attention and the way it feeds her self-confidence. But the society women of Copenhagen do not envy Helga her beauty or notoriety, because "she wasn't one of them, she didn't count at all" (70). Her willingness to embrace her position stems from the fact that the Dahls provide her with a comfortable and coddled lifestyle revolving around teas, parties, concerts, and dinners; the only thing required of her is that she dress expensively and speak rarely. While her beauty seems to give her a sense of belonging in Danish society, that sense of community is predicated upon the fact that Helga doesn't "count at all"; she belongs in Copenhagen in the same way that Chinese vases belong in Anne's elegant living room: as an object that suggests exotic otherness in a thoroughly middle-class and domesticated setting.

The move to Europe shifts the context for understanding Helga's racialization; still isolated, she is no longer seen as a symbol for the improvement of African American people but rather as a symbol of the inherent primitiveness of all Africans. The Danish fascination with Helga as a symbol of African savagery emblematizes western European and American interest in the primitive during the early twentieth century. Helga wishes to escape into the realm of the aesthetic, but the novel reveals the extent to which modern notions of art and beauty are informed by the presence of a racialized other and the inescapability of those notions. *Quicksand* clearly indicts European interest in the image of the "savage" (as embodied by the painter Axel Olsen) by invoking oriental images in relation to Helga's body. The novel suggests that the figures of the savage and the Oriental are constructed along parallel tracks and serve similar purposes: first, to mystify the Asian and the African in order to exclude both from any kind of national body politic, and second, to bolster the Western sense of the individual as a consumer through the realm of the aesthetic.

The impossibility of Helga's project for radical decontextualization is nowhere more evident than in her relationship with Olsen, the celebrated painter who pursues her, artistically and romantically. Helga achieves one of her implicit ambitions when Olsen paints a highly praised portrait of her: she is literally framed as a work of art. His interest in her mirrors modernism's own interest in the figure of the savage. At their first meeting he stares at her through his "heavy drooping lids" and then mutters, "She's amazing. Marvelous," as if Helga herself were not there (71). Axel then asks and receives permission to paint a portrait of Helga

in the romanticized dress of an African savage. At one of the last painting sessions he proposes, expecting an affirmative answer. He is momentarily taken aback when she shrinks from his touch and is then "repelled
by something suddenly wild in her face and manner. Sitting down, he
passed a hand over his face with a quick, graceful gesture" (87). Olsen's
vision of Helga's "wild" face and manner reflects his own anxieties about
the durability of his desirability and power as a white man. Shocked by
Helga's movement away from his caressing hand, he immediately exercises his discursive power over her as a white painter by imagining her
to be wild. His own "quick, graceful gesture" in response covers his momentary discomfort while at the same recentering the conversation onto
himself.

Dispensing with the nicety of not insulting one's beloved when proposing marriage,[18] Olsen then informs Helga that she has "the warm,
impulsive nature of the women of Africa, but . . . the soul of a prostitute":
"You sell yourself to the highest buyer. I should of course be happy that
it is I" (87). His conception of her as primitive informs how he imagines not only their relationship but himself. Her status as a savage is
constitutive of his own consumer status. Her objectification and then
commodification makes clear his role as both a painter and a consumer.
In proposing marriage, he is both the artist and the buyer, and Helga
reinforces the notion that he can own what he creates and create what he
owns. This exchange also brings to light the ways in which art enables
Olsen to disavow the economic and capitalist roots of his consumer status. Consumerism and its disavowal through aesthetics enable him to
express disappointment when Helga tells him she will not marry a white
man. He cannot understand why she insists on introducing race into the
equation, even though his desire for her is based purely on her exoticism.
Her expression of a racialized consciousness does not dovetail with the
aestheticized image of racial otherness that he believes to be natural.

Helga eludes Olsen's objectifying grasp by refusing to acknowledge
his attempts to make her his mistress, by telling him she will not marry
him because he is white, and then by disowning the celebrated painting
of her that he has completed. He insists that her refusal is the result of
Katrina's meddling, bourgeois influence; if left to her own devices, Olsen
implies, Helga's natural sexuality would have led her to accept his offer
to become his mistress.

Olsen represents the modernist movement, with its fascination for
primitive peoples, and he relishes the spectacle of Helga's body in his
painting of her. Larsen's attack on modernism stems from the influence

it had on the American art scene as well as on the African American artists working out of Harlem in the early twentieth century. Modernism seemed to offer a way for black artists and art to be valued by a wider population, but only, Larsen suggests, at a heavy cost. Black artists occupied a position not unlike Helga's. Vetted for their ties to an African or "authentic" blackness, they were forced to play roles that appealed to white patrons. As Michael North writes, "The American avant-garde demonstrated . . . a persistent inability to understand how race fit into its conception of modern America" (129).[19] *Quicksand* rejects modernism's interest in the figure of the savage. When Olsen chastises Helga for following Katrina's bourgeois advice, he does so by asking her what race has to do with his proposal and her refusal, even though his only interest in her is her connection to the African continent. His blindness to his own racism symbolizes the racism embedded in modernism's construction and understanding of itself.

There is one direct but seemingly inconsequential reference to the Orient during Helga's time in Copenhagen that decisively pushes her to return to the United States. Her delight with Denmark is fading; her aunt and uncle are placing considerable pressure on her to make a good marriage, preferably with Olsen. Katrina scolds Helga for her hesitation and tells her meaningfully, "If you put your mind to [marrying Olsen], there's no reason in the world why you shouldn't. . . . Or else stop wasting your time, Helga" (79–80). The veiled threat in Katrina's tone strengthens Helga's feelings of confusion and ambivalence about Denmark. Fru Fischer, a friend of Katrina's, then makes her entrance into the café where Helga and Katrina are talking, and Helga smiles in "self-protection" (80), before feeling disturbed and oppressed by the same unnamable and distant fear that plagued her at Naxos and in Harlem. Fru Fischer comments "that the coffee here at the Vivili was atrocious. Simply atrocious. 'I don't see how you stand it.' And the place was getting so common, always so many Bolsheviks and Japs and things" (80). The invocation of "Japs" at a moment of Helga's profound personal dislocation differs from previous moments. Rather than comforting Helga, Fru Fischer's ceaseless chatter about seemingly trivial matters contrasts with the importance of the preceding conversation between niece and aunt; it also highlights the craven ambition buried under Katrina's pleasant exterior and seeming acceptance of her niece's difference. The connection that Fru Fischer makes between "Bolsheviks, Japs, and *things*" signals the limits of European sympathy for the Far East. Linguistically Fru Fischer dismisses two cataclysmic challenges to Western supremacy in the early twentieth century—the Japanese defeat of Russia in 1905, which signaled Japan's emergence as a world power, and the Russian Revolution of 1917, which toppled one of Europe's last and most powerful absolute monarchies— by making them into objects. Western Europe may admire the clothing and furniture of Asia, but ultimately those from east of Europe are just "Japs" or "Bolsheviks" and therefore indistinguishable from "things." The "thingification" of Japs enables Fru Fischer to constitute herself as a European and as someone who can buy and consume things from the East. The inability to distinguish Japs from things informs the West's fascination with the oriental and Helga herself. Her desire to become an oriental object ends with her desire to reinsert herself in a historical milieu. Her rejection of Olsen, Katrina, and her highly orientalized position within Denmark marks her rejection of chinoiserie as a viable model for being a racialized body in a white world.

The difference between Helga's and the Fru Fischer's relationship to the Orient is that Helga is desperate to find common ground between herself and the "things" that everyone around her wants to possess. Her ultimate rejection of oriental objects does not dismiss or render moot the connections that the novel has implicitly constructed between the discursive practices that objectify African Americans and Asians. To conclude this chapter I want to explore more fully this possibility: that *Quicksand*'s linkage of Helga to chinoiserie works to bring together two communities who are racialized within the United States, African Americans and Asians. *Quicksand*'s representation of the meanings that inform American attitudes toward Chinese *things* asks us to consider the question of the meaning behind Chinese *bodies* in the United States and the nature of the relationship between African bodies and Chinese bodies. In fact, Larsen's creative burst in the late 1920s coincides with the increasing interest in the possibility of Asian-African alliances within urban black communities.[20] Such interest was not peripheral to black political strivings. Du Bois's statement in 1906 that the "color line belts the world" and his lifelong interest in the possibility of an Asian-African alliance was as central to his anti-racist politics as his more famous pronouncements on the double consciousness of black subjectivity in the United States. Though *Quicksand* does not directly comment on this political movement, it does use oriental images to insinuate that common ground can exist between Africans and Asians.

Larsen's use of the Orient as a motif in *Quicksand* coincides with a resurging interest in China and East Asia on the part of Americans in general and African Americans in particular. In the early twentieth century, African American nationalist groups felt an affinity for Asian nations and expressed their solidarity with those nations. These sentiments were not limited to the radical fringes of black politics. Indeed the Japanese victory over Russia—a country that dwarfed it in terms of resources, manpower, and terrain—seemed to deal a serious blow to the ideology of white superiority.[21] Du Bois expressed delight over the outcome of the Russo-Japanese War and declared, "The Russo-Japanese War has marked an epoch. The magic of the word 'white' is already broken, and the Color Line in civilization has been crossed in modern times as it was in the great past. The awakening of the yellow races is certain. That the awakening of the brown and black races will follow in time, no unprejudiced student of history can doubt" (*The Color Line Belts the World*, 43). Like many others, Du Bois viewed the Japanese victory as a victory for all the colored people of the world; the awakening of the "yellow race" was a preview of what the colored peoples of the world could accomplish. Marcus Garvey, implacably hostile to Du Bois, predicted, "The next war will be between Negroes and the whites, unless our demands for justice are recognized. . . . With Japan to fight with us, we can win such a war" (quoted in Deutsch, 195). Various African American Islamic leaders, including Fard Muhammad, the founder of the Nation of Islam, argued that blacks were not Africans but were rather "Asiatic Black men."[22] Some nationalists criticized the emphasis placed on Asia and the Middle East, arguing that this shift away from Africa further splintered the community by confusing African Americans and implicitly denigrating Africa.[23] Nevertheless, theories about the feasibility and effectiveness of an Afro-Asian coalition were in the air. Although Larsen was not explicitly invoking this conversation in *Quicksand*, by identifying her heroine so consistently with Chinese objects and by describing these objects at key moments in Helga's life, she does seem to be gesturing toward the potential similarities that the two communities—African American and Chinese—share in terms of political and social marginalization. Larsen clearly connects the precarious predicament of both racial communities.

Helga's second arrival in New York City differs markedly from her first. Chinese objects disappear entirely from the text. Anne's marriage to Robert Anderson means that Helga is left without a permanent residence and is cut off from the beautiful things that decorate Anne's home. But Helga expresses no regret over the loss of this kind of living. The disappearance of chinoiserie from the novel signifies her abandonment of the notion that she can elude racial signification. She realizes, quite bitterly in the end, that no person can cut herself off from the historical and cultural forces that have shaped her experiences. Having rejected the notion that a self can be disconnected from racial and gender contexts, she kisses Robert in an attempt to express her long-repressed feelings of attraction. His rejection of her precipitates her final move: she marries a minister and moves with him to a small southern town, where nothing more is expected of her than to keep a clean house and bear many children.

The novel's final reference to China occurs before all of these events, while Helga is in New York and confused about what she should do. She notices one day that "a glittering gold sun . . . set in an unbelievably bright sky. In the evening silver buds sprouted in a Chinese blue sky, and the warm day was softly soothed by a slight, cool breeze" (120). This passage is distinctive for two reasons. First, it is one of the few in which Helga is contemplating or describing a natural scene. She is a woman who feels most comfortable and in her element in an urban milieu; the time she spends in the South, away from large cities, stifles her with its social regimentation and narrow-mindedness. Her uncharacteristic moment of contemplation signals the shift that has occurred within herself since her return from Europe.

Second, it is also the only time that the adjective "Chinese" is not used as a direct modifier for a piece of furniture, clothing, or other object associated with domesticated and commodified spaces. Although "Chinese blue" describes a hue often associated with Chinese porcelain, the deliberate choice of this image in a beautiful natural scene and outside of the highly decorated spaces that have characterized Helga's living quarters seems quietly significant. If Helga has abandoned chinoiserie as a model for constructing her own experiences of the world, the novel has not forgotten the transformative potential of such an alliance with its description of a beautiful New York day. The Chinese blue sky—so similar in word choice to the novel's previous descriptions of decorative objects and, at the same time, so utterly different and recontextualized—indicates very briefly that racial difference, although it can never be superseded, can still be reimagined.

Quicksand employs images of chinoiserie strategically as Helga moves from the South to New York, then Denmark, and back again. In Naxos and New York City, chinoiserie represents an ideal of existence for Helga, a way to ignore the painful historical contingencies surrounding black femininity in the United States. By leaving the United States, she believes that she can flee the racial expectations and prejudices (the historical frame) that she endured in the South and in New York and start a new life where she can be appreciated, but the constant and traveling presence of the Chinese objects emphasizes the impossibility of the kind of escape she seeks. In Denmark, she achieves her goal of self-aestheticization: her aunt's financial resources enable her to become a beautiful piece of art, and Olsen's painting materializes that status. Throughout the novel China and chinoiserie are associated with Helga's desire to escape the history of black women's oppression and the black community's response to it. She assumes agency within her own life only when she feels suffocated by the very limited roles that African American women have traditionally occupied. Her lust for Anderson forces her to confront her own desire as well as the historical discourse of black female sexuality, both of which she has tried to avoid. Chinese and oriental objects crop up in Helga's consciousness when she is contemplating freedom, yet they also appear when she feels constrained. They signal the dualities of Helga's own nature, her intense pursuit of happiness that constantly eludes her, even at the moment of its inception. She wants to believe that chinoiserie represents an escape from racialization, but as she learns, even the kind of cultural decontextualization that chinoiserie undergoes is itself a kind of racialization. She realizes that there is no gaze that does not racialize or sexualize her, even if she presents herself (or is presented) as a beautiful work of art. There is no escaping the economy of sex and race in the United States or Europe. Although Helga wants to believe that chinoiserie is without history, her experiences in America and Denmark prove her wrong.

6 / Nation, Narration, and the Afro-Asian Encounter in W. E. B. Du Bois's *Dark Princess* and Younghill Kang's *East Goes West*

What happens when a novel refuses to act like one? What might be the purpose behind such an act of rebellion against the genre of the novel? W. E. B. Du Bois's *Dark Princess* and Younghill Kang's *East Goes West* are two novels that offer ambitious if uneasy answers to those thorny questions. The resistance that both works demonstrate against fulfilling the expectations of genre can be thought of as a meditation on the relationship between literary form and the political possibilities of a global African-Asian alliance. The fluid relationships that both novels build up between African American and Asian characters—and the geopolitical implications that each work represents as emerging from such a relationship—trigger the genre-resisting tendencies in each. Their status as "non-genre literature" (a term I borrow from Jonathan Culler) has everything to do with the political upheavals that they imagine will emerge from the global alliance between Asians and Africans.[1]

I argue that the Afro-Asian interactions depicted in *Dark Princess* and *East Goes West* play an instrumental part in each work's resistance to the primacy of the nation in articulations of Asian and African political identities. These Afro-Asian encounters operate in several ways. First, they reveal the exclusionary ideology that undergirds the United States as a nation-state. Second, they warn against focusing on the nation as the sole location for resistance to racial inequality, while at the same time highlighting the interconnectivity between the domestic racism of Jim Crow and Asian exclusion and anti-colonial struggles abroad. Third, they protest the nationalist and isolationist ideology that tends to pervade anti-racist projects of resistance. In these works, Du Bois and Kang suggest that an intensive commitment to nationalist paradigms of political organization on the part of Africans and Asians *obscures* the connections between minority groups and the colonial projects that transcend national borders. The Afro-Asian encounters in both novels participate in a project of multiscalar engagement that the texts identify as crucial. They drive home the point that anti-racist resistance within a nationalist framework can only be half the battle.

In the past decade, there has been increased attention paid to the transnational elements in Asian American and African American cultural productions. While the United States has imagined itself as an isolated island at various points in its history, seemingly disconnected from and unconcerned with the troubles of the rest of the world, African Americans and Asians living in the United States have never had the luxury of believing in that fiction: first, because there has been a long history of transoceanic movement to this country based on American and European military, economic, and cultural interventions in Asia and Europe, interventions that, of course, continue to this day, and second, because Africans and Asians are often imagined to be two racial groups that can never be entirely assimilated into the nation in the first place. How can you feel insular when you are constantly reminded that somewhere else is "home"?[2] Comparing *Dark Princess* and *East Goes West,* two works that have become increasingly canonized within their respective cultural literary traditions, sheds a spotlight on the work each novel does to imagine panracial alliances and relationships across national borders. *Dark Princess* and *East Goes West* seem to suggest that emphasizing the nation as the privileged site for cross-racial representation reifies racist and potentially violent conceptions of racial purity and cultural authenticity. A doggedly nation-based focus does not recognize the impact of those communities and discourses that are ostensibly outside of the confines of the nation. It also does not recognize how these authors imagined their texts as participating in global political currents. A comparative lens highlights how Asian American and African American cultural formations can be global in terms of the scale of their impact as well as multiracial and panethnic in terms of their political commitments.

Each novel's skepticism toward the nation is most evident in its resistance to genre conventions, and those genre-related subversions can be tracked most effectively through each work's protagonist: Matthew Towns in *Dark Princess* and Chungpa Han in *East Goes West.* Their restless movements within the nation, as well as between the United States and Europe or Asia, reflect their political position; that political position is most clearly delineated when they interact with Asians and African Americans, respectively. Both Matthew and Chungpa are exiles, literal and metaphoric outcasts from their homes.[3] If the nation has served as the justification for African American and Asian exclusion, then both works attempt to de-privilege the nation as the only site that defines subjecthood by imagining an exilic figure as an alternative model for subjectivity to a nationalist narrative of identity, such as citizen. Unlike the cosmopolite or the flâneur (figures that are often associated with transnationality), the exile is forced out of his native land because of some perceived wrongdoing.[4] Matthew Towns initially leaves the United States for Germany in a rage because the medical school where he is enrolled as a student will not allow him to perform physical exams on white women, effectively preventing him from graduating with a degree. Like Matthew, Chungpa Han is a figure of exile and alienation, banished from Korea, resistant to Japanese colonialism, and forced to lead a peripatetic existence in the United States in order to make ends meet. Both novels acknowledge exile's coercive connotation in their recounting of Matthew's and Chungpa's histories, but both works also point to exile as a potentially productive site for cultural expression and political critique. The trope of exile enables *Dark Princess* and *East Goes West* to make intelligible those who have been deemed outside of legible political and cultural boundaries and cautions against the perils of a nationalist discourse that does not recognize its imbricated relationship with globalized anti-racist and diasporic movements. To varying degrees both novels pursue the notion that an exilic subject can find a global racial utopia, where Africans and Asians finally realize how necessary the other group is in the global project to counter colonialism and racism. Matthew and Chungpa become central if uneasy figures in envisioning these just communities for oppressed people of color.

This concept of exile is particularly important in understanding how each work deploys a revisionist genre to challenge the parameters of the nation. Exile as a structuring trope also goes a long way toward explaining each novel's supposed failure to adhere to genre conventions, because each challenges the stranglehold that realism has on capturing ethnic experiences, albeit in different ways.[5] Although its subtitle, *A Romance,* suggests its genre affiliation, *Dark Princess* actually moves between multiple generic modes: from realism to romance to an epistolary novel. *East Goes West* is told entirely in a realist mode, but it has an absence of events that could be called plot in the conventional sense. More significantly, the novel is supremely indifferent to traveling through the stations of the cross that regularly appear in immigrant narratives of the early twentieth century, in which plucky and eager immigrants make their way through various democratic institutions (the neighborhood, school and college, the workplace) in their nearly holy desire to become "American." Chungpa stands out from this cast of characters. Although he is interested in going to college, he does not pursue an education to the exclusion of all else; neither does he repudiate his country of birth, climb a social or economic ladder, or build ties to any one community. His attitude toward Americanization and assimilation is one of amiable confusion at best, and he often seems entirely indifferent to the process of achieving an American identity. Unlike his counterparts within the novel, he alternates between amusement and bemusement as he attempts to eke out a life for himself.

What these subversions of genre suggest is a rethinking by Du Bois and Kang of the link between genre and nation building. If exile is to serve as the starting point for imagining a narrative that cuts across lines of nation and race, then the novel as a genre, which is so intimately tied to the narrative of nationhood and its conventions, must be adjusted. The traditional conception of nation has no room in its borders for the figure of the exile, just as the traditional conception of the novel cannot hold the narratives that exile produces. As numerous critics have documented and theorized, the novel's emergence as a genre coincides with the age of nationalism in Europe. Benedict Anderson maintains that the novel is a literary form that structurally allowed for the concretization of the nation as an imagined community. The intimacy between the novel and the nation can make the novel an ideal vehicle for imposing what Jonathan Culler has called a project of "national homogenization" on its readers ("Anderson and the Novel," 24).[6] Narratives that resist privileging the idea of nation—and narratives about those who are seeking alternative modes of subjectivity outside of the nation—must necessarily be told differently. The multiracial and reciprocal modes of representation partly explain why *Dark Princess* shifts between genres and *East Goes West* has a highly episodic plot. If the novel is the vehicle by which the nation can constitute itself and justify its power, and if both novels want to deprivilege the nation, then they must make changes on the formal level in order to launch this critique. To paraphrase a well-known quotation by Audre Lorde, to dismantle the nation as a house, Du Bois and Kang must use a different set of novelistic tools.

I begin this chapter by examining several key scenes from *Dark Princess* and *East Goes West* that highlight my argument about the links between nation, narration, and Afro-Asian encounters. While these works have similar projects with regard to the novel, their method for carrying them out are quite different. *Dark Princess* shifts genres multiple times; Matthew's political outlook (as symbolized by his relationship to Asian characters) dictates the story's genre. In contrast to *Dark Princess*, which contains an embarrassing wealth of genres, *East Goes West* is conspicuous in that it seems to ally itself with none. The narrative drifts from anecdote to anecdote in much the same way Chungpa drifts from city to city. His distaste for nationalistic projects (whether American or Korean) manifests itself in the alliance he seeks with the African American characters who are his fellow laborers. In both cases, it is the Afro-Asian encounter that prompts and signals the genre and temporal shifts contained in each work.

But it is in the novels' final scenes that we glimpse the kinds of alternative spaces that Afro-Asian relations might create. In the conclusion of this chapter, I will ruminate on whether or not these novels ultimately open up the kind of enunciative space Homi Bhabha ascribes to Frantz Fanon's work (36). Unlike the other works I've examined in this study, *Dark Princess* and *East Goes West* depict the relationships that can be possible between blacks and Asians in some future moment, in a transnational and globalized space. Matthew and Chungpa represent "chiasmatic figure[s] of cultural difference, whereby the anti-nationalist ambivalent nation-space becomes the crossroads to a new transnational culture" (Bhabha, 4). Resistance to genre is made legible both through the protagonist (his movements and his relationships to either African Americans or Asians) and in the way that the finales of both works disrupt the temporal and spatial imperatives embedded within the novelistic project. To varying extents both works reconceptualize the very notion of time itself in order to denaturalize the nation as a kind of political space. It may be a strange thing to consider, but both of these books see America as already beside the point; they are both already trying to imagine another kind of space and another kind of temporal reckoning to undo political exclusions (the nation) and representational hierarchies (the novel). Neither work ever considers the nation a theoretically stable category, and both reveal that accepting the nation as a natural category of political division means making certain kinds of assumptions about the constitution of communities and the movements of peoples, namely, that they are disconnected from and unaffected by international events or colonial histories and that they thus interact solely within national boundaries that are impermeable. But just as the movement of peoples does not necessarily follow geographical boundaries—in fact it often highlights how porous and arbitrary such boundaries are—cultural productions do not always remain within the borders that define a nation. Although the novels critique the exclusionary nature of nationalist narratives and attempt to unsettle the borders that divide races and nations, their finales cannot imagine viable alternative spaces that do not replicate hierarchies of difference.

From the start of his career, as many critics and historians have demonstrated, Du Bois understood that the plight of the African American population was intimately tied to the colonizing efforts of western Europe and the United States in Africa and Asia. His internationalist bent can be seen as early as *The Souls of Black Folk,* where he writes, "The problem of the twentieth century will be the problem of the color line—the relation of the darker to the lighter races of men in Asia and Africa, in America and the islands of the seas" (210). The less-quoted second half of this sentence focuses particularly on the interactions across continents and oceans. Indeed from the earliest stages of his career Du Bois implicitly questions the notion that the nation alone should be the central node for understanding double consciousness. In his early (and most famous) articulation of double consciousness, Du Bois argues:

> The Negro is a sort of seventh son, born with a veil, and gifted with second-sight in this American world,—a world which yields him no true self-consciousness, but only lets him see himself through the revelation of the other world. It is a peculiar sensation, this double-consciousness, this sense of always looking at one's self through the eyes of others, of measuring one's soul by the tape of a world that looks on in amused contempt and pity. One ever feels his twoness,—an American, a Negro; two souls, two thoughts, two unreconciled strivings; two warring ideals in one dark body, whose dogged strength alone keeps it from being torn asunder. (210)

Du Bois implies that the enforced migration of black populations from Africa to the United States and their enslaved condition outside of the realm of the "American world" historically informed double consciousness. It is, in other words, partly because African Americans come from "somewhere else" and can never be incorporated into the American political and social body that they are able to wield double consciousness.

But is double consciousness a curse or a blessing in disguise? That it is the product of racial oppression is not in doubt. But as much as it is historically produced, double consciousness is also a psychological paradigm that offers a form of "second sight." In this passage, Du Bois hints at the possibility of double consciousness as an extraordinarily productive site for black cultural expression and critique. As Paul Gilroy has argued in *The Black Atlantic*, the enforced exile that creates the conditions for double consciousness can transform the experiences of African peoples into privileged sites of critique. Du Bois suggests that being denied full participation in American political, economic, and social life has given blacks a kind of "second sight" into the nation and into themselves. Contrary to the conventional racist wisdom that an innate inferiority or centuries of oppression have rendered African Americans unfit to be citizens of the United States (or, for that matter, any modern nation), Du Bois takes the attitude that the African American community's endangered and yet entrenched position within American history transforms African Americans into the best critics of that culture's past.[7] In this framework, African Americans' historical link to an African past—the "dark" continent that has traditionally been the source of all their woes—offers them the source of their greatest potential.

But Du Bois argues in *Dark Princess* that double consciousness is not a nationalist phenomenon. Indeed the novel takes to task those characters that look only to ameliorate black life domestically by working within a corrupt political system, without worrying about the relationship between white racism at home and the West's colonial enterprises in Africa and Asia. The novel's protagonist is a brilliant African American intellectual whose changing attitudes about African America's place in a global struggle against oppression is reflected in the novel's multiple genre shifts, which the following plot synopsis should make clear. Early in the novel, while in Berlin, Matthew Towns meets Kautilya, a princess and the ruler of a country on the Indian subcontinent and the organizer of a United Nations–like conference for the colored nations of the world. She invites the disgruntled Matthew to join the organization as a representative of the "African American nation," over the protests of other countries (most notably Japan) who think African Americans are not yet advanced enough to engage in global politics. As part of his research Matthew returns to America and becomes a Pullman porter in Chicago in order to gather information from the working class about increasing African American interest in global issues. The politics of the local rears its ugly head in a horrific fashion when he witnesses the lynching of one of his friends, a fellow porter. This crime convinces Matthew to abandon the global dream that he had imagined with Kautilya. Enraged and disheartened, he allows himself to become involved in a plot to bomb members of the Ku Klux Klan as they ride on his train to Chicago. At the last minute, after seeing Kautilya aboard the very train that is destined to be destroyed, he stops the disaster from happening and goes to jail rather than give up the name of the other conspirator. His release is secured by Sammy Scott, the African American political boss in the Chicago machine, and his efficient executive assistant, Sara Andrews. Embittered by his experiences Matthew agrees to work for Sammy and then run for office himself, eventually rivaling Sammy in political clout and popularity. Matthew's experiences as a cog in the Chicago political machine further cement his belief that African Americans should have nothing to do with the wider struggle against white domination. His ascent up the Chicago political and social ladder is crowned by his election to the state house as a senator and his loveless, society-page marriage to the ambitious, efficient, and cold Sara. Kautilya reappears in his life, working as the head of a female labor union (she has given up her royal trappings to see how the working class live). Instantly Matthew recovers his passionate interest in improving the race and leaves Sara and his political career to become a manual laborer. After another, brief separation, Matthew and Kautilya are reunited and married near the Virginia home of his mother; the son that Kautilya has borne in the interim will become the leader of a great Afro-Asian nation, presumably the "Dark Prince" of the Hollywood sequel.

Arnold Rampersad and Claudia Tate are two critics who have paid close attention to the novel's genre gyrations. Despite the differences in their approaches, Rampersad and Tate both see the novel's genre bending as a sign of its failure to reconcile the binaries that constitute African American life: the sacred and the secular for Rampersad and the sexual and the political for Tate.[8] In a more recent essay, Dohra Ahmad has productively examined these issues of genre by focusing on how shifts in the novel's geographical setting (from Chicago to India to the American South) coincide with shifts in its narrative style: from realism to orientalism to romance. Ahmad argues that *Dark Princess* offers a prehistory of the nations that we would now call the "Third World." The literary form that *Dark Princess* takes reveals the problems of this "global South" as Du Bois imagined it (Ahmad, 776). The premise of Ahmad's argument is that "geography dictates genre" (777); *Dark Princess* represents Du Bois's attempt to grapple with the question of how to represent linguistically and formally different parts of the world.

Like Ahmad, I argue that attention to literary form offers us a key for unlocking *Dark Princess*'s racial dynamics. Du Bois simultaneously inflates and punctures the boundaries of the novel in order to expose its links to the political agenda of the nation-state. The novel's genre shifts are pegged to the protagonist's conflicted and merging attitude toward a global panracial alliance that in and of itself is informed by the state of his romantic interest in the novel's titular Indian princess. In order to track the novel's changing genres, one needs to track the level of interest Matthew has in placing African American experiences within the context of a global movement *as well as* his heterosexual desire for Kautilya. Matthew's encounters with other Asian characters, and the kinds of relationships he imagines might exist between all of them, thus crucially link the novel's formalistic innovations with its political agenda. My reading of *Dark Princess* focuses on a few key scenes in which Matthew interacts with East Asian characters and the princess herself. In these moments of interracial encounter, his attitude toward a global anti-racism campaign becomes transparent; this attitude in turn determines how the novel is working from the perspective of genre. The exilic paradigm, as embodied by Matthew Towns, cannot be captured within the conventions of genre. Throughout *Dark Princess* Du Bois upsets the narratological conventions of linearity and space that form the heart of the novel as a genre.

The genre swings begin with Kautilya's first appearance in the text. Matthew's abrupt but understandable departure from the United States because of the racism he encounters is grounded in history; his initial meeting with Kautilya is mostly fantasy. Matthew sits by himself in a Berlin café, feeling utterly "lonesome and homesick" and desiring more than anything else to "clasp a dark hand, . . . to kiss a brown cheek. And then—he saw the Princess!" (8). When Kautilya is accosted by the unwelcome attentions of a racist American, Matthew proceeds to knock him down on the street. Kautilya responds by telling Matthew, "It ha[s] never happened before that a stranger of my own color should offer me protection in Europe" (17). Her arrival on the scene like a deus ex machina, at the very moment when Matthew is longing to see black people, and Matthew's gallant rescue of her from an obnoxious American's advances, make a point that the rest of the narrative will take pains to hammer home: that Destiny plays a hand in bringing the princess and Matthew together and that they thus share more culturally and physically than might be anticipated.

Kautilya herself constantly undoes notions of racial purity, even though she herself is of royal blood. By resisting a definition of race as a hermetically sealed biological category, she suggests that Africans and Asians may share more in common, culturally as well as politically, than anyone has realized. Undermining the notion that racial purity somehow legitimates political power, she proudly points to the similarities between dark-skinned Indians and Africans:

> "Ah! mixed blood," said the Egyptian.
>
> "Like all of us, especially me," laughed the Princess.
>
> "But, your Royal Highness—not Negro," said the elder Indian in a tone that hinted a protest.
>
> "Essentially," said the Princess lightly, "as our black and curly-haired Lord Buddha testifies in a hundred places. But"—a bit imperiously—"enough of that. Our point is that pan-Africa belongs logically with Pan-Asia; and for that reason Mr. Towns is welcomed tonight by you, I am sure, and by me especially." (19–20)

Kautilya's startling pronouncement that Buddha was "black and curly-haired" and that her own royal ancestry undoubtedly includes Africans presages the tropes of polyculturalism that we see in the works of Robin D. B. Kelley and Vijay Prashad. The Indian princess's embrace of an unknown black ancestor reinforces the novel's argument that to a certain extent we are *all* mulatto. As Kautilya's embrace of a black Buddha suggests, histories and peoples are never pure manifestations of biologically distinct racial groups; there is a complicated and heretofore unacknowledged history of exchange that dates back centuries.[9]

This idealized and hybridized notion of identity is immediately made problematic by the novel's insistence upon Kautilya's distinctly regal presence, which seems to be rooted in her long and noble heritage. She "imperiously" ends any further discourse on the possibility of her multiracial identity by pointing immediately to the logic behind an Afro-Asian alliance. It is a fascinating moment, coming in the midst of a discussion that decries racial purity, since Kautilya is essentially reasserting her royal rights,—a right that is based, of course, on her bloodline. Even Matthew's initial description of Kautilya suggests that she is a symbol of something other than a global laboring movement: "She had the air and carriage of one used to homage and yet receiving it indifferently as a right. With all her gentle manner and thoughtfulness, she had a certain faint air of haughtiness and was ever slightly remote" (14). Later, when the members of the conference displease her by trying to dissuade Matthew from joining their group, she exercises her royal prerogative to the hilt: "[The princess] threw one glance at the Indians, and they bowed low with outstretched hands. She stamped her foot angrily, and they went to their knees. She wheeled to the Arab. Without a word, he stalked out. The Japanese alone remained, calm and imperturbable" (33). These images of a princess accepting the unquestioning obeisance of her servants seem irreconcilable in a novel that is working so hard to undo certain kinds of narratives of biological essentialism. We could read these scenes as part of a larger redemption narrative, the kind we often see in modern romantic comedies: Kautilya acts the part of petulant princess who will eventually be humbled and made more worthy of her role as leader. This familiar narrative, however, does not account for the fact that Kautilya never loses that imperious quality, and that in fact the more she labors to understand the working classes, the more transparent her royalty becomes. I think Kautilya's behavior presages what Du Bois ultimately will elevate over racial bloodlines and nationalist belonging: the idea of bloodlines based on royalty and a messianic vision of community.

Even more troubling than Kautilya's seemingly contradictory mix of racial equality and royal prerogative is her belief in the "logic" of a pan-African and pan-Asian alliance. The moment suggests the extent to which the novel is tangled in its own construction of race. Kautilya never states the case directly, but why does she imagine that Africa "logically" belongs to Asia? Do these two peoples share a history of oppression, or, more problematically, is Kautilya suggesting the two groups share an obscured biological heritage? These are questions I attempt to answer more fully at the end of this analysis; here I want to suggest briefly that *Dark Princess* replaces the nation as an organizational principle for a notion of communal belonging more akin to kinship. By its conclusion, the novel presents a vision of community based on a principle of alliance and political organization that supersedes that of nationhood: a premodern understanding of kinship.

The Afro-Asian interracial romance that is at the heart of *Dark Princess* reflects Du Bois's well-known and wide-ranging interest in Asia and the potential relationship that Africans and Asians might have politically as well as culturally. Du Bois's initial attempts to connect the plight of Africans and Asians revolved around excavating a history of "great names" that the two groups might share as common ancestors. It is in this earlier phase of his career that Du Bois insisted on an ethics of civil rights and political equality within the framework of the nation-state. As the century progressed, and as the plight of African Americans and the colonized around the world were ignored by world governments and their governing bodies, Du Bois began to understand that the relationship between Africans and Asians is based on the exploitation of their labor. In fact, he argues that African Americans have lost their place as leaders of "the colored peoples of the world" because of their American-bred suspicion of socialism and lack of understanding of global events. Du Bois sees countries like China, Indonesia, and India—places with strong nationalist and anti-colonial projects—as potential role models for African Americans. By learning from movements in Africa and Asian, Du Bois argues, African Americans can "vote for the welfare state openly and frankly; for social medicine, publicly supported housing, state ownership of public power and public facilities; [and] curbing the power of private capital and great monopolies" (*W. E. B. Du Bois on Asia,* 55).

Du Bois's belief that African America has something to learn from global anti-racist struggles is prevalent throughout *Dark Princess*. Matthew's openness to learning the lessons of this cause determines not only the novel's representation of Afro-Asian relations, but the very form that the narrative will take. The novel's shifts in genre depend on Matthew's exilic status. Ironically Matthew is most disillusioned with global race work at a time when he seems to be the most politically involved. *Dark Princess* shifts into a realist (and therefore more identifiably novelistic) mode after he returns from Berlin, signaling that he has given up his exilic subject position—temporarily—in order to become more rooted in traditional notions of politics, citizenship, and the nation. It is only when Kautilya and Matthew are reunited and their romance and dreams for a panracial future are in full flower that the novel becomes extravagantly nonmimetic.

Matthew's meetings with Asian characters, which occur throughout the novel, act as a barometer of his political commitment to global struggle. When the Japanese statesman from the Berlin conference visits Matthew to try to induce him to participate in a global conference of darker peoples, he confesses that at the time of the conference he had doubted "intelligent cooperation between American Negroes and other oppressed nations of the world might sensibly forward" the political goals of both groups. His doubts, he implies, have been swept away with his time in the United States. Matthew scoffs at the diplomat and at the earlier views he expressed to the princess.

> "I have been wondering," said the Japanese with the slow voice of one delicately feeling his way—"I have been wondering how far you have unified and set plans—"
> "We have none."

> "—either for yourselves in this land, or even further, with an eye toward international politics and the future of the darker races?"
>
> "We have little interest in foreign affairs," said Matthew.
>
> "Some time ago . . . at a conference in Berlin, it was suggested that intelligent cooperation between American Negroes and other oppressed nations of the world might sensibly forward the uplift and emancipation of the darker peoples. I doubted this at the time."
>
> "You may continue to doubt. . . . The dream at Berlin was false and misleading. We have nothing in common with other peoples. We are fighting out our own battle here in America with more or less success. We are not looking for help beyond our borders, and we need all our strength at home." (150)

Matthew's insistent and repetitive use of the pronoun "we," with its simultaneous connotations of plurality and community, is striking here. The "we" that constitutes the subject of these sentences does not suggest alliance or communal identification; instead it signifies a kind of monolithic construction of the black experience that the text consistently deplores. The "we" that Matthew constructs is not a diverse, politicized community, but a narrow cadre of self-interested, opportunistic middlemen and power brokers whose idea of "uplift" is to enrich themselves in the same corrupt ways that white people have. His insistence on devoting himself to a domestic agenda seems a practical one, given the number of obstacles that African Americans faced in the early twentieth century; indeed in his narrow rhetoric, born of despair, we can perhaps hear Du Bois taking a final dig at Booker T. Washington and his "casting your bucket" program of building up black economic self-sufficiency at the expense of political equality. But this "we"-based focus is intensely nationalistic and isolating; it cannot imagine seeking alliances from other quarters of the wider world and in fact refuses to see that the problems of blacks in America might be connected to issues outside of the United States. Matthew's response to the diplomat—spoken in the name of the African American community—is steeped in the myopic notions of national sovereignty and racial purity, which in this novel are always linked and to be resisted.

Matthew's refusal to see the connection between racial struggles at home and colonial struggles abroad is nowhere more apparent than in the conversation he has with a Chinese diplomat working to rid China of Western influences. When this diplomat boasts that the Chinese in America have contributed $2 million in six months to the support of independence movements back home, Matthew groans, "Our NAACP collected seventy-five thousand dollars in two years and twelve million damn near fainted with the effort" (135). The "Chinaman" responds sympathetically:

> "Ah," he said hesitatingly. "Doesn't it go so well here?"
> "Go? What?"
> "Why—Freedom, Emancipation, Uplift—union with all the dark and oppressed . . . "
> "There's no such movement here." (135)

Matthew's confusion ("Go? What?") indicates the extent to which he has removed himself from the goals that began the novel; he is so far removed from Kautilya and her conference that he does not even share the same vocabulary with these global pioneers. The diplomat then exhorts him to support the cause of "Freedom, Emancipation, Uplift—union with all the dark and oppressed," which Matthew caustically dismisses by insisting, "There's no such movement here." The novel figures Matthew's dismissal of "union with all the dark and oppressed" as an act of cynicism and despair and an admission of defeat. "The Chicago Politician" section of *Dark Princess* paints a portrait of the local at its absolute worst, built on a system of patronage and narrow, parochial interests.

The character most consistently and visibly associated with this idea of the political is Sara Andrews, Sammy Scott's executive assistant who marries Matthew and quietly engineers his rise through the Chicago machine. Within pages of introducing Sara, the novel makes repeated mention of her physical appearance. Recalling his first meeting with her, Sammy describes her as looking "unusually ornamental, in her immaculate crepe dress, white silk hose, and short-trimmed hair. She had intelligent, straight gray eyes, too, and Sammy liked both the intelligence and gray eyes. Moreover, she could 'pass' for white—a decided advantage on errands and interviews" (111). A few pages later Sara runs an errand for Sammy "appropriately garbed in a squirrel coat and hat, pearl-gray hose, and gray suede slippers. Her gloves matched her eyes, and her manner was sedate" (117). When she is on her way to win Matthew's release from prison, the novel makes a point of announcing that Sara "had on a new midnight-blue tailor-made frock with close-fitting felt hat to match, gay-cuffed black kid gloves, gun-metal stockings, and smart black patent leather pumps. On the whole she was pleased with her appearance" (119). The detailed and specific descriptions of Sara's dress are in stark contrast to the majestic but nonspecific language used to describe Kautilya's body. For example, upon first seeing the princess while sitting in a café on Unter den Linden, Matthew notes a "hint of something foreign and exotic in her simply draped gown of rich, creamlike silken stuff and in the graceful coil of her hand-fashioned turban. Her gloves were hung carelessly over her arm, and he caught a glimpse of slender-heeled slippers and sheer clinging hosiery" (8). The princess's broadly anti-racist and anti-colonial project is reflected in these descriptions of refinement; the contrasting way the two women are described physically echoes the diametrically opposing viewpoints that they possess toward the idea of "uplift." In its adherence to realist genre conventions in "The Chicago Politician" section, the novel links a nativist focus on domestic racism to Sara's obsessive interest in rigorously maintaining and policing her outward appearance and behavior, both of which the novel outright rejects. If Kautilya represents romance—with her heaving bosom and electric sexuality expressive of her commitment to global alliances and justice for the laboring class—then Sara is the most prosaic of prose, with her careful trading of political favors, budgeting of income, and fashionable if practical mode of dressing.

More than anything else Sara defines power by her ability to attain the American Dream of economic upward mobility for herself: "Sara was neither a prude nor a flirt. She simply had a good intellect without moral scruples and a clear idea of the communal and social value of virginity, respectability, and good clothes. She saved her money carefully and soon had a respectable bank account and some excellent bonds" (114). The qualities of womanhood that society values are merely seen as commodities or capital by Sara. Without them her position is compromised; with them she can climb the highest heights. In this regard, she is the exact opposite of Kautilya, who has a kind of natural nobility that is above the daily need to make money, even when she has none. Sara has a "clear idea" of what community is too, but her vision is of a community that is able to acquire influence, power, and money. It is, in a sense, a perversion of Booker T. Washington's program that emphasized black economic uplift over social and political equality.

In the novel's world, Sara's most unforgivable sin is perhaps her complete lack of physical interest in Matthew, whom we've been told repeatedly is a handsome man. Her inability to reciprocate heterosexual love parallels her lack of interest in the general advancement of black people: "Behind Sara's calm, cold hardness, [Matthew] found nothing to evoke. She did not repress passion—she had no passion to repress. She disliked being 'mauled' and disarranged, and she did not want any one to be 'mushy' about her. Her private life was entirely public; her clothes, her limbs, her hair and complexion, her well-appointed home, her handsome, well-tailored husband and his career; her reputation for wealth" (153). Her unwillingness to be the object of Matthew's sexual desire is a signal of her narrow-minded political commitments. Although Matthew knows he does not love Sara when he proposes to her, he does, at various points, entertain the hope that he can learn to love her. What becomes clear is that Sara has no interest in love; for her, married life is about helping Matthew attain higher political heights so that she ensures her own social position and shore up her political influence. It is this quality of lovelessness that the novel condemns most resoundingly, and again, it is connected to Sara's lack of political vision and reflected in the very language in which her life with Matthew is described. As this passage indicates, Sara exemplifies African America's interest in its material and political position within the United States. The shortsightedness of her political goals is emblematic of the way nationalism limits the goals of racial justice to a set of concerns circumscribed by the nation. As Matthew says in Berlin, before his embitterment, "the white middle class" is able to buy its luxuries because people in the "dark colonies" are being oppressed. And yet his lack of a global vision and his intense focus on the materialist concerns of domestic politics prevent him from seeing himself as part of a global project that millions of others are engaged in.

Matthew's refusal to see the connection between racial struggles at home and colonial struggles abroad is all the more striking given the number of times that Asian characters serve as his interlocutors, symbols of the Afro-Asian global alliance about which he seems so conflicted. After Kautilya leaves him near the novel's end, Matthew rediscovers his dream of racial progress in, of all places, a Chinese restaurant.[10] This scene reminds the reader of Matthew's previous encounter with a Chinese diplomat, in which he scoffed at the willingness of the Chinese living in America to support anti-imperial causes in China. Both scenes bookend Matthew's transformation from local party cog to global race leader. The proprietor of the Chinese restaurant dreams of an independent China free of Western influence:

> "But we must push on always—on!" And then pausing she said timidly, "And you, my friend. Are you pushing—on?"
> I hesitated and then arose and stood before her. "I am pushing— on!" I said. She looked at me with glad eyes, and touching her forehead, was gone. And I was right, Kautilya, I am pushing on. (292)

There is a touching quality to this scene for the modern reader, especially given the way that Afro-Asian relations have been portrayed in the national media in the past several decades, and most especially given the way the two groups have been pitted against each other in the zero-sum political and economic game that defines domestic policy in this country. The direct contact between Matthew and the Chinese woman (he stands to talk to her; she responds with "glad eyes"; they both use almost the exact same phrase and hesitate at the same moment to describe their respective struggles) suggests a certain kind of sympathy between the two and a mutual understanding about the cost involved in "pushing on."

Chungpa Han's exilic subjectivity in *East Goes West* follows a different trajectory than Matthew Towns's.[11] Unlike Matthew, Chungpa realizes from the start that ethnocentrism and isolation lead to violence. His experience of Japanese colonialism and Korean patriotism—both a result of intense nationalistic feelings—makes him an outsider to the Korean expatriate community in the United States. As a Korean man living in the United States he is doubly persecuted and vulnerable: as an Asian national he can never hope to become a citizen of the country where he lives, and as a citizen of Japan he belongs to an empire that has attempted to obliterate his place of birth. With Japan's official annexation of Korea in 1910, Korea as a national entity ceased to exist; Koreans were considered Japanese citizens, paid homage to the Japanese emperor, were forbidden to speak or write Korean, and were given Japanese names to replace their Korean names.[12]

Despite his distress over the Japanese occupation, it is the Korean nationalism of his fellow expatriates that upsets Chungpa the most. His troubled relationship to the Korean nationalism that burns around him constitutes a recurring motif in a novel that is strikingly disengaged from Americanizing narratives. Whereas the genre shifts of *Dark Princess* reflect Matthew's shifting political priorities, the reluctance of *East Goes West* to follow novelistic conventions concerning plot and structure manifests in an episodic plot in which Chungpa—unlike most ethnic immigrant protagonists—shows little interest in Americanizing himself. The novel, in other words, questions the stranglehold that realism has in capturing ethnic experience in America. According to Thomas Ferraro, immigrant writers of the early twentieth century had three genre options for writing about their experiences: "autobiography, the social science treatise, and fiction in the realist tradition" (382). Ferraro goes on to note that the "ethnic novel" might reconstruct "the earlier years of settlement

('the ghetto narrative' and its rural equivalents)" or depict "more recent dramas of passage out of the colony into the middle classes (the
'up-from-the-ghetto' narrative and equivalents)," and thus draw upon
"the writer's continuing struggle for cultural rapproachement" (382).
These were the kinds of expressions of ethnic immigrant identity that
the publishing world and the American reading public expected, and
they constituted the dominant genres in narratives of ethnic experience.
These immigrant bildungsromans reinforced the idea of the nation as
the goal for every aspiring citizen. Incorporation into the nation signaled
the character's maturation and arrival into a new and more complete
identity.

East Goes West is the story of an immigrant coming to America in
order to escape the perils of life in his homeland. When reduced to a
thumbnail sketch, the novel seems like the hundreds of others that have
been published in the United States recounting the experiences of immigrants. But *East Goes West* is notable in that it follows none of the
rules that govern the immigrant's tale. Chungpa arrives, gets various
jobs in New York City, meets a variety of Korean expatriates (including
George Jum, a likable bon vivant, and Kim, a scholar from a well-to-do
family who has fallen in love with Helen, a young white woman from a
socially prominent family), moves to a missionary college in the remote
regions of Canada, quits college with little regret, and works odd jobs
in New York, Boston, and points west. The meandering nature of the
narrative, although not at all similar to Du Bois's, does suggest a cor-
relation: the story of the Afro-Asian exile is one that cannot be told in
the ways we have come to expect from ethnic, immigrant, or racialized
fiction. Kang's novel does not participate in naturalizing the immigrant's
tale with which most Americans were familiar. Chungpa's story ends
with thoughts about the Old World, not the New. If the novel as a genre
imposes a linear order upon narratives that creates an image of coherent subjectivity for its readers, then Chungpa's "beyond-time" bonds to
America wreck the logic of the traditional immigrant's tale and the novel
itself.

Chungpa's discomfort with nationalist narratives of inclusion, whether Korean or American, permeates the novel. The novel shows that the
supposedly insuperable lines dividing racial groups are erected in the
name of social order and are always permeable and difficult to read
reliably. Upon arriving in New York, Chungpa ventures with friends
into Harlem. One of his fellow Korean expatriates, George Jum, has a
girlfriend who dances in a show in one of the nightclubs. Chungpa is

intrigued by the fact that Park has a girlfriend, whom he assumes is African American: "[June] wore some warm brown stain all over her body. That was all in the nude except for a small net on the breasts, and a small piece of cloth on the hips. Still, she did not look very naked, for the brownness clothed her as she danced. She had the most elastic body I had ever seen . . . just like a rubber band" (75). Chungpa's description of June depends on how her body simultaneously submits to a regime of male heterosexual desire and seems to deny her male observers the very images they seek. She is naked and at the same time hidden from view; despite her lack of clothing, "she did not look very naked," perhaps because the "brownness clothed her." Chungpa's portrayal suggests that bodies are not as transparent as we want to believe; the legibility that we assume rests on the surface of the skin is merely interpretation, informed by social context. The body itself is something that covers an individual, like clothing, revealing no more to the viewer than June does. Her skin color seems to be a part of the costume that she dons when she dances; it is part of her performance of desirable, available femininity. The novel drives this point home even further by revealing to us June's racial identity. Her body is not the only thing that is elastic; as it turns out, June wears blackface, or in this case blackbody. She is, as Chungpa puts it, "not black but white, white as chalk" (76). But the certainty of this pronouncement is again undercut when Chungpa learns later that June might be partly of African descent. The more he attempts to place June in one of the two racial categories available to him, the more she eludes any kind of certain categorization.

As I stated earlier, unlike in other immigrant tales, in which characters receive an education, develop social and professional networks, renounce the "old ways" of life, and embrace the new identity and possibilities that America offers them, Chungpa remains curiously indifferent to the American Dream, and his description of certain landmark experiences that other immigrants mark as central in their Americanization is almost always conflicted. The one moment of spontaneous friendship comes while he is traveling in Canada. After a demoralizing semester at school Chungpa boards a train that is overrun with a group of French schoolboys. He has little in common with the group, and yet a friendship is instantly formed, despite the fact that they "had no language contact." Despite their mutual incomprehensibility, the boys are enthusiastic about interacting with Chungpa: "One after another they drew me into their group, asking questions, exclaiming, and nudging each other eagerly. As the night progressed, we gathered into one end of the cold car and sang

French songs in unison. I lost my feeling of alienness experienced earlier in the day. I was caught back again into a common humanity" (108). Chungpa's sense of joy over his "common humanity" with this group of young men points to the possibility that connections can be forged across racial, geographic, and language barriers. But his feeling that he finally belongs *somewhere* is also incredibly short—it lasts only as long as the train ride itself—since he cannot take that kind of instant community with him.

The novel dwells on this concept of exilic movement in its description of Chungpa's romantic(ized) relationship with the oddly, if appropriately, named Trip, whom he hopes one day to marry. His love for Trip is mentioned in passing, though, and there is no indication that Chungpa's feelings for Trip will ever lead to marriage, or even that he will ever see her again: "It was the thought of Trip that comforted and contented me throughout this loneliness. . . . And the study I had undertaken, partly in libraries, partly in weaving a pattern of hitchhiking over the face of the land, appealed to my nature. In one way I was repeating the life of my grandfather, a geomancer, in another existence, a roving life of ever new contacts and scenes" (344). In this passage, Trip is not just a person, but also a trope: the idea of meeting Trip one day and trips themselves comfort Chungpa. He remains attached to his family and his cultural heritage through his grandfather, whose life of movement and exile he is now repeating, although over a different landscape.

Chungpa's determination to find and feel himself at home in North America is most consistent during his sojourn at Maritime College, but again and again the novel depicts the unwillingness of others to accept him, as well as his own reluctance to abandon his exilic state. While attending Maritime he is bullied by another student who eventually attacks him physically: "[Leslie Robin] snarled and struck me on the cheek. 'Turn the other. You're a good Christian!' . . . . I wanted to get revenge, and I told Allan [a friend] I must fight Robin and he must umpire. But Allan would not let me do this. He took me at once to Ian, and both talked to me, and told me that out of my love for Green Grove [the name of the town where the college is located], I must be too proud to take any notice. I must ignore it" (105). This episode illustrates how various discourses (masculine, religious, nationalist) are completely empty of any of the promises of honor and equality that supposedly inform their creation. Leslie Robin strikes Chungpa in an unprovoked attack and then mockingly reminds him to be a "good Christian," implying of course that one such as Chungpa can *not* be a good Christian. Robin's violent and racist nature is in contrast to the effeminate and gentle connotations of his first and last names. His malicious assault ends with the rather odd (as well as obviously self-serving) reminder that as a good Christian, Chungpa should not retaliate against his aggressor. Chungpa's awkward use of the term "umpire" demonstrates his attempt to conform to Western norms concerning masculine behavior. When men fight they must have an objective observer to preside over the proceedings, so despite his desire for physical revenge, Chungpa understands that he must "fight fair" and so asks his friend to serve as an "umpire."[13] That Chungpa finds himself the object of racist hatred at a missionary college whose students will presumably be sent to Asia, and even possibly Korea, in order to convert the heathen to Christianity is an irony on which Chungpa does not comment. But when he drops out of Maritime to continue his life of motion, the last bastion of American acceptance in the mythology of the American immigrant has been shown to be a fraud. If Chungpa cannot feel at home in college, especially *this* college, the supposed goal and dream for all assimilating immigrants, then he can be at home nowhere.

The total demystification of the American narrative of inclusion occurs most categorically in Chungpa's conversation with Senator Kirby, a politician who has taken a liking to Chungpa and patronizingly offers him advice and bromides. Chungpa cannot make the politician see the hypocrisy of American citizenship laws. Echoing the language of Theodore Roosevelt from three decades earlier, Senator Kirby exhorts Chungpa to say "I'm American" whenever anyone asks him who he is. When Chungpa tells him that Asians are not welcomed in America and are subject to discrimination, Kirby scolds Chungpa:

> "There shouldn't be any buts about it! Believe in America with all
> your heart. Even if it's sometimes hard, believe in her. I have seen
> many countries. But this is still the greatest country in the world
> for youth, for a full life, and ambitious enterprise. This land is like
> Christopher Marlowe's country when he was a boy. Young man,
> it's seldom I see any one with as much of that same spirit as I see in
> you. I tell you, you belong here. You should be one of us."
>   "But legally I am denied."
> Senator Kirby pooh-poohed this objection. (353)

Kirby's unwillingness to see how American laws unjustly exclude reinforces the idea that the inability of Asians to "Americanize" rests squarely on their own shoulders. His pooh-poohing of a truth so significant and utterly unconditional (i.e., that Chungpa cannot become a legal citizen) represents a devastating critique of that narrative's naturalness and inevitability. Kirby's admonition to Chungpa to believe in America with all his heart echoes the argument used by Ozawa in *Ozawa v. United States*: that American identity and citizenship are inextricable from white middle-class values and that whoever conforms to those values should be an American. *East Goes West* seems to be a direct response to the line of reasoning employed in that case to justify Asian inclusion. Kirby laconically and condescendingly rejects the legal barriers that immigrants like Kang faced, as if those were the least of Chungpa's concerns.

Afro-Asian encounters in *East Goes West* reinforce and symbolize Chungpa's discomfort with nationalism, whether it's of the American or the Korean variety. At the novel's start his discomfort is most visible over the issue of Korean independence, a topic that arouses extreme passion from Koreans and Korean expatriates. Lin, a member of the Korean expatriate community in New York, attempts to murder Chinwan, a fellow countryman who is rumored to be a Japanese collaborator. Chungpa cannot participate in the nationalistic fervor that has been stirred around him because of this event: "It was as if I saw Korea receding farther and farther from me. Lin failed to arouse my patriotism; he merely italicized my loneliness and lack of nationalist passion, my sense of uncomfortable exile even among my fellow countrymen, where the homeland was constantly before my eyes" (68). Chungpa's exilic status and ambivalence about national narratives of belonging do not prevent him from feeling a personal stake in Korean nationalist issues, a fact that he freely admits. He takes pride in and thrills to hear the story of "Baron Lisangul," a Korean nobleman who killed himself in front of the Hague Tribunal to protest the Japanese annexation of Korea. But his patriotism definitely has its limits, and he takes no pride in the fact that Lin has stabbed a fellow countryman. Rather than drawing Chungpa closer to the Korean expatriate community, this incident punctuates his isolation and reminds him of his dislocation from his homeland, which recedes further and further from him and his own lived experiences. Lin's attempted murder of Chinwan reveals to Chungpa the extent of his alienation from the Korean community in the United States: "Here in this cosmopolitan city, I saw Lin as living in a narrow world, a small world in a large. No message came back and forth from the large world to the little nor from the little world to the large. The big world did not know the small world, nor the small world the big" (68–69). In this passage, Chungpa evokes some of the vocabulary of cosmopolitanism, although I would argue that there is a vital difference between what he calls cosmopolitanism and his own situation in the United States. Lin's devotion to Korean independence frightens Chungpa; more than that, it also seems incredibly myopic, a sign that Lin is out of touch with the "big world" around him. Lin's attempt to murder Chinwan does not inspire patriotic feelings in Chungpa, nor does it seem to him to counter the oppression that Korea faces as a colonized nation. But this passage also levels an indictment against the "big world" for not paying attention to the tragedies occurring in places like Korea, "the small world." It is not just that the "small" has no understanding of itself in relation to the "big" (read: global), but the mutual lack of knowledge and interest between the two "worlds" that Chungpa decries. Despite his words to the contrary, I would argue that it is Chungpa's desire for greater reciprocity between the global and the local, as well as his interest in both, that reinforces his exilic status.

Chungpa's experiences with African American laborers counters the narrow-minded, nationalist experiences he has with both Anglo-Americans and other Koreans. His exilic movement enables him to have an extensive amount of contact with a wide array of African Americans from all walks of life. While working as a houseboy and butler for a wealthy suburban family in Boston, he meets Laurenzo, an older African American man, who works as the family's cook. The family hires Chungpa because they believe that his presence will signal to their guests and neighbors a certain level of sophistication and, one might say, cosmopolitanism. Laurenzo is a genius in the kitchen and a punctual and conscientious worker; his one vice is alcohol, and on his days off he drinks himself into a stupor, either in town or in his own room. Chungpa and Laurenzo never grow close because of the latter's aloofness when sober and working, but during one drunken binge he admits to Chungpa that "a niggerman's only good to cook and wait, that's all. . . . Not good for anything much . . . that's niggerman" (262–63). Laurenzo's self-alienation is evident in his use of the third person (and a derogatory term at that) to talk about himself and what he does. The only thing a black man like Laurenzo is good for is to satisfy the needs of the white family that he serves; those days when he is not serving are days when he is not living. Laurenzo drinks, the novel suggests, because he has no sense of himself outside of his domestic duties and his relation to his employers, and it would seem that perhaps his employers feel the same way about him: whenever Laurenzo gets drunk the family threatens to fire him, but in the end they are unwilling to let go of a man who cooks so well. Nevertheless, both Laurenzo and Chungpa play out their roles in a domestic space determined by national and then global crosscurrents between the colonized and the colonizing worlds.

While Laurenzo defines himself only in terms of fulfilling the needs of the white people who dictate his life, Wagstaff, whom Chungpa meets at a party near the end of the novel, tells Chungpa that his life is ruled by his hatred for the white society who will not let him earn a living. Wagstaff is extremely well educated, intelligent, and articulate, but he works as an elevator operator because there are no other employment options available to him. Chungpa is sympathetic to Wagstaff's story and attempts to compare his own situation with Wagstaff's, but Wagstaff "would not see it that way": "I was outside the two sharp worlds of color in the American environment. It was, in a way, true. Through Wagstaff, I was having my first introduction to a crystallized caste system, comparable only to India, here in the greatest democratic country of the world. It was seemingly beyond the power of individuals to break through. Thinking about it, I did not see what he could do" (273). Ironically Wagstaff's second-class position within the American caste system does not help to reveal to Chungpa his own marginalized status, just as Wagstaff himself resists making any kind of comparison between the situation of African Americans and any other oppressed minority group. Wagstaff refuses to accept the idea of an Afro-Asian alliance, no matter how tentative. Because he cannot see the global position of the United States in relation to Third World countries he has given up on the struggle altogether. He is, in fact, Matthew Towns before he meets Kautilya: totally engrossed in an injustice that he insists is local but that really has global implications.

The end of this passage from *East Goes West* ("It was seemingly beyond the power of individuals to break through. Thinking about it, I did not see what he could do") also encapsulates perhaps the most essential difference between *East Goes West* and *Dark Princess*: the relative silence in the former novel on what an Afro-Asian laboring alliance might look like and the kind of alternative space where such an alliance might thrive. Nowhere is this more evident than in each novel's finale.

As I mentioned earlier *Dark Princess* ends with Matthew and Kautilya's open-air marriage in rural Virginia, a highly ritualized and ceremonial event with dignitaries from India, China, Japan, and African nations in attendance. The wedding is also a family affair: Matthew's mother is present, and Matthew and Kautilya's infant son is crowned the heir to Kautilya's throne. There is a cultural intermixture here; an African American minister presides over the ceremony but three men—"one black and shaven and magnificent in raiment; one yellow and turbaned,

162 / NATION, NARRATION, AND THE AFRO-ASIAN ENCOUNTER

with a white beard, and the last naked save for a scarf about his loins"—
process to the child to present him with "rice and sweetmeats" (310).
Matthew's mother pronounces a benediction in dialect over the baby
("Jesus, take dis child. Make him a man!") before Kautilya dedicates
her son to "Brahma, Vishnu, and Siva! Lords of Sky and Light and
Love!" (311). Kautilya herself stands under an old tree on Matthew's
mother's land, wearing a "wealth of silk, gold, and jewels" "with a
king's ransom" of rubies and gold on the "naked beauty of her breasts"
and around her "slim brown" waist" (307), but Matthew's mother is described as "straight, immense, white-haired, and darkly brown" (309).
The novel ends (except for a brief prose poem) with the baby Madhu,
swathed in a turban in which is set a "mighty ruby that look[s] like
frozen blood," being held aloft by Kautilya. As she announces the baby
as "his Majesty, Madhu Chandragupta Singh, by the will of God, Ma-
haraja of Bwodpur and Maharaja-dhiraja of Sindrabad," there comes
from the forest the "silver applause of trumpets." Unidentified voices
from the forest shout out:

"King of the Snows of Gaurisankar!"
"Protector of Ganga the Holy!"
"Incarnate Son of the Buddha!"
"Grand Mughal of Utter India!"
"Messenger and Messiah to all the Darker Worlds!" (311)

Jesus Christ himself, whom the text is clearly referencing, did not have a
more portentous or grandiose entry into the world of mere mortals.

After reading hundreds of pages detailing the ins and outs of political
graft in south Chicago, readers are well within their rights to ask what
on earth is going on. What possible purpose could such an excessive finale have in a novel that takes seriously the idea of political action? Paul
Gilroy makes this scene the centerpiece of his argument on *Dark Princess*, claiming that it offers "an image of hybridity and intermixture that
is especially valuable because it gives no ground to the suggestion that
cultural fusion involves betrayal, loss, corruption, or dilution" (144). The
marriage between Kautilya and Matthew is "not the fusion of two purified essences but rather a meeting of two heterogeneous multiplicities
that in yielding themselves up to each other create something durable
and entirely appropriate to troubled anti-colonial times" (144).

Gilroy offers a compelling reading that highlights the extent to which
the binaries described in the novel are mutually constitutive and unsettle

the border that ostensibly divides races and nations. Yet I take serious issue with the utopian reading that he offers here, namely that hybridity and cultural mixture triumph over the ideals of purity and nationalism. What Gilroy fails to address is the fact that we are witnessing the birth of a *royal* prince, in whose body a *different kind* of purified blood flows. The novel describes the ruby set in the turban that Madhu wears like a crown as "frozen blood," and it is Madhu's "blood," the fact that he is the son of Kautilya and Matthew, that is generative of the anti-colonial movement that he will rule and embody. Madhu is a leader whose mandate comes from heaven and his ancestry—not from the people he will lead in the future. The story's turn toward the fantastic and romantic necessitates an acknowledgment of the problematics that these scenes present. *Dark Princess* reminds us that genealogies of hybridity can be just as racialized and hierarchical as those that rely on the notion of racial purity.

Parsing whether or not Du Bois's essentializing of blood undermines the novel's coalitional and global political message is of less interest to me than understanding *how* he arrives at this final scene. Specifically, I want to consider Du Bois's reinscription of blood as one symptom (rather than the goal) of a different kind of political project. This scene represents his attempt to create a community based on premodern notions of temporality in a world that is still trying to find a way to cope with the terrors of modernity. Homi Bhabha theorizes the concept of "another time, another space" that appears in the work of Frantz Fanon. According to Bhabha, Fanon opens up a different kind of "enunciative space" by rejecting the progress narrative embedded in the Hegelian dialectic, which always defines blackness against whiteness and thus posits blackness as a form of belatedness. Bhabha is searching for a "critical discourse that contests modernity through the establishment of other historical sites, other forms of enunciation" (254). This is the kind of project that *Dark Princess* is also undertaking: to strike at the heart of racism, nationalism, and colonialism, the novel undercuts the narrative of time as historical progress that has been the foundation of the nation-state.

It might be useful to think of these final tableaux in the novel as emblematizing to a certain extent what Benedict Anderson has called "messianic time," "a simultaneity of past and future in an instantaneous present" (24). Anderson argues that conceptions of time and definitions of simultaneity, which hinge on "the meanwhile," are instrumental in creating the "imagined community" that defines modern nationhood. In discussing the relationship between the nation-state, genre, and time, Bhabha writes, "Such a form of temporality [the meanwhile] produces a symbolic structure of the nation as 'imagined community' which, in keeping with the scale and diversity of the modern nation, works like the plot of a realist novel" (226). Messianic time, in contrast to the time privileged by the nation and reinforced by the realist novel, is a conception of time that has its roots in biblical typology and religious ceremony; it is an understanding of time that dates back before the modern understanding of the nation appeared.

The wedding scene in *Dark Princess* is one in which the rules of time and space do not apply; it does not rely on any kind of dialectical historical thinking. Past and present are immediate: the past of India as represented by the ancient ceremony, the past of African America as represented by Matthew's mother and her minister. The two pasts are knit together through a ritualized performance of bloodlines that acknowledges the links between Africans and Asians; the birth of a royal son embodies what colonial history has buried and forgotten. This notion of blood is antithetical to the white supremacist ideas of race, and yet it performs the same kind of essentializing move. Du Bois is trying to create a present that can account for the future that Madhu embodies. That future that Du Bois imagines—as embodied by the son—collapses the binaries that it has interrogated. That's why Kautilya can write in a letter to Matthew that by working in America he is contributing to a *global* anti-colonial cause: "The black belt of the Congo, the Nile, and the Ganges reaches by way of Guiana, Haiti, and Jamaica, like a red arrow, up into the heart of white America. Thus I see a mighty synthesis: you can work in Africa and Asia right here in America if you work in the Black Belt" (286). The final scene represents an apotheosis of the novel's vision of an Afro-Asian global alliance: national hierarchies and racial divisions are undone by shifting the temporality that defines those differences. For Du Bois, an alternative to the racism of the nation-state seems to lie in a future that fuses a premodern past with postnationalist community, with its emphasis on kinship (as opposed to national) bonds and sacred (as opposed to calendrical) time. Asia and Africa and America are not knit together just in the body of Madhu, but also in a ritualistic ceremony that acknowledges and celebrates their linked (if distinct) pasts and common future. The hero of this tomorrow—Madhu, Matthew and Kautilya's son—will not be solely African or Asian or European but all three, his body and his leadership denaturalizing discrete racial differences and national allegiances.

The finale of *East Goes West* is far less hopeful and ambitious in what it imagines for Afro-Asian relations. On the last page Chungpa states,

"Once here in America, I had a dream" (368). In this dream he returns to Korea with Trip, and he sees his childhood friends, Yunkoo and Chak-doo-shay. While trying to follow the two boys, who are crossing a narrow bridge, Chungpa falters, and things begin to fall out of his pockets, "especially the key to my car, my American car. I clutched, but I saw it falling" (368). Ignoring the boys he can think only of finding the car keys and of "recovering all the money" that had also fallen out of his pocket. Chungpa's frantic pursuit of money and his keys leads him below ground, into a "dark, cryptlike cellar," where he encounters a terrifying sight: "In that cellar with me—some frightened-looking Negroes. Then looking back, I saw, through an iron grating into the upper air, men with clubs and knives. The cellar was being attacked. The Negroes were about to be mobbed. I shut the door and bolted it, and called to my frightened fellows to help me hold the door" (369). When the mob brings fire to burn Chungpa and the black men alive, he awakens. Chungpa's only explanation of the dream is that "according to Oriental interpretation . . . to be killed in a dream means success and in particular death by fire augurs good fortune" (369). We might read this part of the dream as expressing anxieties about assimilating into nationalist narratives. Rather than pursuing his friends—symbols of his connection to a Korean past and family—Chungpa stops to pick up his money and his car keys, icons of American life and culture. The keys symbolize the material comfort that America offers and Chungpa's own potential position as a consumer in that culture; they distract him as his friends run over treacherous territory, presumably symbolic of the Korean struggle for independence from Japan.

Yet this interpretation does not account for the presence of the black men or the lynching imagery that permeates Chungpa's dream. His childhood past and America's violent racist present occupy the same ground, and I would argue that the superimposition of Chungpa's Korean childhood with the all too familiar tableau of racial violence in America deconstructs the distinction between local and global, with Chungpa's own body serving as the link between both. This alternative space is not as carefully delineated or described as in *Dark Princess*, and it is obviously a space that is under constant threat, internally and externally. And yet, despite this difference, this scene, like the finale in *Dark Princess*, works to undo conventions of time and space, specifically by scrambling what can be depicted in the same textual space and moment. (It is noteworthy, for example, that the geographic location of the lynching is never fixed.) While the ending of *East Goes West* lacks the messianic promise of *Dark Princess*, its depiction of a scene that traverses so many boundaries accentuates the mutually constitutive nature of Asian-African, global-local, diaspora-nation. Whereas Du Bois's narrative is unabashedly future-focused, Kang's seems fixed on the past; the personal history of his childhood in a now-colonized Korea becomes indistinguishable from a national narrative of racist bloodshed in a terrifying and thoroughly modernized America.

I want to emphasize that although *Dark Princess* and *East Goes West* insist upon the links between the global and the nation, neither novel is necessarily setting up a strict binary between the diasporic and the national. In fact, although the novels highlight the costs of emphasizing the nation over the diaspora, their finales anticipate the extent to which the binaries described in the novel are mutually constitutive. Those binaries are undone in the finales of both *Dark Princess* and *East Goes West*, but that does not mean that the Afro-Asian relations that end these novels are unencumbered by the burdens of history, violence, and exclusion. While the splendid royal wedding that ends *Dark Princess* offers us an idealized, "hybridic" model for Afro-Asian relations, it does so at an obvious cost. The novel celebrates racial alliances and cultural hybridity, but in imagining an alternative political space for those alliances and hybridity *Dark Princess* winds up reinscribing certain gender hierarchies and privileging the heterosexual, nuclear family. It protests vehemently against the idea that worth should be attached to blood, and yet ends with the birth of a royal prince. The color line has been shown to be a violent fiction, but lines of descent, it would seem, still matter.

The final moment in *East Goes West* lacks the sweeping and celebratory tone of *Dark Princess*; it does not seem to know what to do with the black and yellow bodies crowded in a cellar, waiting to be burned alive. What is particularly striking about the ending of *East Goes West* is that Chungpa undercuts the radical potential of his dream by interpreting it strictly within a nationalist paradigm (as an example of Korean folk wisdom). As his dream suggests, Chungpa understands that the Korea of his youth and the African American men hiding from the lynch mob are connected, but the montage-like quality of the images he presents precludes the possibility of knowing what the future holds for this group, much less celebrating its possibilities, as Du Bois does. The price of national narratives, which rely on the labor of racialized bodies, can be measured in the imprisonment, violence, terror, and poverty that African Americans and Asians must endure.[14]

Ultimately, these scenes indicate the extent to which *Dark Princess* and *East Goes West* are obsessed with the question of time and its significance in writing against prevailing narratives of race, nation, and the novel. In *The Location of Culture*, Bhabha emphasizes the "temporal dimension in the inscription of . . . political entities," which so often rely on historicized progress narratives to solidify their power and naturalize their existence. What postcolonial critics need, Bhabha asserts, is "another time of *writing* that will be able to inscribe the ambivalent and chiasmatic intersections of time and place that constitute the problematic 'modern' experience of the western nation" (293). Bhabha emphasizes the act of "writing" in this passage, but I would put equal weight on the notion that what is needed is not another kind of narrative but another kind of *time*. Perhaps this is what Du Bois and Kang are attempting to offer in their anachronistic and astonishing finales. In blurring the lines between past, present, and future, or rather, in undercutting the logic of a temporality based on "the meanwhile," *Dark Princess* and *East Goes West* offer the kind of alternative of which Bhabha speaks. As contingent and problematic as those enunciations may be, they nevertheless do the important work of targeting the times and spaces of the nation as deeply implicated in the marginalization and exploitation of peoples of color.

By adopting a conception of time that defies the imperative of modernity, both *Dark Princess* and *East Goes West* warp the genre conventions of the realist novel and present a counter-history to the modern nation that questions or overthrows its geopolitical fictions and acknowledges the permeability of borders, histories, and cultural productions. As I wrote earlier, the most important distinction between the way the two texts handle their critique of the purity of nation is in the ways they construct an alternative space; this difference is also evident in the contrasting ways that Du Bois and Kang construct temporally disjunctive final scenes. Du Bois creates a projective past that can account for the fantastic (if vague) messianic future that Matthew and Kautilya's son embodies. Kang, on the other hand, cannot imagine a past that can easily explain the immediate and violent present in which he finds himself. In their finales, the novels represent not just the past of the characters' own lives but a past that is intimately linked to the histories of domestic racial oppression in the United States as well as to the global histories of conquest and colonization. It is appropriate, then, that the finales puzzle readers and refuse to follow novelistic practices; in re-conceiving time, they modify the contours and the rhythms of the novelistic narrative as well.

I want to end with these final images—one of hope, the other of horror—to remind us how intimately linked are the bodies of Africans and

Asians (whether those links are imagined as familial or through a shared history of violence.) *Dark Princess* and *East Goes West* present a vision of culture that cannot be contained by national borders with protagonists who can never be citizens, in forms that can never be comfortably labeled "novels." These narratives find a way to overleap the borders that have been deemed safe, categorical, or commonsensical.

7 / Coda

East Goes West and *Dark Princess* show us that re-imagining racial relations means restructuring the political space in which they operate; this reconfiguration of the relationship between racial difference and the nation-state necessitates the writing of a different kind of novel to tell a different kind of story. These novels make clear that time—the relationship between the past, present, and future—matters in articulating the significance of Afro-Asian connections over the span of a century. The purpose of this coda is to ruminate briefly on the present of Afro-Asian relations, but I would like to begin by thinking about what connections exist (if any) between the past that my book describes and the present in which African Americans and Asian Americans find themselves. I chose to focus on the early twentieth century as a way to complicate the widespread, late twentieth-century belief that Afro-Asian relations have always been and will always be fundamentally hostile because of essentialized cultural differences, a perception that reached its apotheosis with the Los Angeles Riots of 1992, the first day of which also happened to be the day that I took the oath of U.S. citizenship. It seems appropriate for me to close this book by meditating on the continuities and discontinuities that a century of African American and Asian American interactions present.

In thinking about the relationship between these two time periods in Afro-Asian American history, it is tempting to conceptualize the earlier period as the ground from which the roots of Afro-Asian dynamics sprung. It is perhaps equally tempting to take the opposite tack and argue that Afro-Asian relations back then were something wholly and radically different from what is going on currently. However, as I hope my work suggests, these attempts to characterize definitively the ebb and flow that make up the history of Afro-Asian relations seem misguided. Any progress-oriented view of this history, which constructs our contemporary moment as more progressive than the earlier one and that imagines race relations on an ever-upward trajectory toward harmony and mutual understanding, would be inadequate in accounting for how the relationship between these two groups has changed and shifted over the century. This history cannot be constructed along causal lines; we cannot look to the early twentieth century as a way to explain the state of Afro-Asian relations in the United States today. It seems to me that the most helpful way to understand the long span of Afro-Asian American history is to think of the past as a corrective that complicates a heretofore unquestioned account of that history and as a gloss that explicates and contextualizes that relationship for us.

It might seem strange to insist that Afro-Asian relations are not progressive in their movement through the century, especially in light of the historic election of Barack Obama to the presidency in 2008. The euphoria it unleashed throughout the nation—even from those who did not vote for him—certainly contributed to the sense that "things are getting better."[1] Obama's election also seems to represent a high point in the history of Afro-Asian relations, a triumphant counter to the narrative of hostility and resentment that reached its nadir in the early 1990s, with the Red Apple Boycott in New York City, the acquittal of Soon Ja Du for the murder of Latasha Harlins in Los Angeles, and the Los Angeles Riots.[2] According to the Asian American Legal Defense and Education Fund, more than 75 percent of the Asian American voters they polled in several states voted for Obama, although only 58 percent of those voters were registered Democrats.[3] The *Los Angeles Times* reported that Asian Americans in Los Angeles County voted in record numbers in 2008 and that 63 percent of them voted for Obama.[4]

While many segments of the population, not just Asian Americans, voted for Obama in order to make a clean break with the previous administration, it is undoubtedly the case that the details of Obama's personal life—his birth in Hawaii, his exposure to Indonesian culture as a child, and the visible presence of his half-sister, Maya Soetoro-Ng, and her husband, Konrad Ng, throughout the campaign—appealed to Asian American voters and contributed to the sense that Obama is sympathetic to Asian American issues. Indeed his biracial background and scholastic achievements lead the journalist Jeff Yang to wonder, "Could Obama be the first Asian American president?" Explicitly invoking Toni Morrison's famous 1998 *New Yorker* article that "granted cadet membership [to Bill Clinton] in the grand cultural narrative of black America," Yang marvels at the possibility that an "actual black person" might be elected president and argues that many aspects of Obama's life echo those experienced by Asian immigrants and Asian Americans, from the familial emphasis on education to the mockery he endured in school for his exotic-sounding name. Yang insists that calling Obama the first Asian American president "doesn't obscure or invalidate his other identities. . . . If anything, it simply highlights the fact that his diverse heritage uniquely invites those around him to project on him a full spectrum of hopes and dreams." With varying degrees of seriousness, Yang's claiming Obama as Asian American was picked up by other Asian American commentators. In a satiric article titled "Our First Asian President," Alex Chavez called Obama a "rice brother" and bestowed upon him the label "honorary Asian American." Since the election, Obama's appointment of several Asian Americans to his cabinet and his attention to relations with other Pacific Rim nations (particularly China) had led the Asian American journalist and author Helen Zia to echo Yang's sentiment: "[Obama] is the most Asian-American president that we will have" ("Obama the First Asian American President?").

The historic nature of Obama's election is unquestionable, and yet the experiential affinity between the Asian American community and the president that Yang and other prominent Asian Americans are claiming is actually nothing new; indeed, the notion that Asians and African Americans share a common ground built on the experience of racism has been articulated by many public figures and is a persistent trope that spans Afro-Asian relations throughout the twentieth century. To say, however, that Obama's election means that African Americans and Asians have reached a Promised Land of racial amity and cooperation is to ignore the racism, political inequities, and material privations that many African Americans and Asian Americans still endure; it also short-circuits the possibility of a more radical political alliance between the two groups and other racial communities.

While Obama's election may not stake out new ground in the relationship between African Americans and Asians, it does highlight an important if underexamined aspect of Afro-Asian relations: the way in which Asian Americans rely heavily on the discursive strategies of the African American community, writers, and public figures in order to articulate their own minority status. This is an aspect of Afro-Asian relations that has not received much scholarly attention, perhaps because it asks us to consider what links exist, if any, between Asian America's referencing of African America in politics and culture and the historical co-optation and erasure of African American cultural practices, labor, and community experiences by European Americans. While my study focused on the dialectical nature of early twentieth-century African American and Asian American cultural histories, it is important to remember that in terms of political engagement and in the articulation of a nationalist identity, the African American community has been the model for Asian Americans to copy or to rail against for the past half-century.

The vision of Afro-Asian relations riding the edge of an ever expanding horizon, which Obama's candidacy emphasized, stands in sharp contrast to the vision painted by Vijay Prashad, whose research brilliantly examines the historical intersections between black, brown, and yellow peoples. In an essay titled "Bandung Is Done," which serves as a foreword to the edited collection *AfroAsian Encounters: Culture, History, Politics* (2006), Prashad makes a provocative argument that seems to deflate the hopeful tone surrounding Obama's election. He argues that the radical politics that fostered the anti-colonial movements of the early and mid-twentieth century have been "compromised," mostly because of the "cannibalization" of the "national liberation state" by the economic inequities of globalized capital (xiii). The nationalism of this earlier era, which Prashad characterizes as liberatory and radical, has been replaced by a "cruel cultural nationalism that [draws] on forms of social solidarity provided by either religion, reconstructed racism, or undiluted class power" (xiii). He makes the somewhat startling claim that, given the fact that Africa and Asia seemed interested in each other only for the capital and natural resources each has to offer, the current "excavations of AfroAsian solidarity might be nostalgic, anachronistic, or even aesthetic" (xiv). Speaking of his own earlier work, which looked at the historical interactions between Africans and Asians, Prashad acknowledges that it was partly inspired by a nostalgia for that early political radicalism, when history seemed to be in "motion." Prashad tacitly recognizes the dangers of a scholarship based on nostalgia, but he defends his motivation by arguing that his "nostalgic pessimism" is a far more honorable and intellectually legitimate entry into Afro-Asian relations than the "commodification" that he suggests is the current model by which this particular interracial relationship is being constructed. Citing Hollywood and the film franchise *Rush Hour* as a particular example, Prashad seems to suggest that the Afro-Asian relationship in the late twentieth century has been tainted by the logic of global capital.

For Prashad the possibility of Afro-Asian relations is located in a past in which Africa and Asia were still on the verge of a radical Third World political alliance, whereas Yang and others like him are fixed on a future in which Afro-Asian relations will continue to improve. Prashad's equation of aesthetics with nostalgia and his dismissal of popular culture as merely a symptom of commodification overlooks the formative role that text and representation have played and continue to play in the dynamic between African Americans and Asian Americans and the political power that such narratives can have. While I take issue with the broadness of Prashad's assessment of culture, I agree with his critique of the troubling commodification of racial identities and communities in the age of global capital. The encounters on the train between African American and Asian figures trigger a renegotiation by William Miller in Chesnutt's *The Marrow of Tradition* and by Wu Tingfang in *America through the Spectacles of an Oriental Diplomat* of their sense of selfhood; interacting with the other calls into question the identity that each has crafted throughout their texts. The text that serves as Prashad's straw man, *Rush Hour*, with its titular allusion to mass transportation, presents us with a different tableau of Afro-Asian relations and mobility. Set in Los Angeles, the film pairs Jackie Chan's Hong Kong police detective with Chris Tucker's LAPD officer as the two try to solve the kidnapping of a Chinese diplomat's daughter. *Rush Hour* intersperses dialogue that humorously highlights the cultural, linguistic, and stylistic differences between Chan and Tucker with fight scenes that showcase Chan's martial arts prowess. Bearing in mind the differences in medium and audience between it and works like *Marrow* and *America*, the film nevertheless represents the Afro-Asian relationship as based on complementary and interlocking stereotypes, with both actors taking on a whole gamut of cultural tropes associated with African Americans (Sambo, ghetto, hypersexuality) and Asians (kung-fu, filiation, asexuality). The laughter that the film elicits does not contain within it a sense of unease, nor do the performances suggest even the remotest whiff of irony; in an age when racial identity has come to mean value, the audience can laugh comfortably at the racialized buffoonery not merely because they have paid for that right but also because they know that Chan and Tucker (executive producers of the films) are enriching themselves mightily with that laughter.

Prashad and Yang are not explicitly in dialogue with each other regarding the present of Afro-Asian relations. Despite the fact that both are approaching the relationship from a politically liberal perspective, their divergent opinions regarding the current state of that interracial relationship echo a tendency of the late twentieth century to present these two minority groups in a disaggregated manner. The relationship between African Americans and Asian Americans is constantly imagined to be one of extremes: they are perpetual combatants, separated by essential cultural differences, or the quintessential partners for any kind of radical project; their relationship signals that radical politics is all but dead or that the best days between racial minorities are yet to come. In this book, I intervened into a binaristic narrative that constantly figures African Americans and Asians as oppositional groups or that imagines any sign of partnership between the two communities as the epitome of radical change. Looking at the early twentieth century, I argued instead that Afro-Asian relations are historical and always the result of a certain kind of calculus regarding politics. This look back also revealed the length and breadth of Afro-Asian encounters, hopefully making it impossible to categorize that relationship easily.

The historical and political climate of the early twentieth century, which saw the "Asiatic" and the "Negro" as the Janus-faced symbol of the nation's pending racial apocalypse, laid the groundwork for the rich dialogue undertaken by and between African Americans and Asian Americans that I have attempted to trace and theorize. The specific dialogue between African Americans and Asian Americans that this book analyzed cannot be consistently traced throughout the entire twentieth century; interracial dynamics in this case does not follow a continuous path, and the cultural terrain that African Americans and Asian Americans share is often uneven and constantly shifting as a result of U.S. policies domestically and abroad. Kandice Chuh writes, "In conceiving of multiple kinds of difference, we must of course recognize that they do not exist independently of each other. Rather, they converge and conflict and thus participate in shaping each other" (148). My goal was to trace these convergences and conflicts, but I found that the writers were already writing that counter-history, already anticipating the early twenty-first century's obsessions, even as they struggled to imagine a present or future without them. If we as scholars seek alternative narratives of American literary history that look beyond traditional field markers, then how much more empowering is it to realize that, at times, Asian American and African American cultural productions prefigure this in their very composition.

NOTES

1 / Introduction

1. As Chesnutt's speech suggests, "dominant white identity in America operates melancholically—as an elaborate identificatory system based on psychical and social consumption and demand" (Cheng, 11).

2. The Los Angeles Uprising in 1992 is perhaps the best-known example of the ways that the mainstream media reduce interracial relations and conflicts into an easily digestible narrative of cultural antagonism. King-Kok Cheung argues that such a "master narrative" enabled the city and nation to disavow collectively its abandonment of the inner city and the practice of institutional racism ("[Mis]interpretations and [In]justice," 5). Edward Chang notes, "The media has continued to portray the 1992 riots as an extension of the ongoing conflict between Korean merchants and African American residents, despite the fact that more than half the looters arrested were Latinos" (110). As well, nearly 10 percent of those arrested were non-Hispanic whites, and 40 percent of the torched businesses were owned by Latinos.

3. Kenyon Farrow's blistering online attack of a forum about Asian Americans in hip-hop, moderated by the critic Oliver Wang of San Francisco, reveals how quickly celebrations of Afro-Asian connections as liberatory and politically progressive can be interpreted as a form of racism. Although Farrow's claims of hip-hop's role in black identity can be perceived as nationalistic and the effectiveness of his critique is hampered by its intensely personal tone, his scorn for the self-congratulatory atmosphere of the panel seems entirely on point. For the text of Farrow's critique, see http://kenyonfarrow.com/2005/06/02/we-real-coolon-hip-hop-asian-americans-black-folks-and-appropriation/.

4. I have struggled mightily to find a term that is historically accurate and at the same time recognizable to a twenty-first-century reading audience to describe collectively the writers of Asian descent I discuss in this book. Ultimately, I have chosen to stick with the familiar appellation "Asian American," but I do so with some trepidation. The term "Asian American" is anachronistic for my purposes in two ways. First,

because of a slew of legal actions on both the state and federal levels dating from the first days of the republic through World War II, Asians could not become naturalized citizens of the United States. Various exclusion, anti-immigration, and anti-miscegenation acts also guaranteed a numerically small American-born Asian population; there were therefore very few Asians living in the United States who could legally claim to be American citizens. Second, the term "Asian American" itself emerged out of a particular historical moment, a product of the race-consciousness and "yellow power" movements of the 1960s and 1970s. Like many others, I see the term as serving a strategic purpose: it maximizes the visibility and political clout of the people whose ancestry can be traced back to the land mass known as Asia. The writers of Asian descent in this book would not have used the term "Asian American" to describe themselves, but that does not mean that they were unaware that various Asian nationalities were (and are) seen as interchangeable or indistinguishable. Winnifred Eaton chose to pass for Japanese at a time when the Chinese were reviled, and Chungpa Han, the Korean protagonist of Younghill Kang's *East Goes West*, is constantly mistaken for either Chinese or Japanese.

5. Both Najia Aarim-Heriot in her study *Chinese Immigrants, African Americans and Racial Anxiety in the United States, 1848–1882* and John Torok in his article "Reconstruction and Racial Nativism: Chinese Immigrants and the Debates on the Thirteenth, Fourteenth, and Fifteenth Amendments and Civil Rights Law" argue that the perception of Chinese alienness informed the congressional Reconstruction debates after the Civil War. Aarim-Heriot points to similarities between anti-Chinese and anti-black rhetoric and the fact that during the Reconstruction debates the Chinese question was considered at length by both proponents and opponents of the Thirteenth, Fourteenth, and Fifteenth Amendments. Torok argues that the Reconstruction debates reveal that Congress "perceived the threat posed by Chinese immigrant suffrage to 'republican institutions'" because of their "cultural and 'racial' differences."

Authors of Chinese descent wrote all of the Asian American texts examined in this book, with the exception of *East Goes West* (1937) by Younghill Kang. Kang was born and educated in Korea during the time of the Japanese colonial occupation of the peninsula (1910–45). When Japan formally annexed Korea in 1910, Korea as a national entity ceased to exist, and all Koreans became subjects of the Japanese crown. The Japanese project of Korean cultural annihilation (called *naisen ittai*, loosely translated as "Korea and Japan are one") did not begin in earnest until the 1920s, just before Kang left the peninsula permanently for the United States. My rationale for including Kang is based on the geopolitics of the day. American attitudes toward China and Korea were similar; both were seen as premodern nations who benefited from Japanese colonialism. Although Japan was America's competitor for influence in East Asia, its status as a modern colonizing nation meant that America accorded it and its citizens a kind of respect not granted to China and Korea. For example, the Gentleman's Agreement of 1907 was a mutual accord between the United States and Japan in which the Japanese government agreed to limit the number of exit visas it approved for its citizenry, and the United States agreed to allow Japanese wives and children to be reunited with husbands living in America. Although the Agreement limited the number of Japanese who could enter the United States, the fact that the pact was bilateral and included concessions from the U.S. government is an indicator of the care with which the United States approached Japan's increasing global clout.

Ultimately, the Japanese were excluded from the United States in the same way as the Chinese had been for decades, but their continuing military might in the Pacific meant that they occupied a significantly different position within the nation, culturally and politically. For example, when Cecil B. DeMille's film *The Cheat* was released in 1915, the villain was Tori, a wealthy Japanese man. Complaints from the Japanese consulate led DeMille to change the nationality of the villain to Burmese for the film's subsequent releases. Current copies of the film reflect that change. For this reason, I have made the conscious decision not to include any of the writers of Japanese descent (Etsu Sugimoto and Yone Noguchi being the most prominent examples) who were published during this time period.

6. For the text of the first Chinese Exclusion Act, see the appendix of Andrew Gyory's *Closing the Gate*.

7. This point is the crux of Lisa Lowe's *Immigrant Acts*. She argues that a racially stratified nation such as the United States must reconcile the competing demands of the state, which requires unified "abstract citizens," and capital, which depends on "abstract labor," without regard to race or place of origin (13). The exclusion of the Chinese in late nineteenth-century America achieved that reconciliation: "Capital could increase profit and benefit from the presence of a racialized and tractable labor force until the point at which the Chinese labor force grew large enough that it threatened capital accumulation by whites. At that point, by excluding and disenfranchising the Chinese in 1882, the state could constitute the 'whiteness' of the citizenry" (13).

8. Writing about the same period in American history, Amy Kaplan notes that as much as the nation attempted to bifurcate cleanly the national "domestic" space from the global "foreign" space, "the dynamics of imperial expansion cast them into jarring proximity" (1).

9. In examining Hisaye Yamamoto's portrayal of the links between the African American and Asian American communities, Hong states bluntly, "To say that African Americans and Japanese Americans have a common history is false; in fact, the opposite is the case" (292). Nevertheless the fact that both African Americans and Japanese Americans suffered economic privations in the form of property ownership restrictions in Los Angeles after World War II enables her to examine Yamamoto's stories in a way that acknowledges the complicated intersection of race, history, and economic disenfranchisement.

10. Moon Ho Jung, Evelyn Hu-DeHart, Lok Siu, Aisha Khan, and Viranjini Munasinghe are just a few scholars who are pursuing this kind of research in fields outside of literary studies.

11. Brook Thomas's work on Charles Chesnutt and Chinese exclusion is a notable exception. For works that survey the field and focus on the question of how notions of race emerged out of the interrelations between blacks and whites, see Bederman, *Manliness and Civilization*; Michaels, *Our America*; Moddelmog, *Reconstituting Authority*; Sollors, *Neither Black nor White*; Stocking, "The Turn-of-the-Century Concept of Race"; and Wald, *Constituting Americans.*.

12. In his influential study of nativism, *Strangers in the Land*, John Higham states explicitly that the reaction of Americans to the Chinese was a "separate phenomenon" from the antipathy aroused by the arrival of eastern and southern European immigrants in the early twentieth century. Asians, Higham notes, are "historically tangential to the main currents of American nativism" (iii).

13. The Eaton sisters represent a unique challenge to a critic looking for a manageable label to capture the multiplicity of their identities. They were born in England to a white Englishman and his Christianized Chinese wife. When the girls were still children the family moved to Quebec, where they received their schooling. After brief stints in the Caribbean, both sisters settled permanently in the United States to pursue their writing careers. While most critics consider the sisters to be Eurasian (although Tomo Hattori calls them "Anglo-Chinese Canadian [228]), I include them under the broad rubric of "Asian American" because the United States serves as the setting for the works I examine and also because the sisters seemed to consider themselves permanent residents of the United States.

14. Although they are not widely known, the poems inscribed on the walls of Angel Island Detention Center in San Francisco Bay are a notable exception. See Lai, Lim and Yung, *Island*.

2 / The "Negro Problem" and the "Yellow Peril"

1. The concept of amalgamation overlaps with the concept of miscegenation, but with important differences. The former refers to the "homogeneous union of previously distinct elements" (according to the *OED*), whereas the latter emphasizes the sexual intermingling of people from different racial groups. All *OED* citations are from the website www.oed.com and were accessed 5 Mar. 2005.

2. For more information on this series of court cases, see McClain, *In Search of Equality*, particularly the chapter "The Laundry Litigation of the 1880's" (98–132).

3. The Thirteenth, Fourteenth, and Fifteenth Amendments (also called the Reconstruction or Civil War amendments) expanded who the government could recognize as "citizens." The Thirteenth Amendment, passed in 1865, prohibited slavery; the Fourteenth, which was ratified by Congress in 1868, entitled all persons born or naturalized in the United States to citizenship and equal protection under federal law; and the ratification of the Fifteenth Amendment in 1870 guaranteed the voting rights of all male citizens. Albion Tourgée, the lead lawyer for the plaintiff in *Plessy v. Ferguson*, invoked the equal protection clause of the Fourteenth Amendment ("No state shall make or enforce any law which shall abridge the privileges or immunities of citizens of the United States; nor shall any state deprive any person of life, liberty, or property, without due process of law; nor deny to any person within its jurisdiction the equal protection of the laws") in arguing against the constitutionality of segregation. Tourgée contended that whiteness had a value, and the conductor, by calling Plessy a black man, was essentially depriving Plessy of the property value of whiteness without due process.

4. The terms "white" and "whiteness" are themselves historical , as several critics have convincingly argued. Toni Morrison in *Playing in the Dark* and David Roediger in *The Wages of Whiteness* put "whiteness" under a critical lens. They argue that ignoring its historical emergence and context means reifying it as the privileged subject position within the United States. Susan Koshy argues that the interest in "whiteness" studies has reaffirmed the centrality of the black-white binary in accounting for race and identity in this country; she argues that "both blacks and Asians helped make the liminal European groups white, an identity that would have been less tenable in their absence" ("Morphing Race into Ethnicity," 165–66). According to Koshy, Asian immigration *and* African American enfranchisement inspired a legislative reconsideration

of who could be identified as white. It is particularly in the area of the law that whiteness (over and against other identity markers) became codified into the "natural" or "default" subject position for Americans. Cheryl Harris argues that the "right to exclude was the central principle . . . of whiteness as identity, for mainly whiteness has been characterized not by any inherent unifying characteristic, but by the exclusion of others deemed to be 'not white.' The possessors of whiteness were granted the legal right to exclude others from the privileges inhering in whiteness. . . . The courts played an active role in enforcing this right to exclude—determining who was or was not white enough to enjoy the privileges accompanying whiteness" (1736).

5. During this period, African Americans and Asians countered the racism they faced in the United States in nonliterary ways as well. There were public demonstrations and denunciations by groups like the Urban League and the NAACP and other grass-roots political organizations. For example, Paul C. P. Siu chronicles in *The Chinese Laundryman* (1953) the attempts of Chinese laundrymen in New York to protect their economic interests and fight for better working conditions and more equitable treatment from the city. Evelyn Brooks Higginbotham argues in *Righteous Discontent: The Women's Movement in the Black Baptist Church, 1880–1920* that black women's involvement in black churches helped make the church the most "powerful institution of racial self-help in the African American community" (1). African American women were instrumental in the campaign to pass anti-lynching and temperance laws.

6. Michaels considers the examples of Robert Cohn from *The Sun Also Rises* and Louis Marsellus from *The Professor's House*. Both Cohn and Marsellus are legally American citizens but eagerly seek the approval of their "true" American counterparts, Jake Barnes and Godfrey St. Peter, respectively.

7. Sutherland goes on to argue, "With the conclusion reached in these several decisions we see no reason to differ. Moreover, that conclusion has become so well established by judicial and executive concurrence and legislative acquiescence that we should not at this late day feel at liberty to disturb it, in the absence of reasons far more cogent than any that have been suggested."

8. *Ozawa* was not questioning the nation's ability to refuse admission to people on the basis of race or skin color but was only seeking to shift Asians from the "nonwhite" to the "white" category.

9. Ian Haney-Lopez, however, argues that "the Supreme Court's elevation of common knowledge as the legal meter of race convincingly demonstrates that racial categorization finds its origins in social practices" (6). He goes on to say that the racial prerequisite cases "compellingly demonstrate that races are socially constructed. More importantly, they evidence the centrality of law in that construction. . . . Put more starkly, law constructs race" (9–10). I certainly agree that laws and court cases are instrumental in constructing a "common-sense" definition of race, but I find the more dialectical model described by Omi and Winant to be more useful for my purposes.

10. Multiple discourses, with roots in religion, political science, the social sciences, and biological sciences, appeared, disappeared, and reappeared to justify the exclusion of African Americans and Asians. For example, Sandra Gunning chronicles how the nation's anxieties about black male suffrage manifested in "an epidemic of violence that lasted throughout the post–Civil War era and well into the early decades of the twentieth century" (7). The nation's violent paranoia about the figure of the black male rapist is one symptom of a pervasive anxiety that the historical link between whiteness

and national belonging was crumbling. According to Gunning, the "spectacle of violated white womanhood [was] proof of the devastating results of black citizenship" (65). These spectacles—mirages though they were—served as the justification for disenfranchising and terrorizing African Americans. Lynching became a vehicle for justifying black exclusion by invoking the animality and criminality of black men.

11. Gunning argues that highly sexualized and criminalized images of menacing black masculinity "have been accompanied by some of the most horrific eruptions of white violence this country has ever known" (3). Lynching was a punishment meted out to both whites and blacks in the years leading up to the Civil War; in the post-Reconstruction era, however, the number of whites who were the targets of lynching decreased, while the number of black victims steadily rose. Between 1882 and 1930, there were 3,386 known black victims, the majority of whom were male. These numbers are almost certainly low since many lynchings were not reported to authorities. In particular, the 1890s and 1900s witnessed a horrific spike in white-on-black violence; black victims were often tortured, burned, dismembered, and castrated. The NAACP estimated that between 3,337 and 10,000 blacks were lynched in this twenty-year span (Gunning, 5).

12. Page wrote the bestseller *Red Rock: A Chronicle of Reconstruction* (1898), which sympathetically portrayed southerners and slavery in the Reconstruction era, and helped to popularize nostalgia for the Old South through his many short stories.

13. Later in the article, Page claims, "During the whole period of slavery, [the raping of white women] did not exist, nor did it exist to any considerable extent for some years after Emancipation. During the [Civil] War, the men were away in the army, and the Negroes were the loyal guardians of the women and children. . . . Then came the period and process of Reconstruction, with its teachings. Among these was the teaching that the Negro was the equal of the white, and the white was his enemy, and that he must assert his equality." While Page deplores the "barbarity" of lynching, he cites numerous examples of black men raping and butchering white women and children and calls upon black leaders to stop focusing on the lynching of black men in the South and instead turn their attention to controlling the savage nature of black people.

14. See also Degenhardt, "Situating the Essential Alien."

15. Colleen Lye provides a genealogy of the "yellow peril" in the first chapter of *America's Asia*. She argues that the Asiatic figure became the symbol for an increasingly global capitalism and free market forces and "modernity's dehumanizing effects" (11). Asian exclusion stemmed from the anxiety that these economic forces elicited in the labor and political arenas.

16. For more depictions of the Chinese in popular periodicals, see Choy, Dong, and Hom, *The Coming Man*. This volume is an invaluable resource of primary materials about American attitudes toward the Chinese.

17. Other discourses proved potent in rationalizing Asian exclusion. The accusation that the Chinese were infidels was particularly potent in a nation that fervently imagined itself as Christian (and continues to do so). African Americans residing in California worked to distance themselves from the Chinese in a state that was experiencing more anxiety about Chinese emigration than black migration from the south. Philip Alexander Bell, the editor of the black San Francisco newspaper *The Elevator*, echoed the sentiments of many white nativists when he wrote, "[The Chinese are] unacquainted with our system of government, adhering to their own habits and

customs, and of heathen idolatrous faith." The Negro, on the other hand, was a "native American, loyal to the government and a lover of his country and her institutions— American in all his ideals; a Christian by education and a believer of the truth of Christianity" (quoted in Johnsen, 61). Americans recoiled from the Chinese because they were perceived as unclean, un-Christian pagans; it was their lack of Christianity, many argued, that made them undesirable as potential citizens.

18. Nast witnessed the draft riots that swept New York in 1863, when he saw the mob invade a "colored orphan asylum" in which several blacks had taken refuge (Paine, 92).

19. The same kind of interracial dynamics can be seen in the cartoon "Difficult Problems Solving Themselves," which is also from an 1879 issue of *Harper's*. African Americans and Asians are linked by the fact that they are the most visible victims of America's hypocritical "Republican Form of Government."

20. *Birth of a Nation* stirred up a tremendous amount of controversy. Several critics argued that the film introduced a cinematic language for racism that other films, such as *Gone with the Wind*, have gone on to perfect. In 1919, Griffiths released *Broken Blossoms*, a film that critics sometimes invoke when defending him from the charge of racism. Based on the story "The Chink and the Child" by Thomas Burke, *Broken Blossoms* recounts the unlikely friendship between Lucy, a young girl (played by a child-like Lillian Gish), and Cheng (played by a white actor, Richard Barthelmess, in yellowface), the Chinaman who tries to save her from her abusive pugilist father, Battling Burrows. The Chink initially meets the Child as she wanders the streets after having been whipped by her father. As the Child sleeps in his bed, the Chink watches, and his attraction to her is evident. He approaches her menacingly, she cringes as he draws nearer, and then he presents her with . . . a doll. Kneeling before her and kissing her bedclothes, the Chink's sexual desire is sublimated into feelings of protection. When the father finds out that his daughter has been in the Chinaman's bedroom and received gifts from him, he drags her home and savagely beats and kills her. The Chinaman arrives too late to save the girl and shoots the father before shooting himself. Some point to this film as proof that Griffiths's racism was limited to blacks and that his antipathy was a natural result of his childhood in the American South. Susan Koshy convincingly argues that, despite his apologists' protests to the contrary, *Broken Blossoms* enacts the same kinds of racial anxieties and is based on the same fear of racialized bodies as the more incendiary *Birth*. According to Koshy, the hypersexualized black man in *Birth* performs the same kind of cultural work as the desexualized Chinese man in *Broken Blossoms;* both work to foreclose forever the possibility of interracial union ("American Nationhood," 59).

21. Hayakawa was initially offered the leading role in *The Sheikh* (1921). He turned it down, and the part eventually went to Valentino, making him an instant international film star and sex symbol. Hayakawa went on to appear in films in the United States and Japan and was nominated for an Academy Award for his portrayal of a Japanese camp officer in *The Bridge over the River Kwai* (David Lean, 1957).

22. Koshy cites the films *The Yellow Menace* (1916), *The Perils of Pauline* (1919), *Patria* (1919), and *Crooked Streets* (1920) and the Fu Manchu series as examples of the "bad" Asians that populated American popular culture during this time ("American Nationhood," 66).

23. I use the character's original name, Hishuru Tori, from the 1915 release, rather than Haka Arakau, the Burmese name used in subsequent reissues.

24. Just as the lynching scenes represent attacks against black and yellow male bodies, so do the scenes of attempted rape represent attempts to control potentially transgressive white female bodies. Both Elsie and Edith are remarkably headstrong characters who flout, however mildly, the gender conventions of their time and society.

25. In fact, Plessy was one-eighth black and could easily pass for a white man. His white skin color was crucial to the legal challenge: Tourgée wanted to center the case on a light-skinned mulatto, presumably to emphasize the arbitrariness of legal racial classifications. For a thorough and fascinating discussion of the history behind the case, see Lofgren, *The Plessy Case*.

26. Of the nine justices on the Supreme Court, only eight actually heard the case (Thomas, *Plessy*, 31).

27. In *Yick Wo*, the Court declared unconstitutional an ordinance passed by the city of San Francisco that required laundries to be located in non-wooden buildings. Although the language of the law did not specifically target the Chinese, the practical effect of the prohibition was to drive Chinese laundries out of business. Ninety-five percent of the city's laundries could be found in wooden buildings, and two-thirds of the laundries in the city had Chinese owners. Furthermore, the board of supervisors granted dispensation from the ordinance to all but one of the non-Chinese owners but to none of the more than two hundred Chinese petitioners. Yick Wo, a Chinese laundry owner, was one of the rejected petitioners; when he continued to operate his laundry in a wooden building in defiance of city laws, he was arrested and convicted. As both Alexander Saxton and H. T. Shih-shan note, the Supreme Court had no quarrel with the city of San Francisco's right to pass such ordinances; rather, they reversed the decision of the lower courts because of the discriminatory fashion in which the law was enforced. It is also worth noting that *Yick Wo* marks the first time that the Court inferred the existence of discrimination based on data about a law's application, a technique that would be used again in the 1950s to strike down statutes discriminating against African Americans.

28. Specifically Brown states, "Every exercise of the police power must be reasonable, and extend only to such laws as are enacted in good faith for the promotion of the public good, and not for the annoyance or oppression of a particular class" (Thomas, *Plessy*, 49)

29. *The Marrow of Tradition* by Charles Chesnutt, with its depiction of Captain McBane deliberately smoking in the colored car, ridicules the notion that a white man would be arrested for sitting in a segregated train car.

30. See Gotanda, "A Critique."

3 / Estrangement on a Train

1. The train figures prominently in the plots of several canonical American cultural works of this time: films such as *The Great Train Robbery*; fiction such as Theodore Dreiser's *Sister Carrie* (1900), Willa Cather's *A Lost Lady* (1923), and Stephen Crane's "The Bride Comes to Yellow Sky" (1898); and the poetry of Hart Crane, Walt Whitman, and Emily Dickinson. Several works of African American literature include key scenes on trains: Nat Love's *The Life and Adventures of Nat Love* (1907), James Weldon Johnson's *The Autobiography of an Ex-Colored Man* (1912), W. E. B. Du Bois's *Dark Princess* (1928), and Nella Larsen's *Quicksand* (1928). The felicitous link between blues

as a musical form and trains as a subject can be traced to the earliest days of the genre. Indeed, legend has it that the blues musician and impresario W. C. Handy "discovered" the blues one day at a train station in Mississippi and that the song he heard used train routes as its subject. The contemporary Asian American writers Frank Chin (in autobiographical essays such as "Riding the Rails") and Maxine Hong Kingston (in her nonfiction work *China Men*) have also seen the train as an important trope in reclaiming a martial tradition of Asian American masculinity.

2. In Soviet iconography of the Communist Revolution, Lenin is often depicted emerging from a train, ready to lead the proletariat to their socialist future.

3. Streetcars were considered to be even more "classless" than trains. But few cities had them, and they too "exemplify the interlocking relationship between technology, economy, and social norms" (Welke, 256). The distinction between a train and a streetcar will come up later in my close reading of Wu.

4. The economies behind the railroad industry also informed the kind of racial segregation that these writers depict and that took place on railcars. From the railroad industry's perspective, following the social conventions that required subdividing people beyond black and white meant increasing costs and decreasing profitability. The railroad industry quietly supported Homer Plessy's bid to overturn the Louisiana statute ordering separate cars for blacks since adding an extra car onto a train for black passengers added to the cost of every trip.

5. Neither Chesnutt nor Wu explicitly engages with the question of gender segregation on trains, although it did exist. The "ladies' cars" of the day were reserved for those women traveling alone or with one companion who did not wish to mingle with the rest of the riders. The ladies' car depended on caste distinctions more heavily than it did gendered ones. While a gentleman companion to a lady might be allowed to enter the ladies' car, a woman who was not a *lady* most certainly would not have been. (Presumably those women who were not ladies need not have their sensibilities protected and could ride with the rest of the population in the second-class cabins.) Although my reading is not explicitly focused on gender, the question of gender plays a central role in my argument, precisely because I examine how trains as spaces create Americans by relying on the logic of segregating whites from blacks, first class from second class, and men from women. For more information on ladies' cars, see Ely, *Railroads and American Law,* 145–46.

6. *The Autobiography of an Ex-Colored Man* (1912) by James Weldon Johnson contains a scene on a train in which several passengers of various racial, religious, and geographical backgrounds discuss the problem of racism in America.

7. This beautiful impartiality—to borrow the conductor's own language—fails to recognize the material difference in the appearance, sanitary conditions, and levels of safety between the two train cars. The writer George Washington Cable wrote, "The safety, uncleanness, and discomfort of most of these [colored cars] are a sham to any community pretending to practice public justice" (quoted in Gossett, 275). The railroad car to which Miller must move has "faded upholstery, from which the stuffing projected here and there," an unswept floor, grime on the windows, and "stale water which had made no recent acquaintance with ice" (Chesnutt, *Marrow*, 56). Chesnutt emphasizes the distance between the content of what the conductor is saying (i.e., that the system is a "beauty") and the reality of the railroad car to which Miller must move (dirty, noisy, and uncomfortable).

8. For more on streetcars, see Welke, *Recasting American Liberty,* 256.

9. Cheryl Harris notes that Homer Plessy based his challenge of the Louisiana state law partly on the idea that "the refusal to seat him on the white passenger car deprived him of property." In other words, being thought of as white has a particular financial value attached to it; blackness then becomes a liability or deficit. Although it did not directly address this aspect of Plessy's challenge, the Court ultimately lent credence to the notion of "race reputation as a property interest" by "subsuming . . . those like Plessy, who phenotypically appeared to be white, within categories that were predicated on white supremacy and race subordination" (1749).

10. Priscilla Wald, for one, has reported that urban tenements and ghettos were characterized as the breeding grounds for contagious diseases; the fear of physical infection manifest a "less tangible fear of social or ideological contamination" (654).

11. It is interesting to note that while the *New York Times* in 1890–1920 generally reports favorably on the Chinese (the exceptions being descriptions of violent crimes committed in Chinatown by Chinese men), the *Los Angeles Times* is decidedly more circumspect. Of the two dozen or so *Los Angeles Times'* articles I was able to locate that focused on China or the Chinese, the vast majority depicted the Chinese as either exotic curiosities (e.g., "Dope Smokers," 17 Mar. 1896; "A Chinese Slave," 3 July 1896; "Oriental Obsequies: Strange Ceremonies at Wong Chee's Funeral," 3 Aug. 1896) or lawless, "slant-eyed" criminals (e.g., "Assaulted by a Chinaman," 31 Jan. 1892; "Racial Antagonists," 7 May 1913). Even in these newspaper articles, the plights of the Chinese and African Americans are often compared or contrasted. An article on 24 January 1921 mocks a Japanese editorial that asks why the United States will not assimilate the Japanese when it has allowed African Americans to become citizens. Other articles seem to be exercises in racist wish fulfillment. An article on 29 March 1902 titled "Chance for Negroes in the Philippines" details why so many black soldiers have elected to remain in the Philippines after the end of the Spanish American War (reason: the Filipino women find them more attractive than Filipino men) and enthusiastically predicts that other black Americans will join the trend.

12. Western Europe's fascination with China in the seventeenth century led to the popularity of oriental tales. In some, Europeans authors passed as Chinese in order to level veiled critiques of the decadence and corruption of their own societies. Perhaps the best-known work in this genre is Oliver Goldsmith's *Citizen of the World* (1762), in which the Chinese narrator, Altangi, touches on a wide range of topics pertaining to British society and government. The popularity of the oriental tale stemmed from the belief that the foreign narrator could provide objective insight into English life as well as satisfy English curiosity about exotic realms.

13. Wu's memoir was just one in a line of works penned by East Asian writers who were hoping to create greater understanding between their respective nations and the United States. Some of the best known of these kinds of works are Yan Phou's *When I Was a Boy in China* (1887), Yung Wing Lee's *My Life in China and America* (1909), New Il-Han's *When I Was a Boy in Korea* (1928), Huie Kin's *Reminiscences* (1932), Park No-Young's *An Oriental View of American Civilization* (1934), Lin Yutang's *My Country and My People* (1935), and Chiang Yee's *Silent Traveler in New York* (1948).

14. Dominika Ferens's book on the Eaton sisters, *Edith and Winnifred Eaton: Chinatown Missions and Japanese Romances,* also focuses on their roles as ethnographers.

15. Here we have striking proof that a panethnic Asian American identity is the

product of the late twentieth century. Singling out the Chinese for exclusion did not mean that Americans possessed a fondness for or tolerance for other Asian nationals. The Supreme Court handed down decisions in 1922 and 1923 barring Japanese and Indians, respectively, from citizenship. In 1924, all Asian immigration was ended by the Albert Johnson Immigration Act, which created the "Asiatic Barred Zone." The law decreed that the annual immigration quota for any given nation could be no higher than 2 percent of foreign-born citizens living in the United States based on the 1890 census. (The act also effectively shut down immigration from eastern and southern Europe.) Japanese nationals, who had previously been exempted from various Asian exclusion acts, were included in this piece of legislation. *Asian Americans: An Interpretive History* by Sucheng Chan and *Entry Denied: Exclusion and the Chinese American Community in America, 1882–1943*, edited by K. Scott Wong and Sucheng Chan, offer thorough histories pertaining to Chinese and Asian exclusion.

16. Wu was the guest of honor at this annual dinner and was received warmly. The theme for the banquet was "Old Folks at Home," and the hall and tables were decorated with cards and images depicting plantation life, while "plantation melodies were interspersed with national and popular airs" ("Southern Society Dinner").

4 / The Eaton Sisters go to Jamaica

1. In her spirited biography of her paternal grandmother, Winnifred Eaton, Diana Birchall recounts their only meeting. When told by her maternal grandmother that the "jolly, laughing lady" in the room was also her grandmother, Birchall, who was a toddler, promptly replied, "No . . . you're my good grandma" (1). Even as a grandmother, it seems, Winnifred was an also-ran.

2. For a history of the critical narratives surrounding the Eaton sisters, see Ferens's *Edith and Winnifred Eaton*, 3–5.

3. Hattori argues that ethnic nationalism sees race as "the standard measure that makes human bodies and racial culture commensurable and equal to each other" (230). This kind of transformation of human bodies into exchange value reveals how capitalism can infiltrate ethnic critical studies. Thus, the critical debate surrounding the Eaton sisters "exposes the capitalist project of equivalence" (230).

4. Viet Nguyen claims, "Asian American critics tend to see texts as demonstrating either resistance or accommodation to American racism. Not willing to read for ideological heterogeneity, the critics betray their own ideological rigidity. The primary consequence of such rigidity is that critics tend to evaluate resistance as positive and accommodation as negative, without questioning the reductiveness of such evaluations" (7).

5. To avoid confusion I refer to each sister by her first name throughout this chapter. All citations of Edith's work are to the collection *Mrs. Spring Fragrance and Other Writings*.

6. It should be noted that both pen names (Sui Sin Far for Edith, Onoto Watanna for Winnifred) are essentially nonsense syllables and would not be recognized as names in either China or Japan. Birchall quotes a letter from a confused Yone Noguchi (the Japanese literary critic and essayist and the father of the famed designer Isamu Noguchi), who asks Frank Putnam, a mutual friend of both writers, "You say Onoto Watanna? Such is not Japanese name. Is she a real Japanese lady?" (49).

7. As Robert Lee notes in *Orientals*, in the aftermath of Pearl Harbor, the Chinese

went from being hated by Americans as the embodiment of the "Yellow Peril" to being embraced as an ally in the fight against Japan's empire. Lee rather sardonically notes that the alliance with the Chinese meant that "for the first time, being able to tell one Asian group apart from another seemed important to white Americans" (147).

8. According to Katherine Hyunmi Lee, part of the publicity for the book's publication included signs and advertisements posted around New York City that queried "Who is the author of *Me*?" Published anonymously, the memoir raised eyebrows for its depiction of Nora's multiple romantic entanglements. Using clues from the text, the *New York Times Book Review* eventually published an article that revealed the author's identity. For more information on the reception of Winnifred's memoir, see Katherine Lee, "The Poetics of Liminality and Misidentification," 181–82.

9. I refer to "Nora" when discussing the actions that happen in *Me,* and "Winnifred" when discussing the narrative or the author and the textual choices she makes.

10. Diana Birchall makes the most concerted effort to confirm or deny certain facts about her grandmother's life. She writes in her biography that although five years passed between Winnifred's departure from Jamaica and her arrival in New York City, *Me* shrinks that period to one year. Nora is seventeen at the time of her departure from Canada; Winnifred was twenty, and she cut three years from her age for the rest of her life.

11. It is within the context of ethnography that Dominika Ferens reads both Eaton sisters, who she believes subvert the conventional ethnographic dynamic between observer and observed or subject and object. Ferens claims that Edith had to negotiate her gendered and racialized position within her writing: "On the one hand, the role of cultural mediator and writer of ethnographic fiction enabled her to define herself as a middle-class professional woman in spite of the stigma of race. On the other, her ambivalent racial status sensitized her to the politics of ethnographic investigation, so that unlike contemporary white ethnographers, she did not leave unproblematized her own position and authority as purveyor of knowledge about the Chinese" (97). The stories justify this switch between observer and observed by conflating "cultural differences in an idealized diverse but integrated middle-class culture" (104)—in other words, by representing class to trump race or culture. According to Ferens, the question that the story attempts to answer is this: If Americans can authoritatively observe other cultures because of their outsider status, then who can authoritatively write about Americans? Ferens explores how Edith, as a Chinese person, established the authority to write about Chinese and American responses to the Chinese.

12. In Genesis, Ham, Shem, and Japheth, the sons of Noah, survived the Flood along with their father. Noah cursed Ham and his descendants to servitude because he saw his father naked. The Bible does not explicitly describe what the nature of this physical curse was, but interpreters have tended to assume the curse was racial in nature, and the story was used for centuries to justify the oppression of dark-skinned peoples.

13. Edith's radical potential in terms of her representations of racial hierarchies can be found in stories that do not seem overtly to deal with race, whether Chinese or African, at all.

14. *Ozawa* did not specifically challenge the Naturalization Act of 1790 that reserved naturalized citizenship for whites; instead, it asked the Court to consider people of Japanese descent to be white as well. The Court decided that by "white"

the lawmakers meant "Caucasian" and that the popular link between "whiteness" and Caucasianness should stand. According to the majority, "The test afforded by the mere color of the skin of each individual is impracticable as that differs greatly among persons of the same race, even among Anglo-Saxons, ranging by imperceptible gradations from the fair blond to the swarthy brunette, the latter being darker than many of the lighter hued persons of the brown or yellow races. Hence to adopt the color test alone would result in a confused overlapping of races and a gradual merging of one into the other, without any practical line of separation."

15. One need only look at works such as Douglass's *Narrative of the Life of Frederick Douglass* or the rags-to-riches stories written by eastern European immigrants (e.g., Mary Antin's *The Promised Land*) in the early twentieth century to have an inkling of what this transformative process entails.

16. Both "Mrs. Spring Fragrance" and "The Inferior Woman" are striking because they present a portrait of Chinese life in the western United States that seems unbelievably idyllic. Unlike the other characters in the collection, Chinese men and women who struggle to understand how their racial and cultural difference affects their lives in America, Mrs. Spring Fragrance and her husband live happily in their Seattle home and move easily between the society of their Chinese friends and their white neighbors. As Viet Nguyen notes about the collection, the other stories depict the injustices of racism but at the same time affirm the benevolence and naturalness of the middleclass, patriarchal family (55). The genial but mockingly ironic tone evident in these two stories differs markedly from the more earnest and sentimental style of the rest of the volume. It is the stories' more light-hearted tone and seemingly happy endings that I argue make them more powerful critiques of America than the more straightforward and indignant narratives of racial injustice.

17. The quotation is from Alfred Lord Tennyson's long poem, "In Memoriam," published in 1850.

18. Sean McCann focuses on the relationship between Edith and progressivism; Elizabeth Ammons, Guy Beauregard, and Annette White-Parks talk about Edith's relationship to the Chinese community in the United States.

19. The theory of polygenesis argues that the biblical creation myth describes the origins of the white race. According to proponents of polygenic theory, Africans, Asians, Native Americans, and other darker-skinned peoples are not descendants of Adam and Eve but are the products of creations that took place outside of the Garden of Eden. These groups thus occupy a different, subspecies category than whites. Given its incompatibility with biblical accounts of Genesis, Gossett points out that ironically most southern scientists and natural historians soundly rejected the theory of polygenesis, even though it offered them a "powerful" biological justification for the enslavement of blacks. See Gossett, *Race*, 47, 57, 64–67.

20. Writers, jurists, politicians, and commentators imagined racial differences in terms of biological or physiological qualities. For example, the popularity of blood as a metaphor for measuring one's character and human value explains why there was such a proliferation of terms that attempted to quantify what could not necessarily be seen (e.g., "quadroon," "octoroon," and the "one-drop rule").

21. The cartoon image I analyzed in my introduction ("The Last Addition to the Family") illustrates the notion that the Chinese civilization was dependent on American guidance.

22. Edith's "The Gamblers" was published in 1896 and is the first known story by an author of Asian descent to depict Asian characters in the United States. Her short fiction also appeared in magazines such as *Youth's Companion, Century Magazine,* and *Good Housekeeping*; McClurg's published her only book, *Mrs. Spring Fragrance*, a collection of short stories and essays, in 1912. Annette White-Parks has written a literary biography of Edith Eaton, *Sui Sin Far/Edith Maude Eaton*, which offers readings of Eaton's stories based on her life.

5 / *Quicksand* and the Racial Aesthetics of Chinoiserie

1. *Chinoiserie* refers specifically to the Chinese-inspired, European-manufactured goods that first became popular in Europe in the seventeenth century (Tchen, 6). The *OED* defines the term more broadly as a "Chinese notion" or "Chinese art." Since *Quicksand* most often labels its oriental objects as Chinese in origin, I have chosen to use the term "chinoiserie" throughout this chapter. When I want to refer to objects from Asia but without a definitive national provenance, I use the adjective "oriental." The Orient, according to the *OED*, comprises "that part of the earth's surface situated to the east of *some recognized point of reference*; eastern countries, or the eastern part of a country; the East; usually, those countries immediately east of the Mediterranean or of Southern Europe, which to the Romans were 'the East,' the countries of South-western Asia or of Asia generally" (my emphasis). The *OED* definition dovetails with Said's claim that orientalism "depends for its strategy on [a] flexible *positional* superiority" (7). What both definitions share is a notion that the Orient as a place is defined in relative terms; it always exists in relation to a Western or European home.

2. Of that "amazing young crowd who gathered in Harlem" (Bontemps, 10) in the early twentieth century, Nella Larsen was perhaps the most feted and critically applauded of the novelists. Despite her limited production, her work has received a tremendous amount of contemporaneous and current critical praise. Du Bois famously pronounced Larsen's *Quicksand* to be "the best piece of fiction that Negro America has produced since the heyday of [Charles] Chesnutt" (quoted in Lewis, 23). Modern-day literary critics have been no less appreciative. David Levering Lewis declares *Quicksand* "one of the three novels of the Renaissance" (232). Hiroko Sato calls Larsen a "gifted writer" who "[knew] the craft of fiction: how to write effectively and economically" (84), and Cheryl Wall considers Larsen's novels to be "the best written of the time" (97).

3. The prominent focus on chinoiserie and the Orient can hardly be put down to a stylistic quirk on Larsen's part, since this trope is unique to *Quicksand* and does not appear in *Passing* or her shorter fictional works. One must conclude that the appearance of such images and language serves a specific purpose within the novel. However, descriptions of oriental objects seem to abound in American fiction of the late nineteenth century and early twentieth. According to Mari Yoshihara, the appearance of such Asian objects "is not simply an idiosyncratic literary device but an illustration of the material culture shaping the emerging ideals of femininity in postbellum America. The encounter with things Asian as spectacle and objects of consumption was an index of the expansion of women's/girl's imaginary, if not physical, sphere. It suggested a liberating potential for white, middle-class women whose rights and opportunities were limited by their gender yet whose racial, class and national identities made the world come to them in the form of commodities" (17). Yoshihara offers a

compelling history of how white women played an active role in promulgating what she calls an "American orientalism" (6).

4. See Du Bois's "The Color Line Belts the World."

5. In "Journalistic Representations of Asian Americans and Literary Responses, 1910–1920," Rachel Lee describes the popularity of stories with oriental characters or settings. American companies capitalized on the nation's interest in the Orient by linking their products with the Far East, either through the product's name or advertising.

6. For a fascinating account of the impact of Chinese objects on American national identity and cultural practices, see John Tchen's study, *New York before Chinatown: Orientalism and the Shaping of American Culture, 1776–1882.* Tchen writes that by the time of the country's founding, "'things' Chinese had become one of the forms of currency for gaining cultural 'distinction.' Adapting the European elite's craze for Chinese export items and European chinoiserie, New Yorkers cultivated a taste for Chinese and Chinese-style luxuries" (13).

7. Larsen is not the only writer of the Harlem Renaissance to rely so heavily on oriental images. Both Richard Bruce Nugent in his short story "Smoke, Lilies, and Jade" (1926) and Wallace Thurman in his roman à clef *Infants of the Spring* (1932) make extensive use of oriental imagery, particularly as a means of highlighting "queer" masculinity.

8. Born in 1891 in Chicago, Larsen was the daughter of a Danish mother and a light-skinned West Indian father. After her father abandoned the family, Larsen's mother married Peter Larsen, a fellow Dane. Larsen's stepfather and stepsiblings resented Nella, who recognized from an early age that her dark skin embarrassed her family. (She later said that she chose not to see her family after she left home because "it might make it awkward for them, particularly [her] half-sister" [quoted in Davis, "Nella Larsen," 183]). Like Edith Eaton, Larsen seems to have had a restless young adulthood, enrolling at Fisk University in Nashville, taking classes in Copenhagen, studying nursing in New York City, and then working as a nursing superintendent at the Tuskegee Institute. Dissatisfied with the regimented life at Tuskegee, she returned to New York in 1917, where she married a prominent physicist, Elmer Imes, and landed a job as a librarian in the New York Public Library. With the encouragement of Walter White, Carl Van Vechten, and other prominent figures in the Harlem cultural world of the mid-1920s Larsen published her first novel, *Quicksand,* with the prestigious publishing house Alfred A. Knopf in 1928. *Passing* was published the following year, and Larsen was awarded a Guggenheim Fellowship for Creative Writing in 1930, the first woman to earn the award. At the height of her popularity and creative powers she suffered two devastating setbacks, one personal and the other professional. In 1930, she discovered that her husband was having an affair with a white woman; she was then accused of plagiarizing her short story "Sanctuary," which had been published the previous year. Although she was eventually cleared of the plagiarism charge, Larsen withdrew from public life and returned to nursing. She died in obscurity in New York in 1964. For more biographical information on Larsen, see Davis, *Nella Larsen* and Christian, *Black Women Novelists,* 8–9. For information on the literary and cultural circles in which Larsen traveled while living in New York City, see Lewis, *When Harlem Was in Vogue,* 140–41.

9. Barbara Christian, Ann duCille, Claudia Tate, and Cheryl Wall provide vital

readings of the novel that emphasize how the racial and sexual oppressions facing Helga intersect in the novel. While these four critics praise the novel's depiction of these interlocking identity categories, there are some who view *Quicksand* with a less appreciative eye. Farrah Griffin censures the racial politics of *Quicksand* because it does not represent southern black life or the white-on-black racism that pervaded the United States. Griffin takes Larsen to task for her depiction of the claustrophobic and judgmental southern black community that traps Helga at the end of the novel. She objects to the fact that this section of the novel makes no mention of the racism practiced by whites, and she objects to the novel's general tone of dismissal about black "folk" culture, which she argues is the most authentic expression of black culture. As Griffin rather ominously opines, "There are no ancestors in *Quicksand*" (160).

10. The question of whether artists should represent sexuality in black characters and whether self-censoring is a form of subversion or capitulation has troubled many literary critics. For example, in her article comparing Frances Harper's *Iola Leroy, or Shadows Uplifted* (1892) with Alice Walker's *The Color Purple* (1982), Deborah McDowell argues that the former, in attempting to counteract racist images of black women as inhuman and sexually immoral, avoids portraying any type of sexuality that readers might construe as another example of black moral inferiority. Although McDowell acknowledges the political necessity of advocating such a "countermyth" of piety and femininity, she ultimately suggests that *Iola Leroy* and other novels founder under the weight of their own ideological contradictions precisely because they cannot free themselves from the values of the racist patriarchal system that had enslaved them; the novel takes on the impossible task of both complying with white mainstream standards of literary value and social behavior while simultaneously attempting to present African Americans in an "honest" way (41). For a contrasting view on this issue, see duCille's introduction to *The Coupling Convention*.

11. Several critics have commented extensively on Helga's self-aestheticization, although they have not connected it to chinoiserie. Elizabeth Ammons notes that a "framing" metaphor informs Helga's understanding of her own subjectivity. Barbara Johnson applies this framing metaphor in her reading of this initial scene. She argues that the closed room "symbolizes the issue of the self as a container (of value, positive or negative). . . . The self is utterly engulfed by the outside because there is nothing outside the engulfing outside to save it" (254–55). While Helga searches for a space outside the frame into which she might escape, Johnson suggests that such a space does not exist, that although she does not realize it, the frame is all Helga has for understanding her self and her world.

12. One need only think of the common American practice of using chopsticks as hair clips to understand the kind of radical decontextualization that orientalism depends upon.

13. Martha Cutter echoes Barbara Johnson's poststructuralist reading in her discussion of the novel's representation of passing. Cutter argues that passing can be a "liberating" act only when it allows the passer to escape the conventions of a racist, sexist, and classist society that would otherwise circumscribe his or her conduct or actions (75). Helga Crane passes through a host of subject positions in the relentless pursuit of *one* elusive identity that will satisfactorily unify her disparate experiences and quell the feelings of displacement she has experienced her entire life. Her futile search for an identity "demonstrates the fallacy of belief in a 'true self'" (76); there are only

social roles—or frames, to borrow Johnson's metaphor. Cutter goes on to argue that ultimately, Helga's attempts at passing are less subversive than Clare Kendry's (from Larsen's second novel, *Passing*). Clare does not believe in an "essential self" but instead moves through the roles required of her, thus defying the categorization of society. Cutter therefore considers *Passing* to be more of a "writerly text" than *Quicksand*.

14. An anonymous contributor to the *Independent* on 18 September 1902 expresses the representational burden that Helga herself feels: "When a white man in the South does commit a crime, that is simply one white man gone wrong. If his crime is especially brutal, he is a freak or temporarily insane. If one low, ignorant black wretch commits a crime, that is different. All of us must bear his guilt" (quoted in Lerner, 168).

15. For a discussion of the fabrics and colors in *Quicksand*, see Hostetler, "The Aesthetics of Race and Gender," 35–37.

16. Of course yellow is also used to describe the skin color of Asian and biracial persons.

17. For a discussion of the politics behind black female sexuality, see McDowell, "'The Changing Same,'" 41.

18. As Cheryl Wall succinctly puts it, "Only the spell of racial mythology could lead a man to mistake such insults for gallantry" (104).

19. In his study of modernism, North does not distinguish between American artists residing in Europe (e.g., Pound and Eliot) from those living in the United States.

20. For a discussion of the black communities in Detroit and New York and their interest in an African-Asian alliance, see Deutsch, "'The Asiatic Black Man.'" For a discussion of Du Bois's lifelong interest in Asia, particularly China and Japan, see Martin and Yeakey, "Pan-American Asian Solidarity." For an examination of Du Bois's interest in India, see Ahmad, "More Than Romance." For a discussion of the African American back-to-Africa movements in the early twentieth century, see Redkey, *Black Exodus*.

21. In fact, Japan based its claim of equality with Western nations on its ability to adapt Western modes of government, capital, and organization. Throughout the late nineteenth century and early twentieth Japan positioned itself as the protector of Asian nations who were too dependent and backward to understand a modern geopolitical order. As the United States did with Native Americans at home and Filipinos abroad, Japan engaged in a "civilizing" discourse with Formosa and Korea in order to justify its takeover of those nations. It is perhaps for this reason that the Japanese were often called the "energetic little Yankees of the Orient" (Christ, 684). For more information on Japanese attempts to legitimize its colonization of China, see Christ, "'The Sole Guardians.'"

22. Of note is the power this identity continued to wield into the late twentieth century. Muhammad Ali once proclaimed his allegiance to this identity when he stated, "I am not a negro. . . . I am an Asiatic black man" (quoted in Deutsch, 194).

23. Deutsch points to the problems of a pan-Asiatic African identity. First, although the Japanese victory in 1905 did much to unsettle the assumption of white superiority, the Japanese themselves were carrying out a racist colonialist agenda in other parts of Asia. Second, Deutsch conjectures that the emphasis on Asia and the Middle East as a "homeland" for black Americans arose because of the shameful characteristics associated with Africa.

6 / Nation, Narration, and the Afro-Asian Encounter in W. E. B.
du Bois's *Dark Princess* and Younghill Kang's *East Goes West*

1. Jonathan Culler describes "non-genre literature" as a catchall category for those literary works that seem to defy easy categorization ("Toward a Theory," 52). In point of fact, Culler argues that *all* literature is non-genre literature: "The essence of literature is not representation, not a communicative transparency, but an opacity, a resistance to recuperation which exercises sensibility and intelligence" (53).

2. The back-to-Africa movements that have emerged in various incarnations since the Civil War indicate the hold that the notion of an African home has on the American populace, whether black or white. Robin Kelley notes, "[My own family] has been living with 'the question ['What are you?' or 'Where are you from?'] for as long as I can remember" ("People in Me").

3. Although the *OED* notes that exile might be "voluntarily undergone for any purpose," it seems safe to say that exile is generally understood to be compulsory rather than freely chosen.

4. The cosmopolite's class status allows him to choose a life disengaged from local political allegiances. The flâneur consumes what he observes.

5. Thomas Ferraro argues that one of the motivating factors for early twentieth-century immigrant writers was to contest the stereotypes of their own ethnic communities. According to Ferraro, most of the ethnic fiction of the early twentieth century was produced to "tell representative narratives that either countermanded or contextualized stereotypes, to acknowledge the opportunities but protest the obstacles facing newcomers, and to introduce the public to the debate within ethnic homes and communities over alternative American dreams" (383).

6. The nation as a political unit and the novel as a genre are so well matched that David Lloyd suggests that the novel serves a "regulative function" that "orders internally a hierarchy of belonging of identity within the nation" (quoted in Culler, 23-24).

7. Robin Kelley makes a similar point when he argues that black historians have always had a transnational bent to their work because of the nature of what they studied: the slave trade, expatriate communities, double consciousness, and so on ("But a Local Phase"). According to Kelley, anti-racist and anti-imperialist politics are profoundly a part of black historiography.

8. See Rampersad, *The Art and Imagination of W. E. B. Du Bois;* Tate, *Psychoanalysis and Black Novels.*

9. Vijay Prashad elaborates on this premodern polycultural history of contact in the first chapter of his study *Everybody Was Kung-fu Fighting.*

10. James Weldon Johnson's *The Autobiography of an Ex-Colored Man* also prominently features a Chinese chop-suey restaurant; it exists below The Club, where the unnamed character hears ragtime for the first time. The narrator and his friends go there after long nights of drinking in order to sober up.

11. On the question of whether *East Goes West* is autobiography or fiction, the critics are divided. Elaine Kim calls *The Grass Roof* (1931) and *East Goes West* (1937) "slightly fictionalized accounts" of Kang's experiences in Korea and the United States (33). I have chosen to call *East Goes West* a novel, more or less, because it fits even less well into autobiographical conventions than novelistic ones.

12. Although the United States had granted Japanese citizens living in America

more protection because of Japan's strong position in the Pacific, the National Origins Act of 1924 denied entry to almost all Asians, including the Japanese. Congress had already passed the Asiatic Barred Zone Act in 1917, which prohibited most people from Asia from legally entering the country. While the Chinese were excluded from entering the country starting in 1892, it was not until the Gentleman's Agreement of 1907 that Japanese movement to the United States was restricted. Japan was initially exempted from the Asiatic Barred Zone Act, but the United States finally shut the door in 1924 with the National Origins Act.

13. It is perhaps moments like this that remind us of Stephen Knadler's assertion that Kang's tone has made him a less than popular writer with Asian American literary critics, for as much as the text clearly castigates Robin's behavior, it also gently ridicules Chungpa's, with his misuse of the word "umpire." Again, Chungpa's unwitting use of a term from the sports arena makes it easier for the reader to dismiss the whole incident as more harmless than seriously racist.

14. As Lisa Lowe explains, the United States "naturaliz[es] a universality that exempts the 'non-American' from its history of developments or admits the 'non-American' only through a 'multiculturalism' that aestheticizes ethnic differences as if they could be separated from history" (9).

7 / Coda

1. Obama himself paid homage to this idea of progress in his victory speech on election night, when he narrated the events of the past century through the eyes of Ann Nixon Cooper, a 106-year-old black woman who was born the generation after slavery. A full text of the speech can be found at www.npr.org/templates/story/story.php?storyId=96624326.

2. The Red Apple Boycott was launched in 1990 following the alleged assault by a Korean shopkeeper on one of his African American customers. The boycott drew nationwide attention and lasted for nearly eighteen months. In 1991, a teenager named Latasha Harlins was shot in the back by a Korean shopkeeper, Soon Ja Du, while attempting to buy a carton of orange juice. Du was later sentenced to probation and served no jail time for the murder.

3. The poll was not nationwide. According to the press release, "AALDEF, a 35-year old New York–based national organization, polled 16,665 Asian American voters in 11 states on Election Day: New York, New Jersey, Massachusetts, Pennsylvania, Virginia, Maryland, Michigan, Illinois, Louisiana, Texas, Nevada, and Washington, D.C."

4. The *Los Angeles Times* reported that the Asian American turnout in Los Angeles County was 39 percent larger than in the 2000 election (from 211,000 to 293,000).

BIBLIOGRAPHY

Aarim-Heriot, Najia. *Chinese Immigrants, African Americans and Racial Anxiety in the United States, 1848–1882.* Urbana: University of Illinois Press, 2003.

Abbott, Lynn, and Doug Seroff. *Ragged but Right: Black Traveling Shows, "Coon Songs," and the Dark Pathway to Blues and Jazz.* Jackson: University Press of Mississippi, 2007.

Ahmad, Dohra. "More Than Romance: Genre and Geography in *Dark Princess.*" *ELH* 69 (2002): 775–803.

Ammons, Elizabeth. *Conflicting Stories: American Women Writers at the Turn of the Century.* New York: Oxford University Press, 1992.

Anderson, Benedict. *Imagined Communities: Reflections on the Origins and Spread of Nationalism.* New York: Verso, 1983.

Appiah, Kwame Anthony. "The Uncompleted Argument: Du Bois and the Illusion of Race." *"Race," Writing, and Difference.* Ed. Henry Louis Gates. Chicago: University of Chicago Press, 1992. 21–37.

Baker, Lee. *From Savage to Negro: Anthropology and the Construction of Race, 1896–1954.* Berkeley: University of California Press, 1998.

Bascara, Victor. "'Following the Money': Asian American Literature and the Preface to United States Imperialism." *Jouvert: Journal of Postcolonial Studies* (2000): n.p. Web. 6 June 2001. http://152.1.96.5/jouvert/v4i3/bascar.htm.

Baym, Nina. *Feminism and American Literary History.* New Brunswick, NJ: Rutgers University Press, 1992.

Beauregard, Guy. "Reclaiming Edith Eaton." *Re/Collecting Early Asian America: Essays in Cultural History.* Ed. Imogene Lim, Josephine Lee, and Yuko Matsukawa. Philadelphia: Temple University Press, 2002. 340–53.

Bederman, Gail. *Manliness and Civilization: A Cultural History of Gender and*

Race in the United States, 1880–1917. Chicago: University of Chicago Press, 1996.

Benjamin, Walter. *Selected Writings: 1938–1940.* Ed. Howard Eiland and Michael Jennings. Trans. Edmund Jephcott et al. Vol. 4. Cambridge: Belknap Press of Harvard University Press, 2003.

Bhabha, Homi. *The Location of Culture.* London: Routledge, 1994.

Birchall, Diana. *Onoto Watanna: The Story of Winnifred Eaton.* Urbana: University of Illinois Press, 2001.

Birth of a Nation. Dir. D. W. Griffiths. 1915. Videocassette. Madacy Entertainment, 1997.

Bontemps, Arna. *The Harlem Renaissance Remembered.* New York: Dodd Mead, 1972.

Bourne, Randolph. "Trans-National America." *Atlantic Monthly* July 1916: 86–97.

Brennan, Timothy. *At Home in the World: Cosmopolitanism Now.* Cambridge: Harvard University Press, 1997.

Broken Blossoms. Dir. D. W. Griffiths. 1919. Videocassette. Kino Video, 1993.

Bryce, James. "Thoughts on the Negro Problem." *North American Review* Dec. 1891: 641–60.

Cable, George Washington. "The Freedman's Case in Equity." *Century Magazine* Jan. 1885: 409–19.

Carby, Hazel. *Reconstructing Womanhood: The Emergence of the Afro-American Woman Novelist.* New York: Oxford University Press, 1995.

Cather, Willa. *A Lost Lady.* 1923. New York: Vintage, 1990.

———. *The Professor's House.* 1925. New York: Vintage, 1990.

Chan, Sucheng. *Asian Americans: An Interpretive History.* New York: Twayne, 1991.

Chang, Edward. "America's First Multiethnic 'Riots.'" *The State of Asian America: Activism and Resistance in the 1990s.* Ed. Karin Aguilar-San Juan. Boston: South End Press, 1994. 101–18.

Chavez, Alex. "Barack Obama: Our First Asian President." *Asians in America* 1 Apr. 2009. 5 Dec. 2009. http://asiansinamerica.typepad.com/asians_in_america_magazin/2009/04/barack-obama-is-an-asian.html.

The Cheat. Dir. Cecil B. DeMille. 1915. Videocassette. Paramount Pictures, 2002.

Chen, Constance J. S. "Transnational Orientals: Scholars of Art, Nationalist Discourses and the Question of Intellectual Authority." *Journal of Asian American Studies* 9.3 (2006): 215–42.

Cheng, Anne Anlin. *The Melancholy of Race: Psychoanalysis, Assimilation, and Hidden Grief.* New York: Oxford University Press, 2001.

Chesnutt, Charles. "The Future American: A Complete Race Amalgamation Likely to Occur." *Charles Chesnutt: Essays and Speeches.* Ed. Joseph R. McElrath Jr., Robert C. Leitz III, and Jesse S. Crisler. Stanford: Stanford University Press, 1999. 131–35.

———. *The Marrow of Tradition*. 1900. Ann Arbor: University of Michigan Press, 1969.

Cheung, King-Kok. "(Mis)interpretations and (In)justice: The 1992 Los Angeles 'Riots' and 'Black-Korean Conflict.'" *MELUS* 30.3 (2005): 3–40.

Cheung, King-Kok, ed. *An Interethnic Companion to Asian American Literature*. Cambridge: Cambridge University Press, 1997.

"The Chinese Exclusion Bill." *Harper's Weekly* 16 Apr. 1892: 362.

Choy, Philip, Lorraine Dong, and Marlon Hom, eds. *The Coming Man: Nineteenth-Century American Perceptions of the Chinese*. Seattle: University of Washington Press, 1995.

Christ, Carol Ann. "'The Sole Guardians of the Art Inheritance of Asia': Japan and China at the 1904 St. Louis World's Fair." *positions* 8.3 (2000): 675–709.

Christian, Barbara. *Black Women Novelists: The Development of a Tradition, 1892–1976*. Westport, CT: Greenwood Press, 1980.

Chuh, Kandice. *Imagine Otherwise: On Asian Americanist Critique*. Durham, NC: Duke University Press, 2003.

Cole, Jean Lee. *The Literary Voices of Winnifred Eaton: Redefining Ethnicity and Authenticity*. New Brunswick, NJ: Rutgers University Press, 2002.

Culler, Jonathan. "Anderson and the Novel." *diacritics* 29.4 (1999): 20–39.

———. "Toward a Theory of Non-Genre Literature." *Theory of the Novel: A Historical Approach*. Ed. Michael McKeon. Baltimore; Johns Hopkins University Press, 2000. 51–56.

Cutter, Martha. "Sliding Significations: Passing as a Narrative and Textual Strategy in Nella Larsen's Fiction." *Passing and the Fictions of Identity*. Ed. Elaine Ginsberg. Durham, NC: Duke University Press, 1996. 75–100.

Davis, Thadious M. "Nella Larsen." *Dictionary of Literary Biography*. Vol. 51: *Afro American Writers from the Harlem Renaissance to 1940*. Detroit: Gale Research, 1987. 182–92.

———. *Nella Larsen, Novelist of the Harlem Renaissance: A Woman's Life Unveiled*. Baton Rouge: Louisiana State University Press, 1994.

de Certeau, Michel. *The Practice of Everyday Life*. Berkeley: University of California Press, 1984.

Degenhardt, Jane. "Situating the Essential Alien: Sui Sin Far's Depiction of Chinese-White Marriage and the Exclusionary Logic of Citizenship." *Modern Fiction Studies* 54.4 (2008): 654–88.

Denison, John. "The Survival of the American Type." *Atlantic Monthly*, January 1895, 16–27.

Deutsch, Nathaniel. "'The Asiatic Black Man': An African American Orientalism?" *Journal of Asian American Studies* 4.3 (2001): 193–208.

Dimock, Wai Chee. "Deep Time: American Literature and World History." *American Literary History* 13.4 (2001): 755–74.

Du Bois, W. E. B. "The Color Line Belts the World." 1906. *W. E. B. Du Bois: A Reader*. Ed. David Levering Lewis. New York: Henry Holt, 1995. 42–43.

——. *Dark Princess: A Romance.* 1928. Jackson: Banner Books of the University Press of Mississippi, 1995.

——. "The First Universal Races Congress" 1911. *W. E. B. Du Bois: A Reader.* Ed. David Levering Lewis. New York: Henry Holt, 1995. 44–47.

——. *The Souls of Black Folk.* 1903. *Three Negro Classics.* New York: Avon, 1976. 207–390.

——. *W. E. B. Du Bois on Asia: Crossing the World Color Line.* Ed. Bill Mullen and Cathryn Watson. Jackson: University Press of Mississippi, 2005.

duCille, Ann. *The Coupling Convention: Sex, Text, and Tradition in Black Women's Fiction.* New York: Oxford University Press, 1993.

Eaton, Edith [Sui Sin Far]. *Mrs. Spring Fragrance and Other Writings.* Ed. Amy Ling and Annette White-Parks. Urbana: University of Illinois Press, 1995.

Eaton, Winnifred [Onoto Watanna]. *The Heart of Hyacinth.* 1903. Seattle: University of Washington Press, 2000.

——. *Me: A Book of Remembrance.* 1915. Jackson: Banner Books of the University Press of Mississippi, 1997.

Ely, James W. *Railroads and American Law.* Lawrence: University Press of Kansas, 2001.

Fanon, Frantz. *Black Skin, White Masks.* New York: Grove Press, 1967.

"Farewell to Minister Wu." *New York Times* 14 Nov. 1902: n.p. Proquest Historical Newspapers. Web. 2 Mar. 2010.

Farrow, Kenyon. "We Real Cool? On Hip-Hop, Asian-Americans, Black Folks, and Appropriation." www.kenyonfarrow.com. 2 June 2005. Web. 14 May 2008.

Ferens, Dominika. *Edith and Winnifred Eaton: Chinatown Missions and Japanese Romances.* Urbana: University of Illinois Press, 2002.

Ferraro, Thomas. "Ethnicity and the Marketplace." *The Columbia History of the American Novel.* Ed. Emory Elliot. New York: Columbia University Press, 1991. 381–406.

Fitzgerald, F. Scott. *The Great Gatsby.* 1922. New York: Scribner, 1995.

Foucault, Michel. "Of Other Spaces [1967]." *diacritics* 16.1 (1986): 22–27.

Frazier, E. Franklin. *The Negro Family in the United States.* 1938. South Bend, IN: Notre Dame University Press, 2001.

Gaines, Kevin. *Uplifting the Race.* Chapel Hill: University of North Caroline Press, 1996.

Giddings, Paula. *When and Where I Enter: The Impact of Black Women on Race and Sex in America.* New York: William Morrow, 1984.

Gilroy, Paul. *The Black Atlantic: Modernity and Double Consciousness.* Cambridge: Harvard University Press, 1993.

Goldsmith, Oliver. *Citizen of the World.* 1762. New York: Fredonia Books, 2004.

Gong Lum v. Rice. 275 U.S. 78. No. 29. United States Supreme Court. 1927. LexisNexis Academic. Web. 30 May 2005.

Gossett, Thomas. Race: *The History of an Idea in America*. 1963. New York: Oxford University Press, 1997.

Gotanda, Neil. "A Critique of 'Our Constitution Is Color-Blind.'" *Stanford Law Review* 44.1 (1991): 1–68.

Griffin, Farrah. *"Who Set You Flowin'?": The African-American Migration Narrative*. New York: Oxford University Press, 1995.

Gunning, Sandra. *Race, Rape, and Lynching: The Red Record of American Literature, 1890–1912*. New York: Oxford University Press, 1996.

Guy, Basil. "Ad majorem Societatis gloriam: Jesuit Perspectives on Chinese Mores in the Seventeenth and Eighteenth Centuries." *Exoticism in the Enlightenment*. Ed. G. S. Rousseau and Roy Porter. Manchester, England: Manchester University Press, 1990. 3–20.

Gyory, Andrew. *Closing the Gate: Race, Politics and the Chinese Exclusion Act*. Chapel Hill: University of North Carolina Press, 1998.

Haney-Lopez, Ian. *White by Law: The Legal Construction of Race*. New York: New York University Press, 1996.

Harris, Cheryl. "Whiteness as Property." *Harvard Law Review* 106.8 (1993): 1709–91.

Hattori, Tomo. "Model Minority Discourse and Asian American Jouis-Sense." *differences: A Journal of Feminist Cultural Studies* 11.2 (1999): 228–47.

Hemingway, Ernest. *The Sun Also Rises*. 1926. New York: Scribner, 1995.

Higginbotham, Evelyn Brooks. *Righteous Discontent: The Women's Movement in Black Baptist Church, 1880–1920*. Cambridge: Harvard University Press, 1993.

Higham, John. *Strangers in the Land: Patterns of American Nativism, 1860–1925*. New York: Atheneum, 1967.

Hode, Martha. *White Women, Black Men: Illicit Sex in the Nineteenth Century South*. New Haven: Yale University Press, 1997.

Hong, Grace Kyungwon. "'Something Forgotten Which Should Have Been Remembered': Private Property and Cross Racial Solidarity in the Work of Hisaye Yamamoto." *American Literature* 71.2 (1999): 291–310.

Hostetler, Ann. "The Aesthetics of Race and Gender in Nella Larsen's Quicksand." *PMLA* 105.1 (1990): 35–46.

Husband, Joseph. *The Story of the Pullman Car*. Chicago: McClurg, 1917.

Jacobson, Matthew Frye. *Whiteness of a Different Color: European Immigrants and the Alchemy of Race*. Cambridge: Harvard University Press, 1998.

Johnsen, Leigh Dana. "Equal Rights and the 'Heathen Chinee'": Black Activism in San Francisco, 1865–1875." *Western Historical Quarterly* 11.1 (1980): 56–68.

Johnson, Barbara. "The Quicksands of the Self: Nella Larsen and Heinz Kohut." *Female Subjects in Black and White: Race, Psychoanalysis, and Feminism*. Ed. Elizabeth Abel, Barbara Christian, and Helene Moglen. Berkeley: University of California Press, 1997. 252–65.

Johnson, James Weldon. *The Autobiography of an Ex-Colored Man*. 1912. Introduction Henry Louis Gates, Jr. New York: Vintage, 1989.

Jung, Moon-Ho. *Coolies and Cane: Race, Labor, and Sugar in the Age of Emancipation*. Baltimore: Johns Hopkins University Press, 2006.

Kang, Younghill. *East Goes West*. 1937. New York: Kaya, 1997.

Kaplan, Amy. *The Anarchy of Empire in the Making of U.S. Culture*. Cambridge: Harvard University Press, 2002.

Kern, Stephen. *The Culture of Time and Space, 1880–1918*. 2nd ed. Cambridge: Harvard University Press, 2003.

Kelley, Robin D. G. "'But a Local Phase of a World Problem': Black History's Global Vision, 1883–1950." Internet. Accessed 10 July 2003. *Journal of American History* 86.3 (1999). www.historycooperative.org.

———. "People in Me." *Colorlines*. N.p., 5 July 2003. Web. 2 March 2005. https://www.zcommunications.org/.

Kim, Daniel. *Writing Manhood in Black and Yellow: Ralph Ellison, Frank Chin, and the Literary Politics of Identity*. Stanford: Stanford University Press, 2005.

———. "Do I, Too, Sing America? Vernacular Representations and Chang-rae Lee's Native Speaker." *Journal of Asian American Studies* 6.3 (2003): 231–60.

Kim, Elaine. *Asian American Literature: An Introduction to the Writings and Their Social Context*. Philadelphia: Temple University Press, 1982.

Kim, Hyung-Chan, ed. *Asian Americans and the Supreme Court: A Document History*. Westport, CT: Greenwood Press, 1992.

Kim, Thomas W. "Being Modern: The Circulation of Oriental Objects." *American Quarterly* 58.2 (2006): 379–406.

Kingston, Maxine Hong. *China Men*. 1977. New York: Vintage International, 1989.

Kleingeld, Pauline, and Eric Brown. "Cosmopolitanism." *The Stanford Encyclopedia of Philosophy*, fall 2002. Web. 20 Apr. 2004. http://plato.stanford.edu/archives/fall2002/ethics/cosmopolitanism.

Knadler, Stephen. "Unacquiring Negrophobia: Younghill Kang and the Cosmopolitan Resistance to the Black and White Logic of Naturalization." *Jouvert: A Journal of Postcolonial Studies* 4.3 (2000). Web. 3 Jan. 2003. http://social.chass.ncsu.edu/jouvert/v4i3/knad.htm.

Koshy, Susan. "American Nationhood as Eugenic Romance." *differences: A Journal of Feminist Cultural Studies* 12.1 (2001): 50–78.

———. "Morphing Race into Ethnicity: Asian Americans and Critical Transformations of Whiteness." *boundary 2* 28.1 (2001): 153–94.

———. *Sexual Naturalization: Asian Americans and Assimilation*. Palo Alto, CA: Stanford University Press, 2005.

Krasner, David. "Parody and Double Consciousness in the Language of Early Black Musical Theatre." *African American Review* 20.2 (1995): 317–23.

Lai, Him Mark, Genny Lim, and Judy Yung, eds. *Island: Poetry and History of*

Chinese Immigrants on Angel Island, 1910-1940. Seattle: University of Washington Press, 1980.

Larsen, Nella. *Quicksand [1928] and Passing [1929].* Ed. Deborah McDowell. New Brunswick, NJ: Rutgers University Press, 1986.

"The Last Addition to the Family." Cartoon. *Harper's Weekly* 25 Sept. 1869: 624.

Lefebvre, Henri. *The Production of Space.* London: Blackwell, 1991.

Lee, Katherine. "The Poetics of Liminality and Misidentification: Winnifred Eaton's *Me* and Maxine Hong Kingston's *The Woman Warrior.*" *Transnational Asian American Literature: Sites and Transits.* Ed. Shirley Lim, John Gamber, Stephen Sohn, and Gina Valentino. Philadelphia: Temple University Press, 2006. 181-96.

Lee, Rachel. "Journalistic Representations of Asian Americans and Literary Responses, 1910-1920." *An Interethnic Companion to Asian American Literature.* Ed. King-Kok Cheung. Cambridge: Cambridge University Press, 1997. 249-73.

Lee, Robert G. *Orientals: Asian Americans in Popular Culture.* Philadelphia: Temple University Press, 1999.

Lerner, Gerda. *Black Women in White America: A Documentary History.* New York: Vintage, 1972.

Lewis, David Levering. *When Harlem Was in Vogue.* 1979. New York: Vintage Books, 1982.

Li, David. *Imagining the Nation: Asian American Literature and Cultural Consent.* Stanford: Stanford University Press, 1998.

Ling, Amy. "Creating One's Self: The Eaton Sisters." *Reading the Literatures of Asian America.* Ed. Shirley Geok-Lin and Amy Ling Lim. Philadelphia: Temple University Press, 1992. 306-18.

Ling, Jinqi. *Narrating Nationalisms: Ideology and Form in Asian American Literature.* New York: Oxford University Press, 1998.

Lipsitz, George. *The Possessive Investment in Whiteness: How White People Benefit from Identity Politics.* Revised ed. Philadelphia: Temple University Press, 2006.

Lofgren, Charles. *The Plessy Case: A Legal-Historical Interpretation.* New York: Oxford University Press, 1987.

———. "Training America: Law, Liberty and the Railroad." *Reviews in American History* 31 (2003): 275-82.

Lott, Eric. *Love and Theft: Blackface Minstrelsy and the American Working Class.* New York: Oxford University Press, 1995.

Love, Nathaniel. *The Adventures of Nat Love.* 1907. Lincoln: University of Nebraska Press, 1995.

Lowe, Lisa. *Immigrant Acts: On Asian American Cultural Politics.* Durham, NC: Duke University Press, 1996.

Lowell, A. Lawrence. "The Colonial Expansion of the United States." *Atlantic Monthly,* Feb. 1899: 145-54.

Lui, Mary Ting Yi. "'The Real Yellow Peril': Mapping Racial and Gender Boundaries in New York City's Chinatown, 1870–1910." *Hitting Critical Mass: A Journal of Asian American Cultural Criticism* 5.1 (1998). Web. 17 Dec. 2002. http://ist-socrates.berkeley.edu/~critmass/v5n1/lui1.html.

Lye, Colleen. *America's Asia: Racial Form and American Literature, 1893–1945.* Princeton: Princeton University Press, 2005.

Lyman, Stanford M. *The Asian in the West.* Ed. Don D. Fowler. Reno: University of Nevada Press, 1970.

Marshall, P. J., and Glyndwr Williams. *The Great Map of Mankind: British Perceptions of the World in the Age of Enlightenment.* London: J. M. Dent and Sons, 1982.

Martin, Michael, and Lamont Yeakey. "Pan-African Asian Solidarity: A Central Theme in Dubois' Conception of Racial Stratification and Struggle." *Phylon* 43.3 (1982): 202–17.

Marx, Leo. *The Machine in the Garden: Technology and the Pastoral Ideal in America.* 1964. New York: Oxford University Press, 2000.

Matsukawa, Yuko. "Representing the Oriental in Nineteenth-Century Trading Cards." *Re/Collecting Early Asian America: Essays in Cultural History.* Ed. Imogene Lim, Josephine Lee, and Yuko Matsukawa. Philadelphia: Temple University Press, 2002. 200–17.

McCann, Sean. "The Anti-Progressivism of Edith Eaton." *Yale Journal of Criticism* 12.1 (1999): 73–88.

McClain, Charles. *In Search of Equality: The Chinese Struggle against Discrimination in Nineteenth-Century America.* Berkeley: University of California Press, 1994.

McDowell, Deborah. "'The Changing Same': Generational Connections and Black Women Novelists—*Iola Leroy* and *The Color Purple.*" *The Changing Same: Black Women's Literature, Criticism, and Theory.* Bloomington: Indiana University Press, 1995. 34–60.

McKeon, Michael, ed. *Theory of the Novel: A Historical Approach.* Baltimore: Johns Hopkins University Press, 2000.

Meier, August. *Negro Thought in America, 1880–1915: Racial Ideologies in the Age of Booker T. Washington.* 1963. Ann Arbor: University of Michigan Press, 1988.

Meloney, William. "Slumming in New York's Chinatown." *Munsey's Magazine* Sept. 1909: 818–30.

Michaels, Walter Benn. *Our America: Nativism, Modernism, and Pluralism.* Durham, NC: Duke University Press, 1995.

Miller, Stuart Creighton. *The Unwelcome Immigrant: The American Image of the Chinese, 1785–1882.* Berkeley: University of California Press, 1969.

"Minister Wu in Praise of Lincoln." *New York Times* 13 Feb. 1901: 2. Proquest Historical Newspapers. Web. 3 Mar. 2003.

Miyao, Daisuke. *Sessue Hayakawa: Silent Cinema and Transnational Stardom.* Durham, NC: Duke University Press, 2007.

Moddelmog, William. *Reconstituting Authority: American Fiction in the Province of Law.* Iowa City: University of Iowa Press, 2000.

Morrison, Toni. *Playing in the Dark: Whiteness and the Literary Imagination.* New York: Vintage, 1993.

———. "Talk of the Town: Comment." *New Yorker* 5 Oct. 1998.

Mullen, Bill. *Afro-Orientalism.* Minneapolis: University of Minnesota Press, 2004.

———. "Du Bois, *Dark Princess,* and the Afro-Asian International." *positions* 11.1 (2003): 217–39.

Nast, Thomas. "The Chinese Question." Cartoon. *Harper's Weekly* 18 Feb. 1871: 149.

———. "Difficult Problems Solving Themselves." Cartoon. *Harper's Weekly* 29 Mar. 1879: 256.

———. "Every Dog (No Distinction of Color) Has His Day." Cartoon. *Harper's Weekly* 8 Feb. 1879: 101.

Nguyen, Viet. *Race and Resistance: Literature and Politics in Asian America.* New York: Routledge, 2002.

Ni, Ching-Ching. "Asian Americans in L.A. County Voted in Record Numbers in 2008." *Los Angeles Times* 27 Oct. 2009. Web. 5 Nov. 2009. http://latimes-blogs.latimes.com/lanow/2009/10/asian-americans-in-la-county-voted-in-record-numbers-in-2008–supported-obama.html.

North, Michael. *The Dialect of Modernism: Race, Language, and Twentieth Century Literature.* New York: Oxford University Press, 1994.

Nye, David. *American Technological Sublime.* Cambridge: MIT Press, 1994.

"Obama the First Asian American President?" Google News. 27 Apr. 2009. Web. 3 Mar. 2010. http://www.google.com/hostednews/afp/article/ALeqM5jBuHCupFGHaCv5NY8cxm8EzXdGQ.

Okihiro, Gary. *Margins and Mainstreams: Asians in American History and Culture.* Seattle: University of Washington Press, 1994.

Omi, Michael, and Howard Winant. *Racial Formation in the United States: From the 1960s to the 1990s.* New York: Routledge, 1994.

Osajima, Keith. "Asian Americans as the Model Minority: An Analysis of the Popular Press Image in the 1960s and 1980s." *A Companion to Asian American Studies.* Ed. Kent Ono. Malden, MA: Blackwell, 2005. 215–25.

Ozawa v. United States. 260 U.S. 178. No. 1. United States Supreme Court. 1922. LexisNexis Academic. Web. 5 Aug. 2001.

Page, Thomas Nelson. "A Southerner on the Negro Question." *North American Review* April 1892: 401–13.

Paine, Albert Bigelow. *Thomas Nast: His Period and His Pictures.* New York: Macmillan, 1904.

Palumbo-Liu, David. *Asian/American: Historical Crossings of a Racial Frontier.* Stanford: Stanford University Press, 1999.

Plessy v. Ferguson. 163 U.S. 537. No. 210. United States Supreme Court. 1896. Online. LexisNexis Academic. Web. 10 Aug. 2001.

Porter, David. "Chinoiserie and the Aesthetics of Illegitimacy." *Studies in Eighteenth-Century Culture* 28 (1999): 27–54.

Posnock, Ross. "The Dream of Deracination: The Uses of Cosmopolitanism." *American Literary History* 12.4 (2000): 802–18.

Prashad, Vijay. "'Bandung Is Done': Passages in AfroAsian Epistemology." *AfroAsian Encounters: Culture, History, Politics*. Ed. Heike Raphael-Hernandez and Shannon Steen. New York: New York University Press, 2006. xi–xxiii.

———. *Everybody Was Kung-fu Fighting: Afro-Asian Connections and the Myth of Cultural Purity*. Boston: Beacon Press, 2001.

Rampersad, Arnold. *The Art and Imagination of W. E. B. Du Bois*. Cambridge: Harvard University Press, 1976.

Redkey, Edwin. *Black Exodus: Black Nationalist and Back-to-Africa Movements, 1890–1910*. New Haven: Yale University Press, 1969.

Riis, Thomas L. "Bob Cole: His Life and His Legacy to Black Musical Theater." *Black Perspective in Music* 13.2 (1985): 135–50.

Robinson, Edgar, and Victor West. *The Foreign Policy of Woodrow Wilson, 1913–1917*. New York: Macmillan, 1917.

Roe, Jae. "'Keeping an Old Wound Alive': The Marrow of Tradition and the Legacy of Wilmington." *African American Review* 33.2 (1999): 231–43.

Roediger, David. *The Wages of Whiteness: Race and the Making of the American Working Class*. New York: Verso, 1993.

Rogin, Michael. "'The Sword Became a Flashing Vision': D. W. Griffith's *The Birth of a Nation*." *Representations* 9 (1985): 150–95.

"Roosevelt Bars the Hyphenated." *New York Times* 13 Oct. 1915: 1, 5. Proquest Historical Newspapers. Web. 1 Mar. 2010.

Roosevelt, Theodore. *The Free Citizen: A Summons to Service of the Democratic Ideal*. Ed. Hermann Hagedorn. New York: Macmillan, 1956.

Ross, Michael. "Seat of Honor." *New Orleans Times-Picayune* 25 May 2003: 4.

Said, Edward. *Orientalism*. New York: Vintage, 1979.

Sato, Hiroko. "Under the Harlem Shadow: A Study of Jessie Fauset and Nella Larsen." *The Harlem Renaissance Remembered*. Ed. Arna Bontemps. New York: Dodd, Mead, 1972. 63–89.

Saxton, Alexander. *The Indispensable Enemy: Labor and the Anti-Chinese Movement in California*. Berkeley: University of California Press, 1995.

Schivelbusch, Wolfgang. *Railway Journey: The Industrialization of Time and Space in the Nineteenth Century*. Berkeley: University of California Press, 1986.

Schrager, Cynthia. "Both Sides of the Veil: Race, Science, and Mysticism in W. E. B. Du Bois." *American Quarterly* 48.4 (1996): 551–86.

Shaler, Nathaniel Southgate. "The Negro Problem." *Atlantic Monthly* Nov. 1884: 696–709.

Shih-shan, H. T. *The Chinese Experience in America*. Bloomington: Indiana University Press, 1986.

Shklar, Judith. *American Citizenship: The Quest for Inclusion*. Cambridge: Harvard University Press, 1991.

"Silk Association Dines." *New York Times* 9 Feb. 1900: 3. Proquest Historical Newspapers. Web. 15 Oct. 2004.

Siu, Paul C. P. *The Chinese Laundryman: A Study of Social Isolation*. Ed. John Tchen. New York: New York University Press, 1987.

Sollors, Werner. *Neither Black nor White yet Both: Thematic Explorations of Interracial Literature*. Cambridge: Harvard University Press, 1997.

Somerville, Charles. "Slumming in New York's Chinatown." *Cosmopolitan* Sept. 1909: 818-30.

Song, Min Hyoung. *Strange Future: Pessimism and the 1992 Los Angeles Riots*. Durham, NC: Duke University Press, 2006.

"Southern Society Dinner." *New York Times*, 23 Feb. 1899: 2. Proquest Historical Newspapers. Web. 3 Mar. 2010.

Spillers, Hortense. "Afterword: Cross-Currents, Discontinuities: Black Women's Fiction." *Conjuring: Black Women, Fiction, and Literary Tradition*. Ed. Marjorie Pryse and Hortense Spillers. Bloomington: Indiana University Press, 1985. 249-61.

Stocking, George. "The Turn-of-the-Century Concept of Race," *Modernism/Modernity* 1.1 (1994): 4-16.

Stover, John F. *American Railroads*. 2nd ed. Chicago: University of Chicago Press, 1997.

Sundquist, Eric. *To Wake the Nations: Race in the Making of American Literature*. Cambridge: Belknap Press of Harvard University Press, 1993.

Takaki, Ronald. *Iron Cages: Race and Culture in Nineteenth-Century America*. New York: Knopf, 1979.

Tate, Claudia. "Desire and Death in *Quicksand* by Nella Larsen." *American Literary History* 7.2 (1995): 234-60.

———. *Domestic Allegories of Political Desire: The Black Heroine's Text at the Turn of the Century*. New York: Oxford University Press, 1996.

———. *Psychoanalysis and Black Novels: Desire and the Protocols of Race*. New York: Oxford University Press, 1998.

Tchen, John Kuo Wei. *New York before Chinatown: Orientalism and the Shaping of American Culture, 1776-1882*. Baltimore: Johns Hopkins University Press, 1999.

Thomas, Brook. *American Literary Realism and the Failed Promise of Contract*. Berkeley: University of California Press, 1997.

———. "The Legal Argument for Charles W. Chesnutt's Novels." *REAL: Yearbook of Research in English and American Literature* 18 (2002): 311-34.

Thomas, Brook, ed. *Plessy v. Ferguson: A Brief History with Documents*. Boston: Bedford St. Martin, 1997.

Torok, John. "Reconstruction and Racial Nativism: Chinese Immigrants and the Debates on the Thirteenth, Fourteenth, and Fifteenth Amendments and

Civil Rights Laws." *Asian Law Journal*, May 1996. LexisNexis Academic. Web. 25 Sept. 2001.

United States v. Bhagat Thind Singh. 261 U.S. 204. No. 202. United States Supreme Court. 1923. LexisNexis Academic. Web. 20 Sept. 2001.

United States v. Wong Kim Ark. 169 U.S. 649. No. 132. United States Supreme Court. 1898. LexisNexis Academic. Web. 23 Sept. 2001.

Wald, Priscilla. "Communicable Americanism: Contagion, Geographic Fictions, and the Sociological Legacy of Robert E. Park." *American Literary History* 14.4 (2002): 653–85.

———. *Constituting Americans: Cultural Anxiety and Narrative Form*. Durham, NC: Duke University Press, 1995.

Wall, Cheryl. "Passing for What? Aspects of Identity in Nella Larsen's Novels." *Black American Literature Forum* 20.1–2 (1986): 97–111.

Wallace, Michelle. "The Good Lynching and *The Birth of a Nation*: Discourses and Aesthetics of Jim Crow." *Cinema Journal* 43.1 (2003): 85–104.

"Want Minister Wu Recalled." *New York Times* 24 Oct. 1901: 1. Proquest Historical Newspapers. Web. 3 Mar. 2003.

Weinbaum, Alys. "Reproducing Racial Globality: W. E. B. Du Bois and the Sexual Politics of Black Internationalism." *Social Text* 67.19 (2001): 15–39.

Welke, Barbara Young. *Recasting American Liberty: Gender, Race, Law and the Railroad Revolution, 1865–1920*. New York: Cambridge University Press, 2001.

White-Parks, Annette. "A Reversal of American Concepts of 'Other-Ness' in the Fiction of Sui Sin Far." *MELUS* 20.1 (1995): 17–34.

———. *Sui Sin Far/Edith Maude Eaton: A Literary Biography*. Urbana: University of Illinois Press, 1995.

Williams, Teresa Kay. "Race-ing and Being Raced: The Critical Interrogation of 'Passing.'" *Amerasia Journal* 23.1 (1997): 61–65.

Williamson, Joel. *The Crucible of Race in America: Black-White Relations in the American South Since Emancipation*. New York: Oxford University Press, 1984.

Wong, K. Scott, and Sucheng Chan, eds. *Entry Denied: Exclusion and the Chinese American Community in America, 1882–1943*. Philadelphia: Temple University Press, 1991.

Wong, Shawn, ed. *Asian American Literature: A Brief Introduction and Anthology*. New York: HarperCollins, 1996.

Woodward, C. Vann. *The Strange Career of Jim Crow*. New York: Oxford University Press, 1955.

Wu, Tingfang. *America through the Spectacles of an Oriental Diplomat*. New York: Frederick Stokes, 1914.

"Wu Tingfang Pays Tribute to General Grant."*New York Times* 31 May 1901: n.p. Proquest Historical Newspapers. Web. 1 Mar. 2010.

"Wu Tingfang Tells Us Just What He Thinks of Us." *New York Times* 22 Mar. 1914: SM8. Proquest Historical Newspapers. Web. 1 Mar. 2010.

Yang, Jeff. "Could Obama Be the First Asian American President?" *SF Gate* 30 July 2008. Web. 5 Nov. 2009. http://www.sfgate.com/cgi-bin/article.cgi?f=/g/a/2008/07/30/apop.DTL.

Yick Wo v. Hopkins. 118 U.S. 356. United States Supreme Court. 1886. LexisNexis Academic. Web. 2 Oct. 2001.

Yin, Xiao-huang. *Chinese American Literature since the 1850's.* Urbana: University of Chicago, 2000.

Yoshihara, Mari. *Embracing the East: White Women and American Orientalism.* New York: Oxford University Press, 2003.

Zangwill, Israel. *The Melting Pot.* New York: Macmillan, 1932.

Index

Aarim-Heriot, Najia, 28, 176n5
African Americans, 5–6, 46–47; back-to-Africa movements, 191n19, 192n2; black women authors revisited by feminists, 16–17; *Chinese Immigrants, African Americans and Racial Anxiety in the United States, 1848–1882*, 28, 176n5; citizenship and exclusion for, 4, 29–33; double consciousness of, 143–45, 192n7; literature nadir of, 16–17, 182n1; Naturalization Law of 1790 aimed at, 31; in popular (white) culture, 31–33; Prashad on, 172–74; Red Apple Boycott, 193n2; *Takao Ozawa v. United States*, 26, 31, 100–102, 119, 179n8, 186n14; whites lynching of, 33, 42, 90–92, 94, 144, 165–66, 179n5, 179nn10–11, 180nn12–13, 182n24. *See also* Afro-Asian pairing; American identity; Black men; Black women; Negro Problem
Afro-Asian pairing, 118–19; in *Dark Princess*, 162–64; "Difficult Problems Solving Themselves," 38–39, 58–59, 181n19; Du Bois's pan-African and pan-Asian alliance, 148–54; in *East Goes West*, 164–66; Hong on Yamamoto's portrayal of, 12, 177n9; Koshy on black-white binary, 40, 178n4; *Plessy v. Ferguson*, 5, 6, 18, 26, 33–35, 42–54, 60–80, 107–8, 178n3, 182n26,

184n9; Prashad on, 172–74; reasons for focusing on, 12–13; Wang on, 175n3
Agassiz, Louis, 107
Ahmad, Dohra, 145–46, 191n20
Alien, oriental as, 35–36, 46, 58, 65, 157; Alien Land Laws, 119; in congressional Reconstruction debates, 176n5; Wu Tingfang as, 71
Alien Land Laws (1920), 119
Amalgamation, 24, 178n1
American identity: America's obsession with, 26–27; blood is thicker than water, 5–6, 32–33, 178n4; Chinese Exclusion Act, 27–28, 31, 69, 73, 177n7; Du Bois on, 139–42, 161–63, 165–69; exclusionary discourse about, 4–6, 11, 26, 29–42, 94, 176n5, 178n4, 180n15, 181n20; movies conveying racial ideologies, 39, 181n22; in "Mrs. Spring Fragrance," 17, 19, 85–86, 99–100, 102–5, 187n16; *Plessy v. Ferguson* logic of, 46–47; *Quicksand* on, 118, 122–37, 190n10; as romantic mythology, 102–4; weightlessness of, 7–8; white female as metaphor for America, 42; whiteness as, 26, 28, 31–32, 100–102, 107, 119, 171, 178n4, 179n8, 184n9, 186n14, 187n19
America Through the Spectacles of an Oriental Diplomat (Wu), 18, 48–49, 50–54, 69–78
Ammons, Elizabeth, 190n11

ABOUT THE AUTHOR

Julia H. Lee is assistant professor of English and Asian American studies at the University of Texas, Austin.